Happiness
No Man Required

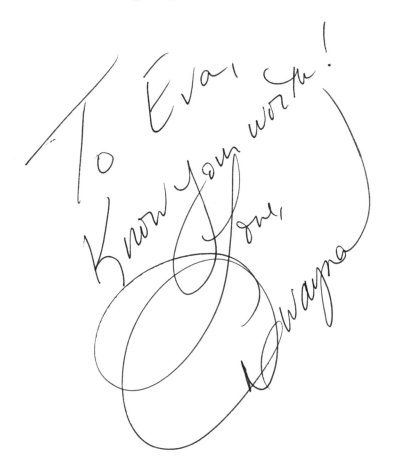

To Eva, on!
Know your worth
love,
Dwayna

Praise for
Happiness
No Man Required

In a day where courtship is rare, many women find themselves in hurtful and abusive relationships with bad men. Weary and broken, these women often feel confused, trapped, and alone. Writing from her own experiences and that of others, Dwayna Litz offers good spiritual and practical advice to help women accept and understand who they are as individuals and empower them to overcome loneliness, sin, and despair through our Lord Jesus Christ, the true Love of our souls.

— CHRISTINE WISNIEWSKI, Crisis Pregnancy and Post-Abortion
Support Counselor

Happiness

No Man Required

50
Tips
for Single
Women
to be Happy
...With or
Without a
Man

DWAYNA LITZ

Graphics, typesetting, and cover design by Rose Yancik at Y Design

Photographs of Dwayna Litz by Eli McFadden

Copyedited by Pam Shoup

Published in the United States by Lighting the Way Worldwide Books

Library of Congress Cataloging-in-Publication Data
Litz, Dwayna
Hardcover ISBN: 978-0-9890809-3-4
Trade Paperback ISBN: 978-0-9890809-4-1
eBook ISBN: 978-0-9890809-5-8
Audio Book ISBN: 978-0-9890809-6-5
Self-help 2. Recovery 3. Addiction 4. Christianity 5. Verbal Abuse 6. Relationships
7. Dating 8. Women's Studies 9. Health 10. Single Women 11. Counseling
12. Rehabilitation 13. Spiritual Abuse 14. Domestic Violence 15. Battered Women

Printed in the United States of America

Order books by Dwayna Litz on Amazon and Barnes and Noble websites

For more information on the author, visit DwaynaLitz.com

To Marilyn Brown—a happily married counselor specializing in addiction, who has worked with me for years to help me fully realize I'm complete in God's love, empowering me to wake up one morning, much to my surprise, happy and whole without a man

To God—for wanting to be everything to me

Contents

Introduction

I've never known "the one who got away." For me, as I look back on all of the men I have ever thought I loved, they were all, without a doubt, wrong for me. Like many of my Christian girlfriends, I have never met a good-looking, impressive, Christian, single man with a stable job, who could be right for me to marry—the *good, Christian men* so many married people presume single women *just find* like a dream come true. The fact that I am still single is not because I am in rebellion from God's plan for my life, as I have been told by a few married Christians who have no idea what single Christians go through to find an appropriate mate. From the time I became an adult, people have said, "It will happen. God has someone just for you." Just as many times I have been asked, "Why are you not married?"

Some women reading this do not want anything to do with God. If that is the case, please stay open-minded and keep reading. Whoever you are, if you are not happy on your own, you have chosen the right book. I address this from a Christian perspective because healing is not possible without a relationship with God. I mean no disrespect toward any woman of any background with any other worldview. But the message is the same to atheists, spiritualists, religious, and nonreligious. There is just one way to really be happy living your life alone. That being said, I hope you won't choose misery instead.

Delight as a single person certainly came as a surprise when it found me. It was more like a beautiful rainbow than any tidal wave of infatuation I had experienced with a man. It didn't look like I thought it would. There was no boyfriend or husband in my life to affirm me, but for the first time I didn't need one. I liked who I was just fine on my own. Happiness had tricked me. When I was off searching for it somewhere else, it snuck up on me. All my loneliness was gone, and I was at ease within myself.

Though I am truly content today alone, this does not mean that I could not also be happy if God were to bring me a companion. Now that I am secure in who I am alone, *I am able* to be true to myself, whether God has chosen a man for me to marry or not. I was never being true to myself all of those years when I would pick a guy who fit with me outwardly but was as different as oil and water from me in character—and this includes the so-called Christian men, too.

No names are mentioned in these accounts. They are all strangers from the men they pretend to be anyway. I could pretty much close my eyes and pick one from the confluence of pretenders I've just so happened to know. There were moments my life felt so exciting in the throes of their charm that it was enough to test a sincere walk with God as boring in comparison. It's not. I would choose it any day over the wrong man.

I've also dated some men of great character who have just not been right for me to marry. Good men worthy of praise are far from extinct. I expound on them in my "Good Men Still Exist" tip. They are roaming the land out in the open with all the clandestine jerks. Living an authentic life is what sets the good men apart and makes them a blessing to know. I cherish the sincere pastors I have known who reflect God's pure love, those who are one-woman-men. It is healing for any woman, married or single, to be around good men. On the other hand, shallow, insincere players are damaging to everyone, especially when they use church—a place women go to feel safe—as their dangerous playground. These tips alert Christian women to red flags, warning them to stay away from so-called "good men" who prey to deceive in churches and on Christian dating sites.

Without realizing it, some Christians encourage single women to idolize marriage, truly believing women cannot be fulfilled without it. Not only is that unbiblical, but thanks to so many wrong men, the label of single women who never marry being called *old maids* has become antiquated. More and more smart single women are being far too productive to let life pass them by without a man. Many are discovering in this day and age they are better off on their own. It is not that they do not want a man, but that they cannot find the right one and are staying single out of wisdom.

I hate to think of all the time I wasted trying to find what so many kept telling me I would (and should) find in order to *settle down*. I foolishly made it my mission more than once to pray for a man who needed saving, both for his sake and mine, because *settling* seemed like my only option. After all, I had been taught by other Christians as far back as I can remember to *pray for your husband*, and this was long before I was even an adult! I used to feel empty on my own, as if it were a man's responsibility to complete me, as if he alone held the power to make my heart come to life. I was told by some well-meaning people that this empty feeling on my own was normal, because I had not yet met *the one*. Who was I supposed to be without *him*? Every man, in and out of church, kept failing miserably from being anywhere close to right for me. I tried to settle but couldn't.

Well, no doubt, my restless soul certainly did need to settle down. God has been so good to do just that. It was one big sigh of relief when the good Lord gave me something far better than a man. He settled me down and made me happy on my own. Now I enjoy every day of my amazing life. I love being single. Every moment is a gift. Hallelujah! No man is required!

This book describes all the ways I tried manipulating a wrong relationship into something right or how I was too vulnerable with deceivers to believe something was real love from God when it never was. The simple truth is there never has been anyone right for me as a mate so far in life. Thank God for the day I finally surrendered! The Bible teaches that God makes a home for the lonely in Psalm 68:6. It is true, because I have finally come home within myself. And what a satisfying place of peace it is.

Happiness occurs when we least expect it, one painful day at a time, living out our convictions. God does not just zap us with happiness. It is a result of choices we make. If you are hungry for love, my prayer is that this book will teach you *how* to be filled with Bread that satisfies. I used to be hungry, too, and it had everything to do with my heart being empty and not my stomach. Now I have enough, only needy for God who has never let me down. And every day I spend living close to Him and away from the false god of *Give Me My Way*, I'm full.

The stories in these tips are not about a perfect girl. Quite the contrary; I used to ache for another person to come along and love me. I was so very lonely on my own. This is about all God has done to heal my deepest wounds, resulting in a happiness that no man can give; a treasure to guard with all my being, so no man can take it away.

Know the Difference Between Love and Love Addiction

*I*n 1940 my grandfather, Claude Pitner, walked into a little country store in Tennessee owned by my great-grandfather, Oscar Burnett. There he met Eloise Burnett, my grandmother, dipping ice cream from behind the counter. At first glance, he thought her red hair was as beautiful as her smile. He ordered a scoop. On top of that he cooed, "I want you to be my sweetheart."

The American culture was much cleaner and easier back then, and so was the love it produced. The charm people experienced in everyday interaction was much more innocent, too. When my grandfather met my grandmother, she had no need for pause before allowing herself to feel infatuated. That's because she was living in a society totally foreign to our 21st century America. In 1940, such a widespread, immoral landscape did not exist to require my grandmother pause to consider some crucial questions about a stranger before falling in love. Today, however, we have come to a virtual end of innocence. We can't assume a man is safe in this Land of the Lost, where there are too many emotional vampires sucking the life (and money) out of women and predators lurking where we least expect to find them.

I've been told there is someone for everyone. I've come to believe there is at least one dangerous person for everyone in this culture to dodge! Of course, good men do exist, but it is too risky to presume the best before knowing the person's character these days. Today's woman first has to stop to ask herself certain questions when she meets a new man, questions that never had to cross my grandmother's mind to ask herself about my grandfather when they first met. In 1940, when my grandfather warmly said to my grandmother behind the ice cream counter, "I want you to be my sweetheart," she never had to brace herself to wonder:

Is he bisexual? Is he bipolar? Does he hope to get married to "escape being gay"? Is he a cocaine, meth, or heroin addict? Is he hooked on prescription drugs? Is he addicted to pornography? Does he hire escorts? Does he visit prostitutes? Does he frequent strip clubs? Is he into orgies? Does he secretly videotape women? Does he have a fetish for dressing like a woman when having sex? Does he want a woman to support him financially because he's a playboy who doesn't want to work? Is my credit better than his? Is he after my or my family's money? Is he chronically lazy? Is he a pedophile? Has he been sexually abused as a boy by a pedophile? Would he define his life by a flow of "7 chakras?" Does he drink Kabbalah water? Does he practice "soul travel"? Does he dabble in occult magick? Is he incapable of beginning his day without first reading his astrological chart? Does he entrust his future to a psychic medium? Has he had metaphysical experiences, which the Bible would define as demonic? Does he pray to Allah? Does he bow to a Buddhist shrine in his home? Would he call himself a Hindu avatar? Is he a thetan in Scientology? Does he spend more time in yoga meditations than he spends making a living? Does he believe in reincarnation and communicate with the dead on a regular basis? Does he have a strong aversion to the Bible as God's Word? Is he into Shamanism? Does he worship education, not realizing the worth of people apart from degrees? Is he a well-educated psychopath? Is he really the man he appears to be on a Google search? Is he on an Internet dating site claiming to be someone else? Does he post photos from years ago on social networking sites, claiming they're recent, to deceive women with whom he flirts in cyberspace? Is he currently married or engaged and just not telling me? Has his bad character stumped even therapists to make them think he has a personality disorder off the charts? Is he incapable of falling in love without sex? Does he only want to get me in bed?

I enjoy watching old movies from the era of Doris Day, Judy Garland, and Cary Grant. Such movies reflect a time gone by in America where men actually had marriage on their minds when they met women instead of just getting them into bed. A good man was defined as a man who wanted a *good girl*, and a good girl was a woman who did not have sex outside of marriage. Can you imagine? A whole culture *was capable* of falling in love and marrying apart from sex outside of marriage. How did they manage to get to know one another without having sex from at least the third date? They managed so well that such platonic dating produced a society where divorce was uncommon, and real love was much easier to experience. It was safe to get excited about meeting a new guy because, more than likely, he was someone nice. Today, more than likely, an extraordinarily charming man on a first date is pathological.

But back in the day of my grandparents, my grandmother had the pleasure of just blushing when my grandfather met her and answered back without thinking twice, "I want to be your sweetheart, too." A few kisses on the cheek later, and they were married. They had a marriage that lasted sixty-four years. My grandmother's family had more money than my grandfather's when they dated, but it never crossed his mind to marry her for that money. As a matter of fact, after they married, he never wanted to take any money from her father, insisting on supporting her financially, even through tough economic times. They saved and never went into debt and owned everything they had outright, from the house they physically built to the cars they drove. Their marriage lasted until death parted them. They were best friends with compatible characters. They knew love.

My dad owns everything he has today in assets, too, but such men are rare anymore. Nowadays, we meet men who are in debt with their toys to postulate a false self, as they parade their lives in one big facade. As soon as one woman figures them out, they are simply off to con another.

One day in 2009, I was talking to my counselor, Marilyn Brown, about the latest wrong man I met and thought I had loved. She was used to hearing stories about the various men I dated over the years. I had come a long way, but I still had a long way to go. When we first began working together back in 2003, she listened as I confessed struggling with overeating at the end of my latest relationship. Back then, it was still hard for me to eat right after telling a man goodbye. The overeating always led to overexercising to remain slim. I would write songs and poetry about how much it hurt after a breakup, because I had *loved* him. Eventually, the pain would subside like an answered prayer when a new man was sent to me. It was inevitable on Internet dating! (The sites send daily matches automatically by email to the members.) I had reluctantly joined a few Internet dating sites in 2003 after a friend said, "I'll bet if you join an Internet dating site, you'll have so many dates you'll be married within a year."

Well, it was true that I had no trouble at all finding a *match* with every digital wink. True love for sale for only twenty-five to fifty dollars a month was a real deal! It was worth every penny with my biological clock ticking to get married and have kids. I could get hundreds of emails in one day. Mr. Right was obviously out there looking for me, too. I always knew I was a unique person, but according to the dating site, I had compatibility with so many! It was enough to *send a wink* to my little profile every morning, noon, and night. Could this go on forever? Well, yes, quite possibly, because all of a sudden I found myself in an endless cyber sea of good-looking fish from all over the world. It was such an ego-boost getting bombarded with so many impressive, handsome men asking me out *online*.

Next thing you know, Marilyn was listening to me rejoice in losing my appetite from the high once again of *being in love*. What a rush it was! I had had a date with a man who initially made me his *favorite* from the overabundance of profiles sent to him as matches, and I had found my way to happiness from love at first sight online. He was moving fast, asking for a commitment on the first date. I liked him so much already! I was hoping he would be *the one*. It was my pleasure to lose my appetite when I met a new guy. It always happened when I felt loved. Such a high alleviated a deep, mysterious angst within my being. I was never hungry, and I always felt so skinny when I was *in love* (or experiencing emotional cocaine, as Marilyn put it). Loneliness was gone. All was well in the world. I had found happiness, and he Googled well!

If only the high could last; if only the *love* could stay. But it didn't. After a lot of prayer, I knew with every single one that I had to say goodbye. So, I kept saying goodbye . . . and saying hello . . . to give love one more chance with someone new . . . only to once again have to say goodbye. . . . and then feel the need to say hello and then goodbye and then hello and then goodbye . . . until finally I moved on, so to speak, in the real world with no one to show for it but me, myself, and I. Believe me, so much dating was tiring!

Marilyn was there listening through the pain of my hunger, as I was determined to stay away from fattening food after I had just let go of another loser. Surely someday I would be the one to win at love with a good man, but it certainly had not happened yet. I just kept *falling in and out of love* with men who were not the people they appeared to be on the surface. At the end of practically every relationship, I found myself trying to understand why the last guy seemed even worse than the one before him. The whole falling in love thing was wearisome. To my credit, though, I never gave up on myself. I never went back to any of the jerks after telling them goodbye. After all, a new jerk always seemed to be waiting right around the corner to offer me the same old story with a different flavor of wrong.

You can imagine my surprise when one day in 2009, finding myself brokenhearted again, Marilyn insinuated that my definition of love had all along been awry. I was complaining about missing a man I had been dating. She had been consoling me for years listening to my bemoaning about the similar scenarios with only the names of the men changing. But on this day in 2009, her response was different. With the tears flowing from my eyes, she stopped me cold in my tracks. She said, "Dwayna, you have never been in love before." She stated it emphatically, without a bit of doubt, like it was an indisputable fact.

I paused, thinking of all the beautiful songs I had written about the men I had met and how much I had felt for them. I whispered to myself what she had told me to let it sink in. *"I've never been in love before."*

She said, "Dwayna, you're a love addict." I had never been told such a thing. I was thankful she finally enlightened me after so many years, but in defense I argued, "I'm not a flirt. I have spent much of my adult life alone. I don't lead men on or say things I don't mean. Why do you call me a love addict?" She answered, "Because you don't think you can be happy without a man. That's a love addict."

She explained that love addiction was great for writing songs, but love addiction is based on a chemical reaction, a baffling pull toward someone. Chemical attraction can even seem mysteriously wicked at times. Real love is different. I did a Google search on love addiction. I was surprised to find that many of the characteristics of love addiction did describe me. I thought about how I had never really known a place of peace and trust with a man due to true compatibility in character. I realized she was right. With so many of the men I had met turning out to be deceivers; with all the tears I had cried in disappointment; with all the intoxicating charm I had experienced from the smooth talkers; with the intense chemistry, worshipful infatuation, and songs and poetry I'd written, I had never really been in love before. I had certainly prayed my little heart out, though, for many a lost man, but that was before the promising honeymoons went south to a place of pity. I came to realize, in hindsight, that none of them had been emotionally available. Marilyn was right. I had never been in love before.

Judging from the American media, it is no wonder most people don't know the difference between true love and love addiction. Most of the popular songs played on the radio are based on love addiction with lyrics like "I don't know what it is but I trust him . . ."[1] If you don't know what *it* is, *it* could be an evil seduction with no love attainable for your soul, and he could be a psychopath! If you want to be happy, with or without a man, don't just go around humming a tune without thinking about the lyrics. Consider the option of getting certain songs *off* your mind if you find yourself feeling lonely without a man after listening to them. It is not worth it if the songs are making you feel sorry for yourself as a single person. There is no reason for you to feel lacking without romance unless you dwell so much on it in distraction from more important things.

I shouldn't have been surprised when I was told at age twenty-one, "Dwayna, you are in love with love," while making my living as an artist on Music Row. The years I spent as a singer and songwriter in Nashville certainly nourished a love addiction to grow within. Still being single at my age today was something totally off my radar in my early twenties. The thought would have terrified me on the inside. I was *oh, so, lonely* without a man. Don't get me wrong; I am thankful for all the songs I have written from my heart about the different men who have touched it. But listening to the songs I have written about men who were not meant for me and focusing on feelings that deceived me is not exactly the best way for me to experience alacrity today. On the other hand, I am continuously uplifted when I hear the songs I have written and recorded about a faithful love that will not let me go. When I listen to worship songs about Jesus, my mind is renewed to a beautiful relationship I have with a God so real that He calls Himself my keeper.[2] And with all of the love I have within me to offer any person on earth, my God loves me more.

---

1   "Trust Him" by Alonzo Mario Stevenson, Tony Reyes, Tiffany Villareal, and Herbert Rooney. Recorded by Fantasia on her *Back to Me* album.
2   Psalm 121:5

HOMEWORK

Homework for this tip is to Google "Love Addiction." Read about it, and get accountability to change if the traits of a love addict are characteristic of you. Too many good women become addicted to men with poor character. Call it bewitchment, "cocaine," chemistry, traumatic bonding . . . but don't call it love. Love is a safe place of trust with a man who is truly your friend. There is no real love without peace. It can't be love when you don't even like the man.

Turn off the depressing music, and get a spring in your step and a new song in your heart. You picked up this book because a holy God wants to introduce you to His love. Should you dare accept it, you will have all you need to be happy on the inside right here and now, with a mansion and streets of gold in a brighter future than you've ever imagined, prepared forever for you before you were even born.

Happiness=an Honest Life

*B*ack in 2009, someone working with me in my Christian nonprofit organization, Lighting the Way Worldwide, had been asking me for months to get in touch with an author he had heard speaking on behalf of conservative values on the radio. He wanted me to ask this author for permission to use a quote from the book he had written in support of standing for truth at any cost. I got in touch with this man, who was revered by many of my Christian friends, via Facebook and sent him a private message asking permission to use an excerpt from his book in some literature I was compiling for my organization. I presumed he was a man of morals. After all, his book was all about *truth* (with that word even in its title) and standing up for what is right. He taught at a Christian college in Manhattan. We had mutual Christian friends through churches and conservative organizations, and he was lauded as a leading therapist. At the time I got in touch with him, I assumed all therapists were kind, trustworthy, empathetic people. (Boy, would I be in for a surprise!) I had done a Google search on his name to find him featured in a prominent Christian magazine as if he were Mr. Morality. He obviously had an audience of Christian sycophants stroking him with adulation for his work. He was well educated with many Ivy League degrees. He seemed like an impressive older man and was nice looking in photos on Facebook. I am thankful, at least, for the "married" status his Facebook profile revealed. At least, that much of his image was real.

From my initial email to him, this man began trying to seduce me for an affair. I would later learn this was something he had done with women many times before behind his wife's back. He immediately began sending me letters, and I immediately began to pray (something, by his own admission, he never did). I prayed for God to help me handle whatever was happening in the right way. Like a drug addict heading for a fix, without one bit of hesitation, he began his smooth pursuit. He was brazen, posting messages on my Facebook wall for everyone to see. No doubt, he enjoyed every minute of this hustle, like it was an easy game he knew he could win. I certainly had no desire to have an affair with a married man, and I was not at all comfortable with so much attention from him. At the time, I was naive enough to think of him as a great man, judging by external credentials alone. I figured he was probably in a bad marriage, and that was that. The thought of him being evil never crossed my mind. He was so nice to me, with an overwhelming slew of long emails right off the bat. He wrote over and over again telling me how beautiful I was. I found myself feeling happy receiving his emails. I knew that since he was married I had to stop this correspondence with my new *friend*. A storm was brewing in the iCloud and heading my way.

Within a day of my first Facebook message to him, which was very formal asking for the excerpt from his book, he began writing me personally telling me that I reminded him of his high school sweetheart and sending me photos of her. He explained that he wanted to introduce me to his colleagues at the Christian college to tell them about my Christian nonprofit organization. I was living in Atlanta at the time, and a week later, I was heading to New York on business previously planned. My counselor, Marilyn, said, "Don't be surprised if he asks you out while you are there." I answered, "Surely, he won't have the nerve to do that!"

Like so many times before, she was right, and I was wrong. I was getting off the plane at LaGuardia and checking my messages when an email came through from him asking to meet at the Algonquin Hotel in Manhattan that night for dinner and jazz music. Conveniently, he was going to be in town without his wife due to working the next day. He had been writing me long letters daily for a week, and I had been praying every day and night for God to help me. At the time, I am embarrassed now to admit, I still had respect for him. So, now this *friend* was inviting me to dinner, without his wife, at one of the most gorgeous and romantic hotels in the world.

His ease made me nervous. I emailed him back with a nice but forthright, "No," and also added that we should lose touch altogether. He had given me his phone number, and I purposely deleted it. I got to my small hotel room, which I had booked through Priceline in the lower part of Manhattan. Meanwhile, this brazen, high-roller-pretender was out carousing like no tomorrow. I thought, *if only he was single.* I had rightly said goodbye to this person who had made me feel understood and appreciated with a week's worth of more compliments than a world of women receive in a lifetime.

I checked into my hotel and looked out my window at the dingy area they were rebuilding where the World Trade Center used to be. My little part of the world was certainly in transition, coming along in repair from the brokenness to stand triumphantly strong again. If I had my choice, I would much rather *not* have been at such a vulnerable place of pain. But there I was. A ritzier place of happiness was simply too high a price for me to pay that night.

From everything I had ever heard about the Algonquin, that destination was completely elegant, where the elite dine. I could have arrived at one of the most pristine places in Manhattan. I could have easily had about a two hundred dollar dinner with a man who seemed so caring, smart, and rich. But it wouldn't have been worth it to me. I couldn't afford the guilt.

I headed out on the rainy, chilly evening and got a fruit bowl at a dirty deli and brought it back to my studio hotel room. The fancy Algonquin Hotel was a place where I had always wanted to go. It was enough for me that night, though, with my bowl of fruit in my little room alone with God. I knew I had pleased Him, and it felt good. Feeling a little lonely, I decided to get down on my knees to pray.

I couldn't help but cry as I asked God for strength to keep living for Him. I asked Him not to let me ever hear from this man again. I thanked God for how far I had come. All alone now, I had gotten to the point where I did not want to overeat; I did not feel the anxiety I used to feel alone, and I realized this was a gift from God. I was in my size 2 clothing without any secret weight fluctuation or need for overexercise from anxiety within, anxiety only men had been able to relieve whenever I had felt loved. I realized my abstinence had come by God's mercy. It was so much easier now for me to eat right on my own, and I didn't want anything or anyone to take away the self-confidence and peace within my heart. I realized I didn't need anything this married man had offered me, including meeting professors at his Christian college to help further my work in Christian ministry. It would not be worth the pain or guilt. As I was praying, God gave me a song. What a gift of happiness to always treasure for my heart! I wrote down the lyrics on a complimentary pad of paper in my room, as they were coming quickly with a melody:

You know where I am when the voice of a stranger comes calling me / And danger knows my name / Keep me near the cross / Keep my life hidden in You / For that's the only life that's true / When I am feeling lonely / The world mocks the road I'm walking / Be my Friend / Fight my battles let me win / One more day of an honest life / Far away from the father of lies / By God's grace full just from the taste / Of Bread that satisfies / Easy to afford so much joy inside / At peace with God as Lord / Sleeping good at night / Keeping my reward what money cannot buy / An honest life . . .

He continued to email, and I continued to pray for it to stop. It did not go on much longer. God answered that prayer in just a little over a week. One fine day I wrote him that I had done a Google search on his wife's name and found out she had a lot of money. That was all it took, and he was gone like the wind. You couldn't have given that guy a million dollars to email me after that. Well, at least not for about another six months, until he sent me an email with "Divorcing" on the subject line.

His wife had given him the boot for his adultery. There was more than enough evidence of his affairs, without her knowing about what he had tried to get going with me! Right after his separation from his wife, he began calling me in Atlanta. I kept thinking about *the great man I thought he was* in the beginning, so it was hard to let go. From just a few phone conversations, I could tell that he knew the Bible enough to twist it pretty well. He tried to convince me that Christians had fallen for a made-up story by believing in Jesus. He would lie to me over little things and then deny telling me what I knew he had told me in an attempt to gaslight me and drive me crazy. His life in rebellion from God had not produced enough income on his own to even afford rent for a Manhattan apartment, he confessed to me by phone. He was hoping to get a big financial settlement from his ex-wife in his divorce, even though he had been the one to cheat on her. As it turned out, he lost his job at the Christian college, and, even with all of his education, he had no stable income. His agnostic life of never praying to God had certainly produced an unholy man behind his unmerited respect from Christians. One day he mocked my beliefs by telling me, "If I ever did pray to Jesus I would probably call him 'Fred,'" suggesting that Jesus did not care about His name. I told my brother that story, and he said, "Dwayna, it's time to lose this guy." The good news is that God intervened and got me out of the entire mess. This sociopathic therapist, respected by so many Christians, wanted nothing else to do with me when I refused to sleep with him on my next visit to NYC. (I write more about this story in Tip #26.)

The ink on the divorce papers was not even dry when someone let me know he was engaged to another woman who was, no doubt, paying his bills. He had picked his next victim very carefully. Being the poster boy for conservative values, at least he married her after getting her pregnant.

All I could think of was, "Bless her heart," as they say in the South. I was so thankful to God that I was not Wife #3 paying his bills. She will probably end up financially supporting him forever while he *falls in love* behind her back with other women. He will enjoy the challenge of having affairs while she works because, after all, *that is his character.* Meanwhile, I have heard reputable, Christian pastors quote from his book as if they know him to be a good man. What a hey-day he must have had, all along duping the Christian crowd, overdosing on the narcissistic supply of attention they went right on giving him *for God's glory.*

If I had met him at the Algonquin that night, his wife would have obviously been the one to finance the fling he wanted with me. I was way too classy a girl to be his cheap date of the month at that expensive place. His image of being filthy rich was like an airbrushed photograph. It was all financed by his wife's money. Nothing about him was real. I was much better off in my hotel room on a lonely, dreary night, writing a song about God's love for me, in my beautiful, honest life.

HOMEWORK

Homework for this tip is to read Psalm 139 in the Bible. Let yourself dwell on this thought: *There is a God who cannot lie who loves you.*

"In the hope of eternal life, which God who cannot lie, promised" (Titus 1:2).

Hitler Was Charming, Too

I recently watched a documentary on Adolf Hitler. He was able to gain control over the people of Germany, bewitching them through deception, hiding his true agenda. It made me think of how I had a similar experience after first moving to Nashville in my teens to work as a singer.

First, I have to explain why I was there so young. I had recorded an album in Nashville at age fifteen, and the man who produced it led me to believe he was a big, influential producer, though he really was not. I moved at the tender age of seventeen, and I hit Music Row right out of high school to work on getting a record deal. To become an artist in the music industry was all I wanted for my life. When I told my English teacher in high school that I only wanted to work on getting a record deal and had no plans for college he said, "Dwayna, there ought to be a law against someone like you not going to college." I never forgot that. I'm thankful for encouraging moments like that from God to give me my true sense of belonging and worth in such a shallow world where people idolize talent, education, looks, and practically anything *except* good character. What I didn't know at age seventeen, so wild-eyed about meeting the bigwigs in Nashville, is that it would be my good character and God's mercy that would prevent me from getting the record deal. It was actually a loving act of God's protection that I never achieved fame. Back then, I was in for such a death blow to my dreams and sense of self-worth, basing who I was on my talent and accomplishments instead of on my character. Who was I apart from a record deal and making money? (Even more surprising, who would I be apart from getting married and having children?)

I was quite the whippersnapper at age nineteen, working on Music Row as a hostess at a restaurant where all of the people in the music industry came. I thought I knew so much more than I did when the most popular hit songwriter in Nashville came into the restaurant. I seated him (as I was often called "the hostess with the mostess" in personality), and he asked his waitress about me. "What is her name?" She answered, "Dwayna Litz." He quipped, "Well, you tell Dwayna that whatever she is running for, she's got my vote."

No wonder this man could write love songs to make a heart melt. No wonder he had been named *Songwriter of the Year* more than once and won numerous country music awards. This millionaire "genius" songwriter had certainly flattered an impressionable, nineteen-year-old, unknown singer who really needed such flattery more than she knew in her flat-broke-financially, broken life. As he left the restaurant, he asked for my phone number, and I was more than happy to give it to him. Maybe love had found its way to me, as one of the songs he had written promised it would.

He began calling me, and right away began telling me he loved me. He said he wanted me to be his wife. I told him that I wanted to be a virgin when I was married, and he argued they did not have marriage contracts back in biblical days. He promised that he wanted to marry me. He kept telling me to trust him and promised he would never lie about such a thing. Being a person of the night (see 1 Thessalonians 5:5-9 for a warning about people "of the night" in the Bible), he would usually call me late at night. He would explain that he was just getting out of a recording session. I found out later that he had been doing cocaine.

I would sit in my little basement apartment, which I rented for two hundred and fifty dollars a month, with old furniture I didn't like one bit, and happiness waiting in his arms for me far away from it all. I'd listen to recordings of this famous songwriter on Music Row, singing his songs and thinking of how he wanted to marry *me*. He painted such a pretty picture, as he promised to get me a record deal by the hit songs he said I would record that he planned to write for me. He called me every night to tell me he loved me. Of course, the fact we had yet to have one date did not stop me from believing it. After all, who would lie to an innocent, loving, sincere, trusting nineteen-year-old girl? He surely would not be making this up. With all of the love songs he had written, I honestly never thought this guy could be the devil coming after me to steal, kill, and destroy my soul. Without much time passing, this charming songwriter would end up being one of the meanest men I had ever known.

The phone would ring, and I would jump up to hear once again how much I was loved from the hit songwriter. He made me laugh and told me I would never have to worry about money again. He was raised in East Tennessee, in the same area of the country where my parents were raised. We seemed to have so much in common. I could hardly pray about it from so much infatuation. I felt so high from the thought of being loved by the man who wrote some of the prettiest songs about love the world has ever known. He was so seductive that his compliments seemed to transport little "no record deal me" right out of my tiny apartment into a mansion of acceptance, affirmation, marriage, and success with him.

Little did I know then that for years and years my time with him would haunt me as one of the biggest nightmares any girl could experience, and I would thank God forever for His mercy on my soul without the man. Thanks to him, I would first hear about the strange teachings of Scientology, though I never became a part of it. True to his *thetan* beliefs in Scientology (which taught him essentially that he was a god), he called other people "earthlings," while at the same time claiming that both he and I were "chosen by God," as he put it. All other people were beneath us as "earthlings." It was strange, but he kept telling me he was in love with me. The late night calls were due to him being crazy in a creative way, he elucidated. Who was I to question this prominent musical genius who wanted to marry me? Maybe it was just his creativity when it came to all of the eccentric things about him that did not make sense, as he was moving so fast in his *love* for me.

I was a girl who always made great grades in school, including an A+ in conduct every single year, so I was used to holding myself to a very high standard. When someone asked me about my morality, I would quickly tell them as a Christian, "I would *never* have sex outside of marriage." I guess it was my pride that made me think I had to be so perfect; plus, as I prayed and my family prayed for me to be a light in the midst of darkness in the music industry, I had underestimated Satan at work against me to make such a strong heritage of faith come crumbling down. Thanks to this horrific experience, I would learn what it means to be broken and realize that I could not boast like the Pharisees in ever being better than anyone else. Just because I grew up as a model Christian, traveling and singing in Baptist revival meetings, I was never saved by God to be perfect. God was teaching me in all of my perfectionism to go a little bit easier on myself. I would see my own capacity for depravity to indebt me to Jesus even more for unconditionally loving me through every single season of my life. I would appreciate Him, to a greater degree, for knowing every mistake I would ever make when He saved me at age five, still deciding to make me His own. I would find myself down on my knees crying out for Him to be everything to me and experience His supernatural ability to keep me as my faithful Shepherd, even when the lying devil comes to steal me away. Thanks to this charming songwriter, luring me with *love*, I would get to know a little better the enemy of my soul.

I used to listen to this guy's recordings and think he had the best voice on earth. I would stare at his photos on his album covers and think, *He wants to marry me. He loves me.* I'm sorry to say it, but he got what he wanted, and then he was gone. I was left alone in my little apartment with the phone never ringing, and I was crying.

Finally, after about a week, I called him and asked, "What about the other night? You said you would call but never did." And like a total stranger, he stormed at me, used language from the gutter, and let me know our night together had meant nothing to him. This was unimaginable. What happened to the songwriter with the sweet words? I had never experienced anything so dark, and no one in my whole life had ever come close to talking down to me the way he had just done. Just like a sicko, he strangely described our night together as "make-believe." It was over. He was done. He said, "Do me a favor and never ring my phone again," explaining he would deny it if I told anyone on Music Row. Getting *me* had just been some sort of conquest and "fantasy," as he called it, nothing he valued at all.

I'd given him the most precious gift I could give to any man, and this is what I got in return. My plan to be a "light in the midst of darkness"[3] as a Christian in the country music industry was not exactly working out. The darkness was bringing *strong-Christian-Dwayna* down instead and way, way down at that. The "hostess with the mostess" could not smile. My self-worth was shattered. Why had God allowed this? He could have stopped it! I stood there crying with all of my heart when this monster hung up on me. The happiness he had brought to me became a living nightmare as I tried to recover.

For the next few months I had trouble even praying, because I was mad at God for allowing this unbelievable downfall to take place. How could He have allowed this to happen to *me*? What had I ever done to deserve this? Why did He even allow the guy to come in the restaurant where I was working in the first place? Maybe there was no God after all.

My pride was on the throne of my heart, and Satan may have thought he was winning. But Jesus had purchased me with His blood, and He was never going to let me go. Satan could not have me because of Jesus. I had done nothing to deserve such undying love for my soul, but I had it all in Jesus' love for me. My Savior was not going to let me be defeated.

---

3   Matthew 5:14; 1 Peter 2:9

I could not forgive myself. God forgave me long before I could forgive myself. How could I have been so stupid? This is not what I had planned for my life. How could I have believed this terrible person had loved me? His *love* had been perverted. And, yet, God was right there all along through this heartache, truly loving me. A few months later I found myself down on my knees crying and telling God, "I am so sorry." Over and over again I would tell Him, until one day in prayer when I could literally feel Him loving me more, far more, than I loved myself. God had forgiven me all along as His child. I was the one who had to forgive myself. He was at work to help me do just that.

I would meet with this songwriter's two ex-wives about six months later for lunch to find he had physically abused them during their marriages, and he had been in rehab many times for alcoholism and cocaine. They were kind, loving women, and they assured me it was for my best that he was gone. If only he could have been the last alcoholic and cocaine addict I met on Music Row, but the hit songwriters who were addicts were a dime a dozen on Sixteenth Avenue.

No wonder that town got too small for me, with all of the bad men wanting to use me on those two one-way streets of recording studios and publishing companies known as Music Row in Nashville.[4] I am thankful for the confidence God gave me not to sleep with the married men who just came right out and told me they wanted to have an affair and would give me a record deal if I would be their girlfriend behind their wife's back. This came from prominent A&R (artist and repertoire) executives, managers, and two heads of record labels. No need to wonder why I never made it. Success in music is not just based on talent. I was a Christian. God had something better planned for me, and it was pure.

God spared me from many mistakes I could have made in Nashville and allowed me to make some I never dreamed I'd make. All along, the

---

4   16th Avenue and 17th Avenue, where the heart of the country music business was at the time

loneliness within seemed never to subside. If only I could get a record deal I would be happy, I reasoned. I would tell God, "If only I could get married and be loved by the right man, I would be happy." I used to get down on my knees in prayer through those broken years, during and in between publishing and production deals, and just cry and cry. I was so sad, and no one understood like Jesus did. My life was not going the way I thought it would, and I was not at all happy. As a Christian I seemed so different from everyone on Music Row, and I had not anticipated how much I would *not* fit in with the world when I set out for a record deal at age seventeen. The world was definitely at war with Jesus in me, and I was thankful to be a Christian, meant to live unlike the system of "making it" in Nashville required. I was often referred to on Music Row as the girl who had never been drunk and who had never done cocaine.

HOMEWORK

Homework for this tip is to watch the BBC documentary, "The Fatal Attraction of Adolf Hitler." He seduced all of Germany with his charm. People loved him and reported that they would have gladly died for Hitler. They had no idea about his plans for genocide. They thought he was their savior. It would do any woman good to watch the documentary and learn how evil works with charm. Seductive men always seem nice, but we must remember, deceivers deceive.

In future tips, I will refer more to what the Bible has to say about Satan. He seduces with flattery in his aim to destroy a person's life. I thank my merciful and loving God for always being honest and for giving me the Bible for my protection against the "spiritual forces of wickedness" and the opponent of my soul.[5] And as for my regrets, well, God has turned them all around for my good. I'm just happy no fatal attraction ever led to marriage for me.

---

5   Ephesians 6:12

"But such men are slaves, not of our Lord Jesus Christ, but of their own appetites, and by their smooth and flattering speech, they deceive the hearts of the unsuspecting" (Romans 16:18).

"His speech was as smooth as butter, but war was in his heart" (Psalm 55:21).

The lesson of this tip is never to trust someone who is *nice* before getting to know his character. Stay pure no matter what he says. Put his compliments to the test by staying in control. Keep reading, and I will teach you how to give it time before *falling in love* and giving yourself too soon.

Purity Is Your Protection

At the end of 2013 I was wrapping up a new music CD of country and pop songs I had written and recorded in New York City. I was looking for promotional marketing quotes from successful writers, as well as endorsements for the press release from producers and A&R people who used to work with me in Nashville. This led to my going out with a man for the first time in well over a decade—a songwriter who was the addiction of my life back when we first met in Nashville so long ago. It was by far the most intense relationship I had ever had. I figured it wouldn't hurt to see him just one more time again after so many years. I figured wrong.

I had met him when I was only twenty-one, and we were dating when he won a Grammy for song of the year. I was working as a singer and songwriter on Music Row, and he totally swept me off my feet. (Two years after it ended with the man I wrote about in the previous tip, I met this man who turned out to be way too much like him. Unfortunately, I was still too vulnerable when I met him to know how to rightly take care of myself.) If I had searched the whole world over, I could have never picked anyone more wrong for me from the standpoint of character. Our relationship was based on chemistry and all that we had in common with music, but it was not based on love or respect or even true friendship. He was not capable of that with any woman, because he was an alcoholic and a drug addict. I didn't know the signs of such things back then. I had never heard of personality disorders. He lied to me all of the time. It was like he could not tell the truth for even a day, but I had never known anyone more charming when he apologized. He had the power to make me feel intensely high and intensely low. I thought those embarrassing, drama-filled years on and off with him would never end. It was really like giving up a bad drug when we finally lost touch.

I know now that men who are inconsistent and dishonest addict women with their inconsistency, but I did not know that when I was only twenty-one. I became caught up in the most relentless cycle of my life with that guy. God taught me one more lesson to last a lifetime, and I never let myself take a chance on getting addicted to anyone like that again by throwing caution to the wind and giving myself too soon. The addiction kept me entangled with him much longer than I ever wanted to stay. It felt like love, the way I could not let him go, and the songs kept pouring out.

When I had moved to Nashville at age seventeen, I knew I was a singer but never dreamed I would ever write a song. It was only after I became involved with this man that many music contracts came my way due to my songwriting. The songs I wrote about him got me every single publishing and production deal I garnered in Nashville. Now, in 2013, I had re-recorded some of those songs I had written so long ago about him. I felt that since he was a Grammy winner, I would compensate myself for all the hurt I experienced with him. After so many years, I decided to call him up to ask him to give me a marketing quote for my music release. It seemed like the least he could do to make up for the pain that had inspired these songs I penned about him years ago, the same songs that would be on my new CD.

God bless the day I finally gave up on the tiring effort of trying to make that man love me in the nineties. It took years, and, believe me, they were long years. I remember he would choose being with "his buddies," as he called them, countless times over being with me. That was a good thing, because everyone in town knew he was doing cocaine with the buddies though he always denied it to me. I never did drugs, and to this day I don't know anything about blacking out from an alcohol binge. But in between writing hit songs, hangovers had become his daily existence from wild nights spent with alcohol. He didn't have a life that anyone with morals could admire. It is both sad and laughable how I honestly thought I was trying to help him get his life together. I never helped him one bit, and he only brought me down. I was someone for him and his drunken friends to mock, because the standards I was raised to have and held as true certainly did not fit with his crowd. I was not living my standards when I was with him, and it came at a very high price. Only God knew how much it hurt that I could not just leave and get over him. (I realized later that this hurt really did not have as much to do with *him* as the hurt inside my heart long before he came along, which he triggered. God was determined to heal that hurt, and how God healed it is what these tips are all about.)

In the fall of 2013, remembering this hit songwriter had always believed in my talent, I called him and asked him to endorse my songwriting and singing for my bio. He had the same phone number he had in the nineties. I still had it memorized, joking with him about how it was surely a sign I had called him way too much back in my starving artist days when he and I had been together. I remembered how my heart was truly starving back then. Time had flown, and I was at a much better place in 2013. We began reminiscing. He told me he had changed, no longer touched drugs, and his drinking days were far behind him. (A mutual friend of ours also confirmed that was true.) I respected him all over again as a talented songwriter. He added, "I never married in all of these years, and I never forgot about you." Then, out of the blue, he let me in on a secret. I was speaking with him by phone at his home in Nashville from my apartment in NYC, casually catching up, when he said, "I always loved you."

I began to cry right there on the spot. I had not anticipated the call affecting me so much emotionally. I was stunned. I paused as I wiped away a tear and said, "You never told me that back then."

He said, "I always loved you from the first time I saw you."

Well, I sat there holding the phone and crying like a baby. I had only called for a marketing quote, but all of a sudden I was twenty-one again on Music Row with him back in the nineties. He told me he had recently been inducted into the Songwriter's Hall of Fame. It felt special catching up with him and hearing about his life, because, after all, he had *loved* me all along.

We decided to meet for dinner for old time's sake in Nashville. He took me out to a beautiful place in October 2013 when I was in town for a photo shoot. At the end of the date we kissed, and it was just like no time had passed. It was perfect. He called me the best kisser in the world, and I had to pause from kissing him to cry. It felt like something very real and deep was going on. What had happened?

Kissing him messed me up. It got me too much attached. We had gone back to his place after our dinner, which was the same place he had lived years ago when we were together. He tried to say everything in the world to get me to go upstairs and go to bed with him. He kept saying, "I love you." I said it back. It was like it used to be, but so much better—including the fact that I had become a little wiser through the years. It was our first date all over again; but this time around, in the heat of the moment, the ruling thought in the forefront of my mind was *Put God first*. It was as if God had given me a do-over, and this time I was going to get it right.

I paused, looked at him, and smiled. He said, "I would do anything for you. I love you," as he was urging me to go upstairs. I replied, "I'm not free." He kept insisting, and I explained further, "I'm a Christian." He agreed that it was not right to go to bed casually, and he even said he was a Christian, too. He argued, "We don't have to have sex. Let's just go upstairs to the bedroom to kiss." I reiterated, "I know my worth. I'm worth way too much for a fling. You cannot have me for free." Remembering vividly how he had gotten me addicted at age twenty-one, I motioned from my head down to my toes as I repeated once again with a smile, "I'm not free." I knew my strength, and it felt good. I was putting God first. I was going to leave the results up to God by doing it His way. I chose in that moment to take God at His Word in the Bible for the true definition of love and not settle for less. And I left his place without going upstairs. The last word he said to me that night was, "Forever." When I got back to my hotel room, I couldn't sleep just thinking about him.

One little detail I should not leave out is that the phone kept ringing off the hook as we were in his home. He explained it was a woman he had been dating who did not mean anything to him. He called her "crazy." He lived on a public street and suggested she could have easily been parked outside close enough to see us come in together. She must have phoned fifty times compulsively while I was there, as he kept letting it go to voice mail. This led to what became the scariest time of my life, because after that one date with him, she began harassing me.

He told her about me the next day, and she started emailing me via my public Facebook fan page, from which I could not block her. She even got my number off his phone the next day and called me! I never once responded to her in any way and blocked her number from my phone. She wrote copious, mean messages with threats like, "You had better never show your face in this town again." I would start shaking from fear reading the Facebook messages from her. They kept coming, usually several per day. Even though I had only been out with him once, she was threatened by the possibility of him having a serious relationship with me.

I was back in New York City, and this man was calling me from Nashville nightly. He swore he had told her goodbye, and he kept telling me she was "nuts" and not to let her come between us. I replied, "A relationship with you is not worth getting killed over!" He obviously had no love or respect for her in the way he spoke about her. He explained that he pitied her and was afraid she would commit suicide without him.

She had never met me or spoken to me, yet she wrote vile things about me in her messages directly to me day and night via Facebook.

Every time I would get another message, my stomach would tighten, gripped by fear. I contacted Facebook about it. On Thanksgiving 2013 (about a month after the date I had had with him in Nashville), I was so scared I could not eat a bite. A friend in NYC told me to go to the police. I went to the NYPD, and they immediately said, "We are going to arrest her." I said, "She does not live here. She lives in Nashville." I explained that she worked for a major airline company, and I was afraid she would fly up to NYC to hurt me. It was by far the most frightening thing I have ever experienced.

The New York detective began calling her, and it would be over a week before she finally called the NYPD detective back. Keep in mind, this man in Nashville—the one who *loved* me—had been calling me assuring me that his relationship with her was over. He said he also planned to report her to the Nashville police for her harassment toward him. You cannot imagine my shock when one night the NYPD detective called and said, "Well, she finally called me back."

I asked in urgency, "Really? What happened?"

He said, "You are not going to believe this. When she called me, she was with him."

The NYPD detective explained that she even handed him the phone to prove they were together. All along, he had been playing both of us. The detective also said that he denied having a relationship with me to the detective when this "former girlfriend" handed him the phone. When I learned this, I realized he was worse off than she was. The two crazy people were certainly compatible. I felt like a fool all over again. The detective let her know that if she ever wrote me again, she was going to jail for harassment. So much for the man who *loved* me. I called him after getting off the phone with the detective.

He said, "Hello," and I said, "You can have her. You all deserve each other."

He asked, "What do you mean?"

I said crying (with the drama stepping up just like it had years ago with him), "I just got off the phone with the detective. He said when she called him back, she was with you!"

He said, "I screwed up."

I fired back, "You sure did. I'm blocking your number from my phone. We're done," and added, "You'll never have anyone like me again."

He said, "I hope you get over this before I do." Before I hung up from the conversation, his last words to me were, "I love you."

I hung up crying and stopped to pray to thank God for protecting me. This guy had not changed a bit and was still just as dishonest as he was when I had been with him years ago. Our long distance relationship lasted only a little over a month since our dinner date in Nashville. I had to thank God for the pure standard He has for my life. The Bible says the Lord is my Shepherd. Sheep are dumb animals, and I sure did feel dumb after speaking with the NYPD detective. This *love of my life* had even been discussing the possibility of marriage with me. I couldn't believe I was stupid enough to fall for him all over again. I wept tears of thanksgiving for God's protection, snapping out of the time warp in my apartment in NYC in 2013, thankful the nineties were far behind me.

The next morning I blocked his number from my phone and never heard from either him or the woman again. I mailed him copies of the police reports I had filed with both the NYPD and the Nashville Police to show I would take more action if I ever heard from that woman again. I also enclosed a letter to let him know I would not be using his endorsement to promote my new CD. I didn't want or need anything from him, including the marketing quote.

In that last phone call, as I was crying, I reminded him there was one bright side to it all. I said, "Well, there is one good thing about this. You didn't get to use me. It makes me feel good to say that. You couldn't get me to go to bed with you after our date, no matter how you tried. I was worth too much for that."

HOMEWORK

Homework for this tip is to look up the word *purity* in a dictionary. Contrast that definition by doing a Google search on *sexual addiction* to learn more about it. Women who are confident enough to say, "No," are women who know their worth. Every time you choose a pure life over sin, the better you will feel about yourself, even if the man leaves you because of it. If he leaves you because you do not go to bed with him, it will be for your protection. When the relationship ends before he proves his love by marrying you, you will have the joy of knowing you were not used. When a man does not get to have you for free, he will never forget you as a woman who is unlike all the others.

Learn the Definition
of a Psychopath

A psychopath is not just some scary looking boogeyman who kills people. A psychopath is, by definition, a person who truly enjoys playing mind games and psychologically abusing others through intellectual domination and passive-aggressive scheming. He knows how to read people well enough to mirror them and tell them what he knows they want to hear. Psychopaths are so coldhearted that they have been described as the walking dead.

I used to think a "personality disorder" was psychobabble. Now, after some scary encounters with these charismatic shysters, I have certainly changed my mind. I can attest firsthand that some people are *not all there*; they don't *get it* and never will. They are, in fact, mentally off. Romans 9:22 certainly warns about such bad "vessels" in the Bible, assuring us that God's wrath is on them. Though darkness will never conquer the light, it does not stop these types from trying. It is a shame they are able to roam freely in this world, often viewed as successful when what they accomplish most successfully is committing crimes of the heart. It is as if they are incapable of even being honest with themselves, much less with God or others. Thankfully, television is profiling psychopaths more to warn the public to be less trusting, exposing them often as well educated with status and upstanding reputations in their community. But look a little closer . . .

Psychopaths go overboard when they are being *nice* to you, and then they swing in a negative direction, going overboard to be mean to you. Nothing is totally sane about them. Yet they will enjoy the challenge of trying to convince you otherwise. Psychopaths and sociopaths are virtually the same in character and operation to the extent that many therapists exchange the terms when describing them.

You may be thinking, *It is too much negativity for me to research psychopaths.* My answer would be that it is better to research them than experience the negativity firsthand! Let me tell you what I mean based on my own experiences. With tales like these stranger than fiction, I have certainly paid my dues for the happiness I have today.

In 2006, a Christian girlfriend set me up with a pastor in California. She told me he had made millions of dollars independently as a doctor and sent me photos of his mansion in Beverly Hills. A *pastor* like this was hard to find (thank God). He had begun a Baptist church, she explained. He called me, and after one conversation, he told my Christian girlfriend, "I don't know whether I'll be walking down the aisle with Dwayna or best friends with her forever." (An excellent counselor and friend, Dr. Sherie Zander, pointed out to me later that that comment alone was a sign of a psychopath. A normal guy would have never said that after just one conversation with me.) The next morning, I did a Google search on his name and found he had been reported for fraud. Women had accused him of conning them out of their money. His *church* was also mentioned in the "Rip Off Report."

The next day he called, and I simply said, "I think God wants me all to Himself right now." He replied, "Got it." He knew I was on to him. I wished him well, truly afraid of his unstable personality, and felt it best to handle things with the least amount of drama possible. I was too afraid to tell him the truth about my Google search. My friend, who had initially set us up, waited for some time to pass for my safety and then called him in my defense to ream him out. "Have you ever Googled yourself?" she asked, challenging him with the reports online. Of course, he said the accusations were false. My friend never heard from him again. Liars leave when they realize they can no longer con people. I ended up reporting the name of his church to the board overseeing Baptist churches in California, alerting them to the fact that this *pastor* had a very bad reputation online for fraud and should not be a Baptist pastor.

In 2008 I was living in New York City when a so-called Christian man working overseas got in touch with me about the possibility of expanding my nonprofit work to Israel. My relationship with him quickly shifted from business to personal as we began emailing. He said he had known me for a few years via my organization's newsletters. He explained how mutual friends had referred him to my work, and he had enjoyed keeping up with it online. He would respond to the e-newsletters from time to time saying he was praying for me and planned to give financially. He said he was on a job assignment in Asia. It came as a shock the day he emailed offering to pay my way to meet him in person in Israel!

Anticipating that I would meet *the one for me* on any given day anywhere in the world, he actually seemed like a viable possibility. His work sounded impressive. What if he was *the one?* I couldn't let the continents come between us. After all, I had been conditioned as a Christian woman to believe God has someone for all of us (although that is not in the Bible). Maybe this guy working on assignment in Afghanistan was the one in a million for me. My mother agreed to go with me if I decided to take him up on the offer. Feeling adventuresome, I agreed, and he paid for my plane ticket and for my hotel stay for ten days in Israel. My mother went with me on the trip, and we had a nice stay in the room he financed. Unfortunately, in my anticipation to meet him in person, I assumed too soon that he was normal.

Walking hand in hand on the streets of Jerusalem, it felt like I had found a friend. He was very handsome. We made a good-looking couple, but it would be confirmed over time that we were no match on the inside. One day he prayed for me in the presence of my mother before a meal, "God, thank you for Dwayna and for whatever You are doing here.

Help us as we move toward marriage." He told me he loved me after only ten days. He was so smooth that even my mother fell for it, though he was unpredictably aloof toward us both at times, not at all acting like a man wanting to marry me. Neither of us imagined when he had initially offered to pay for my trip to Israel that he was not all there mentally. His inconsistency would vex me at moments. That is what he wanted all along. Pathological personalities are abusive. It was contradictory, because he kept talking about a future with me, yet he would be cold toward me for no apparent reason when I least expected it. I knew something was not right. It was a continuous struggle to understand what was going on. I spent most of my time trying to weave together the truth, determined to be smart enough to crack the case of figuring him out. I felt like a detective trying to piece the facts together to make sense of it all. Every time I was sure I had caught him in a lie, he would convince me I had misunderstood. The challenge of understanding what he had up his sleeve was enough to keep me in communication with him for six whole months, and that was six months too long in hindsight.

He was an amazing deceiver. Boy, that guy could really lie. His psychopathy was masked in "getting to know me" and "falling in love." As my dad asked when it was over, "What kind of guy would fly a girl over to the other side of the world on a first date?" If I had only known more about psychopathy it would have made better sense to me from the get-go. He managed to fly to Tennessee to meet my family before our relationship ended. It was a funny moment when he met my dad in Tennessee, and my dad said, "We love to work! We really love it and don't even take time off for holidays. We are successful, because we work, work, work over twelve hour days all the time. Don't you love to work hard?" I can still remember the look on his face. Surely, he knew his little charade was coming to an end. It became apparent he wanted in on my family's business. He felt he deserved money and power without working for it, just like the psycho that he was.

I remember telling my hairstylist in Manhattan about it, and she warned, "He's just like my ex-husband. You will be confused as long as you are with him from all of his contradictions. He deserves someone just like himself, not someone like you." She was the first person I knew to call him a psychopath. (She also went on to tell me she had become happy on her own after her divorce, adding, "You don't need a man," as she encouraged me to become happy on my own, too. Even though I was not at that point yet, I never forgot her advice.)

Before I met him face to face in Israel, he had supposedly emailed Prime Minister Benjamin Netanyahu, blind copying me on the email, asking him to meet with us while we were in Israel, as if he was some big shot who was friends with the prime minister. It was really impressive at the time, sitting in my room in Manhattan reading the email from him to Netanyahu. This joker pursuing me said he worked for the State Department. He told me he was "on assignment" in Afghanistan. I would later find he was simply a civilian police officer who had taken a job in Afghanistan in a mercenary, global police program *funded by* the State Department. (This is the type of job many sociopaths/psychopaths enjoy because it is so high in danger; these people find a normal, responsible life to be boring.) Kudos to me for my detective work when I decided to do a background check on this guy's history. When I confronted him with what I had found, he casually said it was true, as if he had never led me to believe otherwise. He went on to admit that he had been fired from his job as a police officer in Florida due to his alcoholism. He basically took the job in Afghanistan to get away from responsible living in the states. He was also in quite a bit of financial debt. He had exaggerated the truth about his job and lied about practically everything. He spent his life in disguise, pretending to be someone he wasn't. And, in case you are wondering, he never introduced me to Benjamin Netanyahu!

At last, all of the embellishments came to an end, and the truth was revealed. He was an alcoholic, addicted to antidepressants and pornography. When the time came for us to part, he headed back to his sociopathic police job in Afghanistan with his drinking, drugs, and

Christian Internet dating site. He explained he had been on the dating site until he met me in person. I decided to do one last little bit of detective work. Without joining, I checked out his Christian dating site the very next day after we said goodbye. Looking through the profiles of the men, there he was. I saw that he posted the very photos I had taken of him in Israel on his little profile for the next victim looking for love with a Christian man. Back in NYC, I was left reading *The Sociopath Next Door*. It was such a relief to know that he was far away in Afghanistan. I was worn out from the battle. I had dodged a bullet with him in Israel, Manhattan, and Tennessee.

HOMEWORK

Homework for this tip is simple: Google the word *psychopath*. Go ahead and look up *sociopath*, too. They are one and the same in character. Do yourself a favor and learn how they operate by reading books on the subject of psychopathy in our culture today. Read *The Sociopath Next Door* by Martha Stout and *Snakes in Suits* by Paul Baibiak and Robert D. Hare. If you want to guard your happiness as a single woman, it is crucial to know the signs of a psychopath.

Take Care of Yourself, Not His Feelings

An overly sensitive man is a boy who has never grown up. When you are not happy with something a good man has or has not done, guess what? He will actually put in the effort it takes to make you feel better. The difference between a nice man who makes mistakes every now and then and a full blown jerk is simple. A nice guy cares when he hurts your feelings. A jerk does not care one bit when he has hurt your feelings. If he apologizes, it will only be to manipulate you because of something he wants you to do for him (like keep a certain date in the future in order to make him look good, or go to bed with him). In contrast, a good man really cares about you. Making you happy makes him happy. A bad man wants it the other way around. He wants you to work to make him happy all the time.

Women who date intelligently will chase such a *little boy* away more than likely. He will be too immature for taking it slowly in the beginning and getting to know you respectfully. He will find your confidence in knowing how to take care of yourself too intimidating. A real man wants to take care of a woman; whereas, a man who has never grown up wants a woman to take care of him, and this includes emotionally.

I hired a video producer back in 2011, before I knew him personally, after a mutual friend recommended him. It would have saved me a lot of headaches if I had heeded a glaring red flag in the beginning—his excessive charm. After I hired him, it didn't take much time before Prince Charming became cranky and almost too difficult to even work with me on the video project. He was way too thin-skinned artistically. After he sent me the files he had filmed for the shoot, I let him know as nicely as I could that I was not satisfied with most of it. I was challenged to word it in a way that would prevent him from getting so defensive. I could not even tell him respectfully that I did not like something he had done creatively on the video without it hurting his feelings to an abnormal degree. He would text me repeatedly, "You have hurt my feelings. I can't talk to you, because you have hurt my feelings." It was only over work, nothing personal! We finished the project by text and email, because he kept repeating that his "feelings" were too hurt to speak by phone with me about the very project I had hired him to do. My goodness, I thought to myself, *how childish!* I felt sorry for his fiancée. (He admitted that her mother did not like him, and I could understand why.) I was happy to finally get the video files from him, for what they were worth. I kept my word and paid him our agreed upon price, though I was disappointed in the videos overall. My satisfaction had not been guaranteed, because this man was not emotionally whole enough to offer that to me.

When a guy wants you to make him feel good all the time, and you sense yourself walking on eggshells trying to keep from hurting his feelings, this is not a real man. When he cares more about his feelings than yours, you will never be able to love him enough. Do yourself a favor, and say goodbye. He is too immature to make even himself happy over time. What you want is a guy who is sensitive in the right way, with good character, which includes empathy for you when you are hurt. I have seen good men sincerely shed a tear when they pray or when a tender moment touches them. Of course, this is endearing as a trait to be cherished in any man. As an artist working in music circles, I have known wonderful men (true to their wives) who are creative and still mature enough as individuals to handle emotions responsibly. To the contrary, I have to laugh a little when I think of the "therapist" I described in Tip #2.

He would often use the line, "I have tears in my eyes." It was an act, because there were never any tears in his eyes. At first I believed him, but then I had to wonder if he actually thought I was stupid enough to keep falling for this. He once said, "You're very smart, Dwayna," and I thought to myself, *Yes, and that is why all of your contradictions keep me confused! At least I have enough sense to know I cannot trust you.* He kept trying to blame his contradictions on me and how I was simply misunderstanding him. Butter could melt in his mouth when he spoke about love, with all of his flowery language and fake tears. But at the same time, he never acknowledged it was his raw lack of self-control emotionally that made him so quick tempered. That, plus the fact he admitted he had been diagnosed as bipolar, but that's another story!

Sadly, we all have to put on a therapist hat when getting to know men in today's world. It behooves us to pray and stay close to the God "who knows all men" as we need His insight in discerning the difference between the authentic and the counterfeit.[6] If only we could read each other's minds, but we cannot. The number one problem between men and women is communication, and good communication requires confidence. When it comes to communication, ignorance is not bliss. Telling someone the truth is often more respectful to the other person, as well as to yourself.

We have to learn how to communicate respectfully and hold someone we love to that same standard. I learned through counseling that when a man loses his temper, he is overcome momentarily by fear. He feels totally out of control about a situation, and it scares him. Such fear comes out as anger. Learning how to responsibly handle the emotion of fear is part of growing up. It is all about learning how to turn things over to God in life, including our own shortcomings, instead of just hauling

6   See John 2:24.

off and letting another person have it. Anger in and of itself is not wrong when it is justified out of righteous intent and not stemming from an overflow of fear or pride. In contrast, a man who throws temper tantrums on a regular basis is just plain overly emotional. Don't make his happiness your responsibility.

Measure your personal relationships by how men make you feel, and don't let them turn it around. Be the girl; meaning, let him work to make you happy as any real man will. Show him respect for making you feel good. Tell him how he makes you feel. Don't worry so much about *his* feelings. Unless you are asking him to commit a crime or to go against his conscience before God, any real man will enjoy making you feel good and giving you whatever you want. Set the standard by being true to yourself, and let that standard determine whether or not your relationship with him is healthy. It is all about how he makes you feel, not the other way around.

HOMEWORK

Homework for this tip is to practice communication skills. If you are in a relationship that is not going very well, here is an easy tip to alert him that a goodbye may be coming. Just say, "I don't like how you make me feel." It is more powerful than a long rant, which he is probably expecting from you when you are upset, since women are emotional by nature. Even if he is abusive and gets a kick out of hurting you, he will get the message when you calmly state this and let him think about it. If he keeps hurting you, keep saying it over and over again until you have the confidence to leave.

If you have a good man, remind him often, "I love how you make you feel."

Give Yourself
90 Days to Detox

Women can become addicted to men very easily due to a hormone released in a woman's brain called oxytocin. This is scientifically proven. A woman cannot concentrate clearly when this hormone possesses her. Make no mistake; it will do just that to an overwhelming degree in all of its splendor when she is truly in love and in all of its rage when she is not. She has trouble thinking objectively about the man to whom she is chemically bonded, due to the oxytocin at work in her brain to draw her to him. It is much like any other chemical addiction.

There is a reason why treatment centers keep addicts for at least ninety days to detox from drugs and alcohol. You will need at least a ninety-day detox from a wrong man. These tearful, miserable, long days filled with distracted thoughts about Mr. Wrong are reason enough to guard yourself and stop *falling in love* head over heels with guys too soon. As for any *liberated* woman in our neurotic society who believes she can have sex with no strings attached, this hormone makes it impossible for that to be true. Oxytocin has the power to enslave you. Due to oxytocin, a woman cannot even kiss with no strings attached when there is chemistry. If we learn how to be happy on our own and keep our head on our shoulders when dating, the best reward is that we won't have to deal with this wild hormone that intensely and shamefully addicts us to the wrong men. The detox period can be worse than the jerk himself!

Oxytocin is a gift when it bonds us to someone worthy of a strong tie. It is a "here comes the bride" kind of hormone that bonds a wife to her husband for better or for worse. Oxytocin can be a bull in a china shop outside of true love, though. It can keep us bonded to a man we don't even like, so respect the oxytocin! You must fear it for all it is worth in your happy life. Oxytocin can certainly make you confused, distracted, high as a kite on lust, and lower than you have ever been when a relationship ends. Oxytocin was never designed for goodbyes.

Follow my advice to give yourself time for that hormone to leave your body after a breakup. Keep in mind, the more toxic the relationship, the more time you will need to detox from it. If you want to leave even a good man, who you know is simply not right for you to marry, you must also give yourself at least ninety days to get him out of your system chemically in order to get on with your life. At the end of any relationship, the oxytocin is still working in your body to keep you hormonally attached to him, and it takes a minimum of ninety days for it to leave your body chemistry.

When he asks you to stay in touch *as friends*, you must not allow yourself to do that, because: a) You are not compatible enough to be friends in the first place if it was a toxic relationship and he has bad character, and b) You have to have ninety days away from him to think clearly and get back into your own life again. These long ninety days are not a death sentence. With every day that passes, the hormone is leaving your body, giving you the freedom to work through the rest of these tips and experience your life at its best as a classy woman instead of some controlling maniac, high on the pixie dust of oxytocin.

Most of the time it is the men who can thank themselves for making us controlling and possessive, because that is what they get when they want to kiss us too soon, lie to us with excessive charm, and go to bed with us casually. The jerks like it when the oxytocin is at work to make us mistake an average man for greatness. It is magically deceptive. Oxytocin comes with an intense bonding component that men often blame women for having too soon, as if it is our choice. God made women to bond to men through this hormone. Don't give the jerks the honor of being bonded to them. Have the confidence to keep yourself at a chemical distance until a man has time to prove himself.

This book is about *being able* to wait on love. For most women, if we stay emotionally away, we will stay physically away, too, and be able to stay psychologically sober *without kissing* while getting to know the guy. It is your personality, smile, intelligence, and character that a real man will love. You want to be a woman set apart, not just the next one for the next player. See yourself as way too good for a man who meets you and has this sleazy question on the forefront of his mind: *How good is she in bed?* You want a man who instead sees you and thinks, *What a beautiful, sweet, and intelligent woman! I would like to get to know her better.* You have to know that you are worthy of love as a human being; not because you are "putting out," as they used to say when I was in high school, when loose living was not *en vogue* like it is today. To be happy is to know you are worth more than sex. You don't want a man who is incapable of getting to know you platonically. As you are detoxing from oxytocin, take it as an opportunity to learn how to better guard yourself from it next time around.

Here is how you detox: you must not see him, touch him, taste him, smell him, or hear him for at least ninety days. It is just that simple. You are withdrawing from an addiction, and you have to get over the guy in order to move on. To do that, you must become intellectually and emotionally sober. Make your emotional sobriety your number one priority, and God will reward you with more happiness than this man could offer by keeping you *drugged* if you will just give it time. You cannot be the woman God created you to be as long as you are addicted. You cannot be compatible for a healthy man unless you learn *how* to unhook yourself from the unhealthy ones. If you are thinking that good sex will keep a man, please stop to think about yourself, because, more than likely, you will be the one staying longer than you want to stay.

If you are addicted to a bad man, the addiction itself is bringing *you* down, not just him. We have to assume responsibility for the fact that we all reap what we sow in life. We are where we are today based on decisions we made yesterday, and our decisions today will determine where we will be tomorrow. This is especially true when it comes to men. Every time I have left a guy whom I knew I had to leave, I got myself the support I needed and counted the long days and nights with no emails or phone calls or text messages from him. Then I rewarded myself when the ninety days of absolutely zero contact ended. I never got myself to the point of being free by remaining *friends* with him and staying in touch, which is what they all want. Think of the example of Nicole Brown Simpson. The oxytocin traumatically bonded her to O. J. Simpson, and she was so addicted that she could not let go. The co-dependent cycle killed her.[7]

I want to make sure I make myself clear here. You cannot stay in touch with him as friends if you wish to detox. If you have photos of him, don't look at them. If there are images of him you will be tempted to view on any social networking site, disconnect from his profile. Block him, if necessary. Make your freedom from addiction your number one priority, and don't worry about his feelings. After all, this is your addiction, not his, and this is your life we are talking about and your future. Don't see him at all for any reason for this detox period. It will be very, very hard, so tell yourself you can see him if you wish after the detox period is over. (If you see him within the ninety days, the cycle will have to start all over again.) This self-talk will help, because you will be missing *him* so intensely. More than likely, it will be the chemistry that you are missing, not him. The truth is, if he has bad character, you will not want to be around his toxicity after you fully detox. You'll be too healthy for him.

7   "The O. J. Simpson Tapes—7 Shocking Things He Said in Rarely Seen Deposition Tapes," ABC News, Sept. 25, 2015, http://abcnews.go.com/US/oj-simpson -tapes-shocking-things-rarely-deposition-tapes/story?id=33924968

You cannot hear his voice for any reason for ninety days, or it will trigger the oxytocin. If he does not agree to stop calling, you must block his number. Stop counting on him to consider what is best for you. Assume responsibility. Keep in mind he probably wants to keep you addicted, so you will never get over him. Of course, if you are not seeing him, you won't smell, touch or taste him. The oxytocin is released through the senses, so you must cut it off cold turkey altogether for at least ninety days.

Many women get extremely attached to men via the Internet and don't even need a kiss for the oxytocin to have them wirelessly high as a kite. Be smarter than that. When you sense that you are beginning to *like* someone you don't know and have never met in person on Facebook or any other social networking site, stop yourself. Say a prayer, trusting that if God wants you to have a real relationship with this man, the man will jump in his car or hop on a plane and come to you for you to know him in the real world. Don't allow yourself to even be impressed with men online. They post photos that are not recent and often pretend to have a totally different personality than they actually have. They even lie about their marital status, education, and work history. For goodness sake, don't get a chemical addiction going digitally by staring at photos online that are probably years old or not even his.

Get accountability during this ninety-day period. When good memories come (and they will 24/7), take out a pad and write down all the things you don't like about him, things that prove he has bad character. Write down all the times he has hurt you, and read the list to yourself daily. It will help your thinking during your detox and remind you why you must stay away. In truth, you are not *falling out of love* when you feel so much pain through this detox period. It is just the oxytocin leaving your system. Remember, the pain you feel without him is a merciful door to the rest of your life compared to still being with him. The pain is what we all get for *falling* for a man not worthy of our love. True love will not hurt us; deception will. We have to get smarter.

Let at least three months pass to literally get the guy out of your system, and then take a closer look at a photo of the man you once thought was so handsome, who turned out to be so bad for you. The same photos of a jerk I wanted to stare at all day in oxytocin-dreamland don't even look good to me now. What was I thinking? He was not deserving of the pain he put me through, but I thought at the time he was the most handsome man on earth. Good ol' oxytocin was alive and well, reminding me that I am the healthy woman God made me to be, able to bond to a toad, due to this hormone.

Homework

Homework for this tip is to Google *oxytocin*. Study it, and understand its power. The unparalleled use you have for oxytocin is *when you want to be* bonded like crazy to a man, in love with him forever. The only way you will be able to get past the excruciating pain of letting go is if you give yourself at least ninety days to detox. If you have recently said goodbye and are reading this without tears coming down your face, you must have made it through. For a happier life ahead, let's add to the homework putting into practice Tip #16 on your next date. If you do not think you can date without kissing, trust me, there is more confidence waiting to be yours if only you will take it.

Count Your Blessings

When things don't go my way and I feel frustrated in life, all I need to do for everything to get better is to stop and thank God for all He has done for me. As I praise Him, I can feel my heart soften through any disappointment. Getting *my way* does not matter compared to His, because His way is perfect. He is God, and I exist to do His will; He does not exist to do mine. The Bible teaches that God prunes His own to make us stronger.[8] Why do we complain as if we should be entitled to some fairy-tale life when so many others have it worse than we could ever imagine? God is perfect. But my well-meaning strategies, justifications, and myopic dreams are flawed. When I do not get my way, as I live in obedience to Him, He has something better in store. But I will only experience that *something better* if I surrender and stop fighting against it. A strange thing happens when we finally surrender to God. He makes us happy.

God loves me enough to *not* always let me have what I want. As I trust Him, He changes the desires of my heart to delight in His desire for me. He knows me better than I even know myself, because He made me. When I stop to count my blessings, the list is so long that counting my blessings changes me. I can't focus on what I don't have when I am focusing on what I do have, and I have so much! There is no fear in

---

8   John 15:2

surrender, because being wherever God wants me to be, even if it means going through a struggle, is right where I want to be. This is because the God of the Bible has moral character I can trust. He cannot lie,[9] and He loves me as His own more than I could ever love myself.

It is impossible to feel self-pity and be praising God at the same time. God is a perfect heavenly Father to me as His child. He has been good to me, and this includes every time He has not given me my way. He loves me enough to protect me from something I want when it is not best for me. I have experienced this many times when I have prayed about men, asking God to make a relationship last when it was better for me to let it end. One thing He has proven—He is just as faithful and just as good when I don't get my way.

When I was twenty-six years old and living in NYC, I came home to my tiny apartment to find it was flooded. My water heater had burst. The rug was soaked, and everything was musty. I was singing three nights a week around town, and I did not have the time or the money to get rid of the mildew all over my furniture. I was relieved to realize afresh that God, knowing I am allergic to mold and how it would affect my voice, was still just as much in control. It was one of those times when we get tested as Christians. The test is sometimes more about our attitude than anything else.

I had been offered a lead in an off-Broadway musical previously that year, but I had turned it down. I knew the role would have hurt the Lord. It was literally about mocking Christians. Next I had been almost guaranteed the lead in a hit Broadway musical, which was again a mockery of what the Bible teaches. I did not want to act in roles that were dark to me as a Christian, because I knew becoming the character would have demanded all of my time and would have had a big effect on the person I am (for real). If these were tests about whether or not I would remain true to my convictions, I had been winning so far. It was

---

9   Titus 1:2

not easy financially, though, doing the right thing and turning down roles. The entertainment business was feeling more and more like one big testing ground for me as a Christian from my experiences in both Nashville and NYC. It just seemed like every opportunity had immoral strings attached in one way or another. I had been thanking God for the gigs I did have in Manhattan, and for how well they were going, and for how He was taking care of me daily on such a tight budget. But the evening I came home to the water spill in my Midtown apartment felt like a more challenging test. My first reaction was just to let it all out in a panic because of my severe allergy to mold and how it would affect my ability to sing. The question came to my mind, *Are you still going to praise the Lord now?*

I recall looking out a window over the city that night and making the decision to do that very thing. In spite of the sadness of the moment, I whispered a prayer of thanksgiving for all Jesus had done for me instead of complaining. I told Him that I knew He knew about the water heater and had a solution, but I just wanted to take time to thank Him for being so good in the midst of my turmoil. I started softly singing a praise song as I stood there at the end of the hall looking out over the city on a dreary night alone. There I was, broke, with a flooded apartment, thanking God for His faithfulness in my life. Tears of happiness, peace, and thanksgiving rolled down my cheeks, because I could feel His love for me right there in the midst of it all. God provided a good friend who had me stay with her while my apartment was being cleaned. It wouldn't have accomplished anything for me to get angry or upset, but it certainly did help me be content when I stopped to praise the Lord. It was a lesson He was beginning to teach me, as I had been wound too tightly on the inside and a little too easily frustrated in the past. I was offering up a sacrifice of praise, and He was blessing me for it.

In 2012 I sang at a private fashion event in Manhattan, and it did not go the way we had planned. It went God's way. He helped me sing my best, and everyone had a great time. The "important" people we had invited did not show, and my Christian friends from my church came to fill the room, for the most part. The next day I awoke disappointed that the people invited from *Vogue* and *Vanity Fair* did not come. Immediately, I could tell that I needed an attitude adjustment. I was not in a spirit of praise. I recognized once again that my heart is only right before God when I can thank Him for whatever comes (or does not come) my way.

I called a Christian friend who had attended the event to pray over the phone with me. She said, "Dwayna, you have a gift. I could feel God's spirit as you sang, though you were not even singing Christian songs. Maybe someone there needed to know about the love of Jesus." We prayed together, and I could honestly thank God that the event went the way it did. I realized the people who came were very important people to God, and they were more important to me than strangers at *Vogue* magazine. As I prayed, I was grateful to God for every single person who came and told God I was sorry for not having my mind more on His work in the hearts of people through the music I sang. My becoming more known in the world OR My recognition is, of course, meaningless in comparison. I said to God in prayer, "I don't know what I was expecting. I thank You for helping me sing my best and letting people sense Your love as I sang. What more could I want?" And, yes, before long, tears of joy filled my eyes, just thanking Him for everything. As I stopped to thank Him, He made me feel good. As I praised the Lord, He affirmed me by His precious Holy Spirit in my heart. And feeling His pleasure over me and His affirmation was enough. I couldn't be sad praising the Lord.

When days are difficult, the best we can do is stop and praise God in this fallen world. He lifts us up through our praise, and we get the victory when we would otherwise be defeated. We can remain happy and calm and not let any disappointment rob us of our joy in Him when we choose to thank Him instead of getting frustrated. He is sovereign over everything, even our disappointments, mistakes, and hurts. He is at work to accomplish something good, and we can always be grateful to Him for that. It is a blessing alone just to belong to God in a world that rejects Him. Even the mere desire to live for Him is a blessing (and certainly worth more than any man). At least you can be thankful that you are at the place in your life even to read this book. Instead of seeing the glass as half empty, see it as half full.

If you are a woman who is easily irritated, try this little assignment. Take one day and write down every single thing you can remember complaining about from morning until sundown. Do the same thing the next day. Ask God to help you break the habit of negativity. Does your life seem to always go wrong? It will turn around if you stop to count your blessings. Complaining all of the time certainly won't bring you or anyone around you happiness. Every day of your life is a gift from God for you to *live*. How would you feel if you gave someone an immeasurable gift, and all they did was grumble about it? Take your eyes off yourself and put them on others who have so much less, and you will be grateful.

When you pray, don't just bring a long list of all that you are asking God to do for you. Sing praise songs to Him when things go wrong. When we live for Jesus, we do not have to worry about things going wrong, because He has us right where we belong. He has something better than our plans when things do not go our way, as long as we stay close to Him. Saved at age five, I have known Jesus as my Savior all of my life, and I can honestly say there have been times He has disappointed me, but He has never let me down.

If you have a habit of being in a bad mood, raising your voice in anger on a regular basis, and getting frustrated too often at things out of your control in life, you can break that habit. Begin counting the days you stay calm. See if you can make it ten days in a row where you don't lose your cool and learn to deal with disappointments with composure. Before long, you will get in the habit of living in a spirit of praise to God. I promise it will be life changing. (*Caveat:* You can't keep your serenity with the wrong man. If you are dating someone who is bringing you down, leave him. And when counting your blessings, put that goodbye at the top of the list!) When you stop to count your blessings, it will change your whole perspective on life. And that change of outlook may very well be the greatest blessing of all.

HOMEWORK

Homework for this tip is to take out a sheet of paper and write down everything you can think of that God has given you today. Count your blessings. You may be surprised at the length of the list by the time you are finished. For instance, if you can read this you have your eyesight in a world where many people are blind. If you are blind, thank God for the gifts you have, such as hearing when others are deaf. No matter the situation, there is always a reason to praise the Lord. Keep a journal of your blessings on a daily basis. When something goes right, which could otherwise have easily gone wrong, write it down to thank God for it. Read your list of blessings out loud to yourself. Learn to thank God for little things. It will change your attitude and make you a happier person. See every day as a gift. Stop complaining. Praising God is the best medicine for a broken spirit. Let His love heal you and make you whole as no man can.

"This is the day the Lord has made. Let us rejoice and be glad in it" (Psalm 118:24).

"Rejoice in the Lord always. Again, I will say rejoice!" (Philippians 4:4).

"I will rejoice greatly in the Lord. My soul will exult in my God; for He has clothed me with garments of salvation. He has wrapped me with a robe of righteousness . . . as a bride adorns herself with her jewels" (Isaiah 61:10).

"Let us continually offer up a sacrifice of praise to God, that is, the fruit of lips that give thanks to His name" (Hebrews 13:15).

Know You Are Pretty
(Before the Next Jerk Tells You)

*A*ny woman loves to hear compliments from the guy she is dating. I enjoy dressing up to look my best for a date, and it really matters to me when the man I'm dating tells me I look good. When someone means enough to me to make me want to dress to the nines for him when we go out, I like it when he notices. This is true especially in the beginning of a relationship. If he is too inconsiderate to tell me I look nice when I go to so much trouble, one date is enough. There is nothing wrong with a little charm when it is sincere. It has been said that men fall in love with their eyes, and women fall in love with their ears. It certainly makes us feel good when we hear nice things. This tip is not about the importance of hearing beautiful compliments every now and then from the man in your life. It is about *knowing your worth* without his affirmation.

Have you ever dated someone who has hurt you and left you secretly thinking to yourself: *If only my face wasn't broken out he would treat me better . . . If only I could lose ten pounds, he would call more . . . ?* None of these things matter. A jerk is a jerk. It is his character and who he is. If you are dating someone who habitually hurts you, it has absolutely nothing to do with your looks. He would be a jerk with any other woman of any other shape or size. When it comes to jerks, it doesn't matter how pretty you are.

I was living in Santa Monica, California, in 2001, when I met a really nice-looking guy who dressed great and had graduated from the prestigious Cornell University. He was my neighbor. He was from a family that stressed the importance of having a proper education. As I wrote earlier, I had moved to Nashville at age seventeen to sing instead of going to college. I am embarrassed to admit this now, but I struggled back in 2001 with the feeling that I was not good enough for this man. I guess I figured that going to a university had made him smarter than I was. I know now that education cannot make anyone smarter, just more educated. As I got to know him, he turned out to be a very *unimpressive* man who was highly educated but had never grown up. I was too good for him before we met, too good for him while I was in his life, and I am too good for him today. I know this now, because I have learned to judge myself and others based on character. He was the only guy I ever knew who told me he had been labeled a sex addict by some of his business associates who were privy to his lifestyle.

Knowing I was a Christian and did not sleep around, he said he wanted to go out with me, but only as friends. (I wish I had had a book like this to read back then to remind myself of the slippery slope of dating *as friends*, like Tip #42 teaches.) He said he normally did not date a woman without sex by at least the third date, but we could do things as friends since he had other women "for sex," as he put it when referring to his many "girlfriends." He let me know he was an atheist. And, of course, being the caring, Christian friend to him I felt I needed to be at the time, I began praying for him. I kept praying for him as he made jokes about my beliefs. My prayers were answered when God saved me from him. God showed His faithfulness to me by enabling me to eventually leave that guy for good. It took a lot of heartache, though, to get me to that place.

We were both politically conservative. He said he wanted me to meet his friends in California who had worked with Ronald Reagan, and he had a photo on the wall of himself with President Reagan. There seemed to be enough compatibility initially to draw me to him. There were times he showed me respect, as if he really was my friend, and I was more special to him than the women he officially *dated*, which were women who slept with him. But he would also be disrespectful toward me when I least expected it. For instance, he would tell me he would call when he would not. He had a plane at the Santa Monica airport. He took me flying once, which was fun, but another time he said he would take me flying and just flat out stood me up. I can still remember getting all dressed up and waiting for the phone to ring, but he never called. He was not my friend consistently. That's for sure.

The first time I saw him, he looked like he had just stepped out of *GQ* magazine. Though I enjoy staying in shape and looking my best, I have never been skinny like a typical model and wondered if the women he "dated" were taller than my 5'3" self, all with pedigrees of *proper education*. As it turned out, I couldn't have been more wrong. He was a womanizer, who would literally sleep with anyone. All he really cared about was the next woman he could get into bed, not at all about the quality of the woman herself. I was just a "friend" on the side. He even disgustingly bragged to me about getting women in bed he did not even think were pretty. He did not mean the compliments he gave them. He would just tell them they were pretty, because he knew it was what they wanted to hear in order for them to have sex with him. He knew how to make them feel pretty by the things he told them, and that is all it took for him to get what he wanted.

He would mock the women he slept with to me, explaining he preferred women who are not so pretty, because pretty women expected more out of him. He thought that "high maintenance" women, as he called them, were the prettiest, so he preferred "low maintenance" women instead, who required less. He went on to reason that the pretty girls, who expected better treatment by his estimation, were just too much trouble.

Though he had slept with scores of women, he didn't exactly have the modus operandi of treating any of them well, evidently. His game was all about control. What was of foremost importance to the handsome player was his power over women. Whether he thought a woman was pretty or not was irrelevant; what mattered is that he knew how to make any woman *feel* pretty. (I have actually been shocked to meet many *successful* men over the years preferring only to date women they deem as "less than" their equal in both looks and intelligence.) The degree from Cornell left him clueless when it came to cherishing a woman. He was totally ignorant about what it meant to be a real man.

Needless to say, my days spent being his *friend* made me cry a river of tears. As so many times before, I liked who he was on the outside but not who he turned out to be on the inside. I was a much more thoughtful person toward him than he was toward me in our so-called friendship, and he only wanted me as another ego boost in his harem of women. Even though I had lost all respect for him, he had some sort of hold on me. It got to the point that he hurt me so much as a *friend* that a real friend recommended a counselor to help me gain the confidence to break off all communication with him. I scheduled a counseling session with Dr. Sherie Zander in Brentwood, close to where I was living at the time in Santa Monica. She turned out to be another great counselor who helped me tremendously in our brief time together in that little room on Bundy Drive. I admitted to her that when I first met this man, I had not felt good enough for him. I never forgot her response. She said, "That is because you thought that about yourself before you met him." She meant that I felt like I was not "enough" in general back then. I know I am today. I know that whoever gets me gets a good thing.

If you do not feel you are enough on your own without being told you are pretty and smart, it will make you too vulnerable to the bad men who use charm to harm women. You will miss how they make you feel too much to stay gone when you try to leave them because you need their affirmation. You will keep going back for more compliments (and more pain). If you cannot see yourself with the best—meaning, a man who treats you well, who is sorry when he has hurt you—you certainly need this book. If you feel unworthy of a man with great character, it is because you need to work on your own. Being a confident woman is a key trait of having good character. Healing takes time. It is evident that God is at work to do that very thing within you, because you are reading these tips.

Without confidence on the inside, when a jerk comes your way you will not be able to let his compliments go. You will feel that you *need* them in order for *you* to like who you are. This is why women stay with abusive men. It is not for the abuse. Many people do not realize that abusive men are not abusive all of the time. The same man who has made a woman happier than she has ever been is the same one who abuses her. She stays for the good side, for the nice man, not the mean one. Too bad you cannot have one without the other, but it is a package deal with an abuser. A woman who knows her worth will not need the flattery when an abusive man tells her she is beautiful. She can let that compliment from such a precarious guy go, because she does not need to hear it from him to define her own sense of identity. She already knows it is true.

If you Google "sex addicts" to do research in order to avoid them, you will find they are not as much addicted to sex as they are to power. They are addicted to the challenge of saying whatever it takes to have enough control over a woman to use her. If you are confident in who you are on the inside, you will be able to get to know a guy at a healthy pace, not nearly as fast as a dangerous man *falls in love*, racing to get women in bed. A bad man won't be able to hide his true character for long. Just keep your eyes and ears open, and you will see. This tip is about how *not* to let him get the best of you in the meantime.

Work now on becoming your own best friend, before you meet a new guy, before the next one comes to sweep you off your feet. You will be one step ahead in your paradigm to wholeness, with or without a man. The test is this: If you can like who you are when you are all alone without any man's validation, then you are confident. If you need a man in order to feel good about yourself, then you are not there yet. Only when you are confident from within will you be able to take it slowly enough to get to know his character before *falling in love* with him so fast. Do what it takes to like who you are, as I teach in Tip #17. If you do not have a serious illness, you can be the weight you want to be. Work out, eat right, and get there. If you need accountability, I also work as a health coach, and you can read about working with me at an affordable rate on the Health Coach page at my blog, DwaynaLitzBlog.com. Beauty is only skin deep, so work on becoming a woman you like, inside and out. Then you will already have more than any man can give you.

HOMEWORK

Homework for this tip is to look in the mirror and see a woman worthy of love. See a person who was made for more than lust. You are worth loving. As you stand there for a minute, don't be critical. Realize that you are enough today to be loved. You do not need to be more. Don't be so hard on yourself. Show compassion to that nice person staring back at you in the mirror, and learn to treasure your soul.

Realize that God made you beautiful just as you are, probably more than you have ever known. Take this gift of *you*, who is a person like no other, and treat it well. Take necessary steps to get and stay healthy, inside and out. Aim high, but when you make mistakes, offer tender mercy to the one who has tried so hard, overcome so much, and has lived every day of your life: "you."

Remember, no woman is the prettiest, and no woman is the ugliest. Make it your top priority to like who you are. A crucial means of achieving that is to stay away from the wrong men. Today's the day for a new beginning to actually like the one and only you. So go ahead and do it. Look in the mirror and know you are pretty You don't need a man to tell you it's so.

"Indeed my heritage is beautiful to me" (Psalm 16:6).

"He sets me on my high places" (2 Samuel 22:34).

"But as for me, the nearness of God is my good" (Psalm 73:28).

"For the Lord takes pleasure in His people. He will beautify the afflicted ones" (Psalm 149:4).

"You will also be the crown of beauty in the hand of the Lord and a royal diadem in the hand of your God. It will no longer be said to you, 'Forsaken'" (Isaiah 62:3-4).

You Don't Need Anyone Who Has Hurt You

I received an email today out of the blue from a man who used to work with me two years ago. I thought he genuinely cared for me like no other man I had ever known. He turned out to be abusive. The first time he yelled at me, I felt as if I had been hit. Although I told him it hurt, there was no apology. There never is with an abusive man. Evidently, he felt I deserved to be yelled at often. This was to be expected in even my working relationship with him. When he raged at me, he told me it was good for me. He knew how much I cared for him, so I guess he thought I would put up with the abuse. I knew the signs of an abuser, and he had all of them. Little did he realize I had already been through this before (dealing with an abusive man back in 2005, whom I write about in Tip #40) and knew there was nothing I could do to change him. I got my audio files and said goodbye without hesitation. I was proud of myself for being able to leave at the first signs of his abuse and stay gone.

I had never shared more chemistry in my life with anyone, but our characters were not at all compatible. He had deceived me, because I thought he was such a kind and caring man in the beginning. I had fallen in love with the man I thought he was. In all reality, it was as if hurting me made him feel powerful, like he got some degree of pleasure from my pain. He was so perfect when we first met. Then he became very inconsistent. It took quite an effort for me to eventually get myself out of the ordeal. I blocked him from social networking sites. I counted the long days without him. I cried and cried, but I made it to happiness again in due time. After attending a support group in Manhattan for women who left abusive men, I was asked to lead the group. It was a blessing to see something so good come out of such a painful experience. Now two years later, surprise, surprise—he emailed me today, the very day I began to write this tip. After so long, he wants to be friends.

Our musical connection was incredibly rare and special. When I recorded my songs with him, we were one. After I got a dose of his frightening temper, I guess he tried using our musical chemistry to maintain control over me. He said, "You *need* me to help you finish your CD. You *need* someone to keep your audio files. You *need* me to be your producer." He continued to give me reasons why I needed him to co-produce the CD with me in order for it to be a success. I had never produced any CD on my own at that point. I was used to relying on another person to help me make final decisions about production and mixes. I vacillated about it, because it felt like I did need him. But then I thought, *You don't need anyone who has hurt you.*

I finished my CD *I'm the Girl I Used to Know Again* on my own. I produced it myself. Many people said it was the best CD I have ever made. I found I could trust my own opinions. I experienced a new confidence to speak up and define "right" by what I like. I could make my own decisions, and they were good ones. I had it in me all along. Thanks to working with the best musicians and engineers, following my own gut instincts and recording at only the top studios, the CD was a success. It came out just fine, as I finished it on my own, working only with people who respect me and staying away from anyone who has hurt me.

When I say goodbye to a guy, and finally mean it for good, it never fails—something always happens to make me think I need him. When I lived in Atlanta and dated a guy who was an expert in technology, I told him goodbye, and my computer started having problems. I thought, *If only he were here to help me. I need him to fix my computer!* Such coincidences are not about a need as much as they are a test. Life is not easy. When I have faced challenges and not let myself turn to a man who has hurt me, I have found strength within me I never knew I had. I have either figured it out on my own or held out for someone nice to come along to give me a hand. It is not safe to need a man who has already proven too many times to not even be a friend. We have to care about ourselves enough not to give such people a chance to go on hurting us, no matter what the situation is without them. Have faith. Let business and personal opportunities unfold in a credible way that does not go against who you are as a person. Life has a way of working out. Things will get better as we trust God to help us. But that is contingent on staying on the right path. Remember, the right path is always the honest one.

Let taking care of yourself be the number one rule, and just watch how God will take care of you. Hard times can get a whole lot harder when we think we need a man who has the capacity to weaken us even more. There are people in this life who make us better, and there are others who bring us down. Learning how to know the difference is crucial, because we actually become like the people with whom we surround ourselves. Surround yourself with people you like and want to be like. Stay away from people with bad character who hurt others, especially when it is you they have hurt. Think of what happened to poor me in Tip #4 after I got in touch with a man, even after a decade, only for him to hurt me again. You don't *need* the trouble. It's not worth it.

So let's review. You don't need a guy who has hurt you to help you in your career. You don't need a guy who has hurt you to come and fix your sink. You don't need a guy who has hurt you as a date for an event. You don't need a guy who has hurt you to give you a ride when you have car trouble—call AAA! Get stubborn about your happiness and character long term. Only allow yourself to be a damsel in distress with a guy who has it in him to be there for you in support of your wholeness from an emotional standpoint. If there is not a reliable person available to come to your aid, don't underestimate what you can do on your own. You are stronger, smarter, and more capable than you think.

A woman may be reading this hoping the man in her life will change, prepared to keep forgiving and getting hurt and forgiving . . . to make *it* last forever. If that is the case, please ask yourself this: How much hurt is it supposed to take? How much hurt do you think you deserve before you leave? Don't keep living out this axiom the hard way. *Hurt me once, shame on you; hurt me twice, shame on me.*[10]

HOMEWORK

Homework for this tip is to draw two columns on a sheet of paper. At the top of one column write "Prices." At the top of the other column write "Prizes." When thinking you need someone in any situation who has hurt you, make a list of the prices you will pay for getting back in touch with him. Compare that to the prizes you will get, the good things he could offer you. This is a list of the pros and cons of calling him for help. More than likely, you will find the high cost of even the possibility of him hurting you again in the future will not be worth any *prize* on your list that could prove to be abysmal over time. True happiness only comes with self-respect. Be sure to add to the list of prices how it will make you feel about yourself if you weaken and get in touch with him, only for him to hurt you again. Let the urge pass. There is more happiness waiting for you around the corner, and it's a happiness filled with honor—a happiness no man who enjoys hurting you can offer.

"Love is kind" (1 Corinthians 13:4).

---

10 Author of axiom is unknown. For more encouragement, see Rachel Simmons, *Odd Girl Speaks Out: Girls Write About Bullies, Cliques, Popularity and Jealousy,* (Boston: Harcourt Books, 2004).

Reward Yourself

*T*here is no such thing as a successful life without working hard and making time for play. I tend to be a workaholic. Marilyn Brown, the counselor to whom I dedicate this book, used to have to ask, "Are you making time for play?" Now, at the end of every accomplishment I achieve with work, I make the time to reward myself by doing something fun I would not otherwise do. This also includes the emotional work it takes to get over the wrong guy. If you are going through a breakup from a guy, at the end of every thirty days without him, reward yourself. You deserve it. The time will come when you will be so happy that you will stop counting the days. That alone is a great reward.

The rewards I give myself can be as simple as a long walk along the river, going to a museum, or a night out on the town with my girlfriend. You don't need a man to mark your calendar and enjoy an evening to its fullness. You don't need a man to celebrate God's love for you. Meet a friend out for dinner at your favorite restaurant, or learn how to enjoy an evening alone. When you realize one day, after reading this book, that you have become comfortable within your own skin, plan something special for yourself in celebration. Living life to its fullest in your newfound confidence will be worth all of the effort it takes to get you there.

I enjoy my work so much that most of the time it feels like play. It is important, though, to have a healthy escape. Find a way to relax in life that does not hurt you. (This excludes going off on a tangent with the wrong man!) Ask God to help you have fun in ways that make you a better person. For me, it can be as simple as going to a symphony or taking photographs of children or nature. We can't work all the time as single women, though money in the bank account does make us happy.

Let a new guy wish he could join you in your successful life. After all, marriage should be a reward that makes your life better, not worse. The right man is not supposed to be a burden. Keep yourself available for someone who could possibly come along in the future as a blessing instead.

Homework

Homework for this tip is to set self-imposed, realistic goals in your professional or personal life and stay focused until those goals are accomplished. Be proud of yourself for a job well done, and don't compromise giving it your best when it comes to your work.

If you are breaking up with the wrong man, count the days without him, and reward yourself for every ten days of no contact until you reach your ninety-day goal. If you want to lose weight, set a goal for making it ten days without eating addictive foods that are bad for you; then try making it to thirty days, and so on. Reward yourself when you achieve your goals. Experience the confidence that breaking any bad habit can give you. A reward can be as simple as buying yourself fresh flowers to enjoy in your home when you otherwise would not. Stop and smell the roses. They can be yours, with or without a man.

"For I know the plans I have for you, declares the Lord, plans for welfare and not for calamity to give you a future and a hope" (Jeremiah 29:11).

"Lovers" Are *Easy* to Find (Sex Is Not Love)

*I*magine living the rest of your life without ever feeling like you've been used. If you wait to become someone's lover and let the man first prove that he loves you, you would be going against the flow of our present-day society—but you are worth it. "I love you" is easy to say and feel, but it is not so easy to prove. This book is about helping you become confident enough to make him prove his love first. There is a reason loose women are called *easy* by men. They don't mean it as a compliment. Even in today's culture, men still appreciate women who are hard to get.

Personally, I know I deserve more than to be a man's lover outside of marriage. It is less than the woman I want to be. Plus, I don't care for the thought of the pain I would feel from the oxytocin withdrawal after a short or long fling as a mere lover. I like the thought of outsmarting all of the predators out there who are skilled in making a woman think she is loved, only to get her in bed. The bad guys leave women who say, "No," which definitely keeps me happier in the long run. My standards may not be easy for the smooth talkers, but even they will work (to some degree) to meet the challenge of a woman who is harder to get. I am worth too much to let a man use me. And living a pure life keeps me feeling good about myself.

There is a new generation of people hooking up for sex with no strings attached. When women use sex to control, ironically, it only makes them more out of control. Using sex like this (as an escape from yourself) can easily foster an addiction, and addiction is humiliating. Any woman who thinks she needs a lover to *meet her needs* is only fooling herself. What she really *needs* is love.

What an insult hooking up for sex would have been to any lady just a few decades ago in an American culture when women knew they were worth marriage. A mere lover was the vernacular for an adulteress or a prostitute back then. For all you know, when you set out to be someone's *lover*, you will not only end up addicted to the man, but one addiction could beget another and another. You are not only liable to become addicted to a man you don't even like, but other addictions could result, such as the degrading cycle of abuse, an eating disorder, an addiction to alcohol, pain killers, antidepressants, and so on. What if you get so addicted that you marry him, only to find out after the marriage that you have a psychopath on your hands, a different man than you thought you knew? A woman following these tips will find herself living on too high a plane for the bad men, not allowing them to pull her down to their all-too-common, personality-disordered level.

The scariest men with the worst characters don't date in purity. They are too selfish. A bad guy masquerades his evil motives in *charming* immorality. What if your dream man turns out to be Jack the Ripper in disguise? If you have great sex with a man who has no love for you, guess what? You were never really *lovers* after all when true love was absent. You can save yourself all of the turmoil if you will just stay pure. If not, you could end up sadder than you have ever imagined, all because you wanted to be happy according to *your* own standards and refused God's standards for your protection. Because God cares for you, the Bible teaches, "This is the will of God, your sanctification; that is, that you abstain from sexual immorality."[11]

---

11 1 Thessalonians 4:3

Science is even proving the bad effects promiscuity is having on the brains of teenagers. In the book *Hooked: New Science on How Casual Sex Is Affecting Our Children*, by Joe S. McIlhaney Jr. and Freda McKissick Bush, the authors point out there is no such thing as safe sex for the brain in promiscuous teens, even if sexually transmitted diseases are avoided. Over time, the brain becomes unable to bond properly when a young person has many sexual partners. Sex is beautiful, but only when it is used as God intended.

Some women throw themselves at men, thinking that if they are good in bed, the men will fall in love with them. Meanwhile, the men are hooked on pornography. This dynamic fosters neurosis, not love. Some women excuse pornography as acceptable or even expected for men, with every guy having it available to him now on his home computer. At the same time, such women innocently presume that men look at pornography just because they like sex. Sex is not at the core of pornography. Pornography is about the abuse of women. It has changed over time to be far worse than just nude layouts in a magazine or videos of two people in the semblance of making love. Men who watch pornography today are getting a thrill from watching women degraded in torturous sado-masochism. It is an idealization of women as mere objects. Women in pornography are viewed as only good for one thing instead of being seen as human beings with feelings and brains and differing opinions.

Some of the documentaries I tried researching on the pornography industry were too hard to watch. I saw one on Netflix with a snippet of a man literally shoving a woman's head into a toilet bowl, evidently as part of some sick arousal. I had to turn it off. We have an entire subculture of men addicted to porn, who find hurting a woman stimulating. If a guy informs you that hurting you in bed (spanking, slapping, for example) is something he would enjoy, realize this is not just fun and games. There is something deeper going on in his thinking that is abusive. He does not see you as an equal but as someone to dominate, which will also include his desire for emotional domination. Keep God on the throne of your heart, and the bad men will not have a chance. Wait for a man who wants to keep you high on a pedestal in his mind instead of powerlessly beneath him as an object.

Think more highly of yourself. You are worth the best life, and the best life is one of purity. Let the men who are looking only for a lover find a woman who does not have your self-esteem or confidence. Stay set apart where the wrong men cannot hurt you, and keep feeling special. Don't let yourself be used.

The only way you can know for sure that a man won't use you is by opting to stay pure. A pure life is a gift only you can choose to give to yourself. It is a gift like no other. You will be much better off saving yourself for a man who deserves one-in-a-million-you. And when you meet that one-in-a-million-man for you to marry, having *you* will be a treasure, especially when he knows you have not given yourself so easily to so many others and have chosen instead to wait for him.

HOMEWORK

Homework for this tip is to watch the documentary *After Porn Ends*[12] (available on Netflix) to hear testimonials about the abuse of women in the pornography industry, explaining further the difference between sex and love. Realize that if a man is hooked on pornography, you can bet he is hooked on abusing women. Don't overlook a porn addiction in a guy as something easily dismissed. It is a big deal, and the longer he does it, the less he will be *able* to love you or any other woman. Porn robs a man of the capability of caring about a woman's soul.

Read the book *False Intimacy: Understanding the Struggle of Sexual Addiction* by Dr. Harry Schaumburg.[13] If you do not know how to fall in love apart from sex, this is the perfect read.

---

12 A nonrated 2012 documentary, revealing the dark side of the pornography industry and how it impacts people.
13 Published by NavPress, the publishing ministry of the Navigators.

In a society of men addicted to pornography, who don't know how to have a relationship with a woman outside of sex, know that you are worth being loved. Learn to love yourself enough to get to know a man without letting him use you. Stop gambling your essence by sleeping around. The more confident you become, the more you will want to wait for true intimacy and not settle for less.

Leave Mr. Wrong
Without Gaining Weight

*I*t hurts so deeply to leave a man when there is a chemical connection, even when you know he is wrong for you. In the sadness of goodbye, all of us would like to be able to reach for a little something to numb the pain. Well, I have good news and bad news. The bad news is there is really nothing to numb the pain; you must experience the sadness in order to be released from it eventually. There is no way of getting around it. The good news is that *responsibly feeling* your pain today will be part of your happiness tomorrow. You have to let yourself feel it in order to heal.

Resist wallowing in self-pity, and whatever you do, don't pity him after you leave him. Take it easy. Forgive yourself for the embarrassment of trusting him if he was untrustworthy. Love is still a beautiful thing, so pick up your broken heart and move on, hoping the next time you feel love it will be for real. Your heart will heal as long as you stay away from him with zero contact. Cry all day and night. But let this tip help you learn to mourn without hurting yourself even more by binging on too much food (or drinking too much).

Too many women gain weight after a breakup, which leaves them even more depressed. Don't turn to food or any other drug to heal your broken heart. Both sugar and alcohol are depressants. When you are already hurting, compulsively overeating on sugary starches will make you feel even worse. Eating right in the midst of sadness actually has more to do with boosting your brain and renewing your heart than filling up your stomach.

The last time I found myself in the pain of a breakup, I knew that becoming my own best friend (after thinking he was) was crucial in handling my pain responsibly. I made it a top priority to eat right from the moment I told him goodbye, because I was determined not to give him the power to make me gain weight in addition to all the other ways he had hurt me. I reached out and got the accountability I needed to take care of myself through the sadness. Self-pity is at the core of addiction, so start counting your blessings instead. You can begin with the fact that he will not be able to hurt you anymore if you stay gone. See yourself better off and smarter for the road ahead. Being grateful is the key in helping you stay filled up on life instead of on junk food after any man you thought was Mr. Right becomes yet another Mr. Wrong.

Sometimes I look at a woman right after she meets a new man she says she likes (long before he becomes someone she dislikes). She seems to be in her prime, floating on the pink cloud of chemistry from the connection. She eats practically nothing, seemingly on top of the world from how happy he is making her feel. She loses weight and exudes confidence, slim and trim. Then, when reality sets in, and she is back to her old self again after the goodbye, she looks like a different person from the weight she has gained. Even after the guy who hurt her has left her life, she continues to *abuse herself* by not knowing how to feel pain in a responsible way. It is as if he is still there insulting her, the way she is destroying her body by binging on bad starches over *him*.

I know all about it. I have been there. You will not get over the hurt until you learn how to feel it and stop stuffing your feelings with food. Men are only a symptom of the much deeper pain within you. God wants to heal that pain and make you whole. Abstinence from overeating actually works as a tool during sadness to bring to the surface all you have been trying to stuff away. As you feel heartache, there is no greater medicine than abstinence from junk food. It's better than any pill for depression. As you eat right, you will see that you don't really need him that much after all. You're fine on your own. It may sound odd, but the less you eat over time, the less *hunger* you will feel as you learn to tell the difference between using food as a drug and using food for nourishment. It is during the hours that you are not eating that God wants to fill up your heart with life. It is not your stomach that is hungry for food when you are hurting. It is your heart.

If you are a drinker, you can find a bar where everybody knows your name.[14] In contrast, the addiction of binge eating is usually a disease of isolation. I work as a health coach to help women break the addiction of overeating by asking them to turn every single bite of food over to me for thirty days. (As I have written previously, to find out more and read testimonials, go to my Health Coach page at DwaynaLitzBlog.com.) Contact me if you need help, because I would be honored to share in the joy of your recovery. You may have heard the expression, *Love looks good on you.* Let me or someone trustworthy teach you how to let God's love look good on you. You don't have to be wearing your pain in extra weight everywhere you go. One day at a time, you can get past the pain by abstaining from overeating and letting God heal you.

One of the hardest things to do when you are hurting, and probably the most powerful, is to stop eating at night. It can sometimes be harder to get to sleep if your blood sugar is a little off, but not eating a bite past 5:00, 6:00 or 7:00 p.m. is powerful in breaking food addictions. It is also great for digestion and makes you feel really thin in the morning, which will definitely make you happier. If this seems impossible, realize it is not. The first step is to get accountability to break old, harmful habits and begin new, healthy ones. As for skipping meals, science proves that the body does not starve itself for days and even weeks without food. The

---

14 In reference to the television show, *Cheers,* which was set in a bar and aired in primetime from 1982–1993. "Where Everybody Knows Your Name" is the theme song by Gary Portnoy and Judy Hart Angelo.

Mayo Clinic reports that it can take up to forty-seven hours for a woman to fully digest a meal with it passing through the body properly.[15] This means we are used to eating way too much. When I am feeling sadness, I call up a friend to get accountability so I will eat less, not more.

When I am going through a stressful time, I often fast from television. Television can be extremely mind-numbing. I find it helps to keep my mind occupied at night by reading. I also enjoy watching nonfiction documentaries on Netflix or Amazon Prime to help me grow as a person instead of surfing through television shows that are junk food for my soul. It is as if all of the advertising is designed to make us feel less than we are and *hungry*. I have said goodbye to a guy more than once without gaining any weight by keeping my mind occupied and keeping myself busy during the day with work, exercise, and good friends.

Remember, feelings cannot kill you, but trying to escape negative feelings in a self-destructive way can. Addiction affects the brain and your whole personality. Telling a man goodbye when you were so convinced you loved him is supposed to hurt. Let it hurt. Don't eat. Stick to a meal plan, and realize extra food will not help your heart one bit. It will only make you even sadder when you can't fit in your clothes the next day. It is easy to substitute one addiction (the bad man) for another (eating or drinking too much). True and lasting serenity comes when you deal with whatever it is within yourself that has been eating away at you all along and stop trying so hard to escape it in the first place.

HOMEWORK

Homework for this tip is to say this little prayer every day: "God, grant me the serenity to accept the things I cannot change, courage to change the things I can, and the wisdom to know the difference."

This prayer calms me every time I wish I could change something in

---

15 Michael, F. Picco, M.D., *How Long Does It Take to Digest Food.* http://www .mayoclinic.org/digestive-system/expert-answers/faq-20058340

my life that is out of my control. It helps me turn things over to God. No wonder it is called the Serenity Prayer.[16] There is a lot of serenity to be found when we surrender. It has helped me more than once put down the effort of trying to make a wrong man right.

"Keep deception and lies far from me. Give me neither poverty nor riches. Feed me with the food that is my portion" (Proverbs 30:8).

"And we know that God causes all things to work together for good to those who love God, to those who are called according to His purpose" (Romans 8:28).

---

16 "The Serenity Prayer" is the common name for a prayer authored by the American theologian Reinhold Niebuhr (1892–1971).

God Is Love

The Bible teaches in 1 John 4:8 that God is love. I have heard it suggested that since "God is love," it could also be true that "love is God." But you cannot always logically prove something by reversing it. For instance, it is true to say that hamsters are animals. If you turn that around to purport that animals are hamsters, well, that is not totally true. There are more animals than just hamsters. I am glad that love is *not* God. I have thought I was in love many times when I really was not, and I would certainly be without a compass in life if ambiguous, capricious, human love was my God. My God is the author of divine love. Even His justice and vindication on my behalf toward anyone who has hurt me is part of His love.

You may think that God must not be so loving after all because He allowed something very bad to happen to you. But part of God's love for you is His justice. He promises to punish people who "love lying"[17] and commit evils such as molestation, murder, and injustices against humanity with cold hearts and without repentance. The Bible teaches that God's wrath is on the wicked.[18] I am so thankful for a perfect God of love and a perfect God of justice who makes me better, the more I love Him in return.

Do you know how much God loves you? You may think that you have made too many mistakes for Him to love you. That is not the case.

17 Revelation 22:15
18 John 3:36; Romans 2:5

He wants you to come to Him just as you are. Don't worry, because He won't leave you that way. He will begin His great work of making you better for His glory. In any relationship, the more time you spend with a person, the more you become like that person. When we draw near to God by spending time with Him and getting to know Him through prayer and reading the Bible, we become more like Him. That includes learning to accept and forgive ourselves.

The Bible warns about a war going on for your soul between the pure God (the Father, Son, and Holy Spirit) and the impure gods, described in the Bible as deceitful spirits and demons.[19] Satan is called "the father of lies" and "the god of this world" in the Bible.[20] Jesus came to pay the penalty for our sins, so we can be forgiven and be reconciled to the only true and living God. You may think this is all a made-up story, but when you really stop to ponder it thoroughly, you will realize no man could make it up. It is a belief system supported by history, archaeology, and prophecy. Jesus fulfilled over three hundred prophecies from the Old Testament to the New Testament, and the sixty-six books of the Bible were written over a span of fifteen hundred years by over forty different authors. No other *holy book* can compare. No one could ever invent a story like the one the Bible teaches of God's redemptive plan for mankind. No one could just make up a Savior like Jesus.

Jesus came as God in the flesh, and He died for our sins on the cross, and this redemption through His blood comes freely to anyone who wants to leave their old way of living behind and follow Him as Savior. Only then can someone have a personal relationship with God as a loving Father. The Holy Spirit lives within the heart of any believer, so that Jesus is "with us always, even unto the end of the age," just as He promised in the Bible.[21] This powerful Love indwelling in the heart of any Christian gives us joy like no other, as we live in obedience to this God who *is* love. The Bible

---

19 1 Timothy 4:1; 1 Corinthians 10:21; Revelation 16:14
20 John 8:44; 2 Corinthians 4:4
21 Matthew 28:20

explains that God's love is so perfect toward us and so pure that it is a much higher love than we could ever offer to Him in return.[22]

The moral conscience within every human being also is evidence for the existence of a personal, moral God of love. An impersonal *energy force* could not configure this moral compass residing in each of us known as the conscience. It only makes sense with the explanation of a moral God who made us. Also, only Jesus offers a salvation for mankind not based on our works. A relationship with Jesus is based on *His* work that He did on the cross when He died for you. Christianity is the only belief system offering a relationship with God by God's grace alone and through no merit of our own. If you believe you can have a relationship with Jesus, however you define Jesus, and one religion is the same as any other, think about this. If you could save yourself through yoga meditations[23] or reincarnation, Jesus must have died in vain. Won't you get a Bible and read it to find out more about this God who loves you enough to die in your place?

When searching for a new beginning, keep in mind that Jesus is the only God who calls Himself the Resurrection and the Life[24] and proved it as He conquered death. The grave where He was buried is empty today. You cannot say the same for Buddha. Islam teaches in Surah, chapter 4, that Jesus never even died on the cross, which just so happens to be the event contingent on the whole redemption of mankind. You may wonder how to know the truth when so many religions contradict. The first step is

---

22 Isaiah 55:8-9
23 Yoga meditations are not to be confused with merely stretching the body, which is good for us as physical exercise. Yoga meditations (the yoga positions along with the meditations) are a vital part of Hinduism; stretching out, of course, has no spiritual connotation. Due to gymnastics and dance, I became very flexible at an early age, able to do the splits on both legs and other "yoga positions," but I never practiced yoga. The practice of transcendental meditation *involves* yoga stretches, but the "practice" of TM goes far beyond the stretches. Go to this site for more on how "practicing yoga" is far more than just stretches for exercise: http://christiananswersforthenewage.org/Articles_YogaTraining.html
24 John 11:25

to realize that God does not want you to become religious. Jesus called the most religious people of His day snakes and white-washed tombs![25] God wants you to have a *relationship* with Him. Jesus wants to be your Friend.

Either Jesus was a liar and a lunatic, or He was who He said He was—God. Jesus said in the book of John, chapter 10, verse 30: "I and the Father are one."[26] That is just one of many verses to show that the Bible clearly teaches the deity of Jesus. The Holy Spirit is called a Comforter who helps us when we pray and when we are in pain; the Holy Spirit is also God. When you read the Bible, it will be the Holy Spirit who helps you understand it, because His work is to draw people to the love of Jesus. It is the work of the Holy Spirit to convict us when we sin. This is because the God of the Bible is the perfect Judge.[27] When we come to God as a little child in humility, He promises not to turn us away. He resists the proud but gives grace to the humble.[28] It is good news that we have a loving God who came to save sinners. We are all sinners, every single one of us. All you have to do is tell God you are sorry and choose the new life Jesus offers by turning away from your old one. He offers this acceptance to you today, no matter what you have done. No matter your background, you cannot out-sin God's forgiveness.

"By this the love of God was manifested in us, that God sent His only begotten Son into the world so that we might live through Him. In this is love, not that we loved God, but that He loved us and sent His Son to be the propitiation for our sins" (1 John 4:9-10). *Propitiation* means the blood of Jesus atoned for our sins when He died for us on the cross and that we can live eternally because Jesus died in our place. It means that He redeemed us to abundant life through His death and resurrection.

---

25 Matthew 23:27; Matthew 23:33
26 *Caveat:* For people who are not used to reading the Bible, scripture references like "John 10:30" may be hard to understand. The book of the Bible is listed first, then the chapter, then the verse. For example, the book of John, chapter 10, verse 30. That is how the reader can look up the scripture in the Bible for herself.
27 James 4:12
28 James 4:6

Eternal life is available for anyone willing to take up his or her cross of suffering in a world that mocks Jesus by following Him for a greater happiness the world could never give.

There is only one thing that will separate you from a saving relationship with God right now, and that is sin. Every single human being on earth is in need of God's mercy and grace. The good news is no one is better than anyone else when we come to God in repentance. The ground is level at the foot of the Cross where a Savior unlike any other waits for you.

HOMEWORK

Homework for this tip is to read the book *I Don't Have Enough Faith to be an Atheist* by Norman L. Geisler and Frank Turek. [29]

If you have Netflix, watch the move, *The Father's Love*.[30] I am friends with the producer of the movie. I was at its premier in New York City. As I watched it, I could feel God's love. He invites you now to know His love, too.

Read Isaiah, chapter 53, and read the book of John in the Bible. Your whole life and eternity depends on it. Take the time to read some verses in the Bible and you will understand that it is God's love letter to you.

"How lovely on the mountains are the feet of him who brings good news, who announces peace, and brings good news of happiness, who announces salvation, and says to Zion, Your God reigns" (Isaiah 52:7).

"God demonstrates His own love toward us in that while we were yet sinners, Christ died for us" (Romans 5:8).

"Jesus said, I am the way, and the truth, and the life, and no man comes unto the Father except through Me" (John 14:6).

---

29   Published by Crossway Books.
30   *The Father's Love,* directed by Sharon Kon, 2014. (See www.thefatherslovemovie .com)

Bad Character = Bad Man

When I was in Nashville, around age twenty, I performed a song called "If He Could Hurt Me He Could Hurt You." It never became a big hit to my knowledge, but that was one true country song! If you are dating a man who has been mean to his ex-wife or ex-girlfriend, guess what? Your time is coming. If you are involved with a man who is cheating on his wife (and that includes emotionally), it is really not that complicated. He's a bad man with bad character. If he had good character, he would either work on his marriage and stay with his wife or get a divorce; no matter how he tries to convince you otherwise, married men are not capable of falling in love for real with a mistress on the side. When you see a pattern of bad character over time in a guy, this always equals a bad man. No excuses. It does not matter how *nice* he is to you. You are the one being tested if a man like this comes your way wanting to get involved with you, and the only way to win the test is to leave him. He is an adult, and he is responsible for his character. If he wanted to change, he would humble himself before God and become a better person with God's help. Men with bad character are usually not honest with themselves, much less God. They actually enjoy pretending to be good and fooling everyone. But they have never fooled God for even a second and never will, no matter how they try. Stay close to God, and you will see right through them.

What is really scary is that a man's bad character can and will rub off on you to an extent if you stay with him. This may be hard to admit, but it is true. If you are having an affair now with a married man, you also have bad character. Think of the wife. Would you like to have a husband cheating on you? How can you do this to her and his family if he has kids? Get away from him while you still have a heart. He will find someone else to use, because he is a bad man with bad character. Using women is what he does. He is looking for a woman without morals. Please don't let that be you. Good women leave bad men, and bad men leave good women. Let the chips fall where they may. Just keep holding God's hand in life, and you will win.

Men in church are not excluded from this tip. Whether a pastor preaches a great sermon or a priest is worshiped like a god, if he has bad character, he is a bad man. The pedophilia in the Catholic Church among priests, and the pedophilia with any pastor in a Protestant church, for that matter, illustrates the fact that these men are just men. A smart woman will not expect such men to be perfect. The Bible says we are all sinners, including pastors and priests and elders in churches. The test of a *highly respected* man is how well he handles praise. Usually, it is the men who are the least popular who have the best character. God sees the heart. Those who will have the biggest reward from the Lord in heaven are the men with the gifts that only God can give here on earth, such as walking with Jesus closely enough to live an authentic life.

A man is not good because of status, education, wealth, talent, or even because of knowing Bible verses. This is why you must take it at a slow pace when getting to know a guy, even if you meet him in church or on a Christian dating site. Measure his worth by his character. This takes time. It is his character that will matter in the end. If he has good character, guess what? He will actually treat you well and tell you he is sorry when he hurts you for some reason *over time*. (Even the worst of men do this in the beginning, but only in the beginning.) As you get to know a man, if you do not see good character, do yourself a favor and leave. God does not need your help when it comes to helping a lost man find his way. The Bible teaches that God saves us *from* such men, not for them!

After I moved back to NYC in 2011, a man came along who said he wanted to help me get a song I had written about America to the 2012 presidential candidates to be used in a commercial. He said he knew one of the candidates personally. I agreed to meet this political contact at the Harvard Club. He looked like he was about eighty, and it never crossed my mind that he was thinking of our meeting as a date! I just thought this was a business dinner, and he wanted me to meet him to discuss getting my song to various political action committees for a campaign commercial. He was living with a woman, who I assumed was his wife at the time, and I figured she would be with him. I would never have met him if I thought he had anything up his sleeve. Over dinner he told me I looked stunning, kept telling me he liked my perfume and explaining that he had picked the Harvard Club for what he called our "first date." There I was with him at this highbrow club surrounded by the heads of animals on the wall for what seemed like the longest dinner of my life. I wanted to leave early, but it was a five-course meal! It was good to exhale as soon as I got in a taxi on my way back home to the Upper West Side. I had a terrible feeling about having anything else to do with this person. There was something crooked and dishonest about him and the way he went about living his life.

The song I had written was called "America Come Home." Of course, I would like to have seen it used in some way to inspire others during the election. I could have made a fortune in a licensing deal for a commercial with it. This man was my only direct connection, but I chose to steer clear of him. I don't work with anyone who is not straight up, and that is why I am thankful to be satisfied with or without fame in the music industry. There are very few opportunities in the music business for people who want to live good, clean, moral lives. Nothing major happened with the song, but I would prefer it to be that way than to work in a situation that goes against my conscience and does not fit the person I am. Some things, like peace within my heart, are far more important.

"Bad company corrupts good morals" (1 Corinthians 15:33).

HOMEWORK

Homework for this tip is to write down these six questions to ask yourself as you get to know a man to measure his character: 1) Is he trustworthy? 2) Is he respectful? 3) Is he responsible? 4) Is he fair? 5) Is he caring? 6) Is he a good citizen? Go to Charactercounts.org to read more about these six pillars of good character.

Think about your favorite people in life who have good character. Think of your girlfriends who inspire you to be better. Think of both men and women who make you want to be more like them the more you get to know them. Now, compare that to a man who is crooked in his dealings with others (including you). Think of moments when he has shown you who he truly is, moments you realize how different you are ethically from him on the inside. It may sound cruel, but homework for this tip is to break any attachment you have to him. Save your friendships for the people you respect and want to be like. Think about the person you want to be. If you do not want to be like a man, stop spending time with him. This advice applies especially if you are trying to be friends with him after a breakup. It is not honest. You cannot truly be friends with someone whose character is bad and needs changing.

Maybe you are trying to have a close relationship with a business associate who is showing you that he or she is not the kind of person you are. If this person has been disrespectful toward you or others, begin to distance yourself from him or her. Learn to guard your character by becoming more selective in your friendships. Having a true sense of belonging in life has nothing to do with receiving praise from the popular crowd. It comes by living an honest life. Keep your distance from people who have bad morals, claiming instead all that God has in store for your happy future in His faithfulness and love.

"Do not take my soul away along with sinners . . . in whose hands is a wicked scheme and whose right hand is full of bribes" (Psalm 26: 9-10).

Don't Kiss on Dates

I can't blame women who want to laugh at this tip. I would have laughed, too, years ago, until I tried it. It works! Your confidence level will soar the more you do it. The bad guys will be a nervous wreck. It is enough to leave a smooth talker speechless. Try this, and I promise, you will love the power and control it will give you—the power in a relationship that should have been yours all along with every single guy who has come your way.

Marilyn Brown, my counselor, gets the credit for suggesting this tip to me. She was teaching me more about the hormone oxytocin a few years ago and suggested that I stop kissing on dates. (Read Tip #7 for more about this hormone, which can make us feel bonded and attached to a guy way too soon.) Marilyn even went further to suggest I wait a whopping three months after going out with a man before kissing him on dates. She explained this was for my protection, to give myself enough time to get to know him first. She said if I would do it, it would keep me from getting too attached to the wrong men, and it would test the waters with all the nice ones to make sure we are having enough fun together platonically to fall in love for real. It is the best test for true compatibility. I have been dating this way ever since, and I am living proof it works. Before you think it is too crazy an idea, keep reading . . .

If you are a woman who has fallen one too many times for a jerk, get prepared next time around for the tables to turn. It will drive any man of your choosing crazy, as he tries to conquer you. You won't have to worry about being the one he will never forget. Not only that, but you will be the woman of *your* dreams, as any woman should confidently feel about herself, if you will just do it. It is going to take some practice, but the more you do it, the easier it will get. If this seems unimaginable, it is because you don't know your worth. The good news is that with my help, you can begin to experience dating this way and your self-worth will increase. It is powerfully feminine. As a result of dating this way, I have never felt better about myself in my whole life.

I used to be afraid men would leave me if I did not kiss them at the end of a date. When I began putting this tip to the test, I found I was wrong. Most men wanted to keep dating me even more, not less. It was only the jerks who left. Living this way convinced me that I am worth getting to know for my personality and character and soul, and if a man does not want to spend time with me just for who I am with the pleasure of getting to know me better, it's his loss. The same goes for you. There is no one like you in the whole world. What makes you unique is not how good you kiss. What makes you unique is all that you *are* instead of all you can *do* for a man.

Let him fall in love with the woman you are on the inside, which requires him doing what it takes to earn your respect for him as a person. When we kiss too soon, not only do things get confusing in a whirlwind of chemistry, but we can't help but become controlling and attached before even knowing the guy. What is worse is that we become that way before the men get a chance to truly know us. If you do not want to become too clingy, and if you would rather have a guy work a little harder to have you, this one word will do the trick: wait. We date this way, not to be manipulative, but to take care of ourselves. It just so happens, though, as a little added bonus, that a man will never forget a woman who is unique from all of the others with such a remarkable mystique about her.

It is just this simple. On the first date, look your absolute best so that when he sees you, you knock him off his feet. Listen, smile, laugh, respectfully communicate with him, and let him pay for everything. Let your personality come out, and be your sweet self. If you really like him, toward the end of the date, you need to articulate your boundaries in a nice way. Men cannot read your mind. Choose to use your brain in communication instead of taking the easy way out by attempting to control him with sexuality.

The first time you only depend on *you* instead of giving a guy a big kiss at the end of a date may be very hard. No matter how awkward this seems at first, don't give up on yourself. Smile and tell him the truth so he will not misunderstand or feel rejected. After enjoying your date with him, just look into his eyes and say, "I really like you, and thank you for such a fun night, but I need to tell you something. I don't want to kiss you until I have had time to get to know you first. If we enjoy spending time with each other as people, we will know we have something real. I am hoping you will agree to give it some time before we kiss, so we can get to know each other better."

Keep smiling.

If he seems taken aback, you can reiterate, "I am not trying to waste your time or money on fancy dinners. It is just that I really want something real or nothing at all, because life is too short for anything less. Thank you for this night. I really like you. I just want to get to know you and give it some time before we kiss."

Woohoo! You are working it now when it comes to using your brain and outsmarting most of the men on the planet at this point. He is going crazy. No matter what he says, stay strong. He may be used to using women and getting whatever he wants without much effort. All of a sudden, he is faced with a challenge, which puts you in a higher caliber from all the rest. And you are the one in control. If he complains too much about your boundaries (revealing that he has bad character), you will find it much easier to let him go and let the first date be your last. Let him show you sooner than later if he is not deserving of you.

After he learns that you wish to wait before kissing, if he still tries to kiss you, it is not because he is head over heels in love with you on the first date and simply can't resist. It is either because he is manipulative and trying to addict you or just too selfish to honor your boundaries. He could be very mean beneath the charm for all you know. Users use. Con artists con. The right man will let you take care of yourself. Remember, purity is healing for everyone. *Pure* love is also what he needs to find for himself, whether he realizes it or not. Bad men are men without substance. If you know he is attracted to you, yet he never calls again after realizing you wish to date without kissing, it is probably because true intimacy scares him. That is all right because you are looking for someone who knows how to love. After all, you want to be a woman who knows how to love. Dating this way becomes easy and natural for any woman who knows her worth and knows the difference between being used and being loved. This tip will work for any woman of any background who chooses to begin living a pure life. It will work with any man, bad or good, as it will weed out the bad ones and make the good ones want to keep coming back.

Back in 2009 I went out with a man when I lived in Atlanta who happened to be very wealthy and handsome. On our first date, strangers stopped us on the street telling us we made a great-looking couple. As the night ended, I explained to him that I wanted to wait for weeks before kissing him. He looked at me like I was crazy but reluctantly agreed. By the second date, he showed he really did not care at all about what I wanted. He pulled me close and kissed me, though I chided, "I said I wanted to wait, and I am not ready for kissing." Fortunately, I did not enjoy the kiss. The second date was our last date. It was not a good sign that he kissed me before I was ready. I did not know him well enough to call him a full-fledged jerk, but he was certainly acting like a jerk when he kissed me, knowing I did not want to kiss so soon.

A man's reward for spending money on you and buying you gifts simply comes from being in your presence and knowing you are happy when you are with him. A good man will already understand this. Thanks to this boundary of not kissing too soon, you win no matter what. If he likes you and wants to keep dating you in purity, you win. If he never calls, and you never see him again, you win. If you are not compatible, you win. If you don't like him, you win. You are free. No matter what, you can break it off easily. There is no way to lose with purity. Purity gives you a safer life and helps guard the peace you are meant to feel within yourself all alone.

Not long after I first began practicing dating without kissing, I met this guy I really, really liked, or at least I thought I did initially. There was so much magnetism on the first date that we could both feel it as we looked at each other over dinner. If I had kissed him, it would have really been confusing. Though it was disappointing when I realized we were not compatible, instead of the cordial goodbye we had, well, I could have cried for weeks if I had kissed him. That is how much we were chemically drawn to each other. You could cut the chemistry with a knife. We both felt it, and it was amazing. I could tell by looking at him that a kiss would be terrific, but I did not kiss him. On the second date, I gave him my little speech about how I wanted to wait before kissing in order to have time to get to know him. He agreed and really seemed to cherish me as we closed the restaurant down just talking. All was going well until he drove me home. On the way back home he revealed that he was in over his head with financial debt. That was not anything that appealed to me. Though he called himself a Christian, while we were making conversation it came out that he did not believe in the Bible as the Word of God. "It's just a lot of made up stories," he said. Next, he told me that he had already been married three times. On that drive home I knew we were heading in different directions as people.

Even the hug goodnight felt great. I could think about our lack of compatibility clearly because I had not kissed him. We wished each other well and parted with zero drama. The impressive guy with the really nice car (who may very well always remain in financial debt) moved on and is married to someone else today. We are still connected on a few social networking sites, because there was no intensity or heartache to make me feel the need to lose touch with him altogether. After only two dates and a world of chemistry with this man, we ended it as we should have, and we never kissed. No tears were shed. It remains a great memory in my life, even though it was not meant to be. I can only imagine how much the chemistry could have hurt me if I had kissed him. Goodbye would have been much harder.

Going into a relationship for marriage is sort of like a business deal. You have to pick someone who is compatible as a friend and outsmart the con artists. Love does not conquer all when it comes to a degrading cycle of addiction. Believe it or not, going out and having genuine fun with a man platonically is what true love is all about. This no kissing tip is the litmus test, because if you are not compatible as people, you won't have fun platonically. As you get to know him, if you feel yourself more and more attracted, keep holding back your heart. *Wait at least three months before kissing him.* A bad guy won't even last a month without hurting your feelings, and a really bad guy probably won't even make it to the second date. Just don't kiss him, and you will see. This is the way it is supposed to work. It helps you find out who someone really is a whole lot sooner. Let him wonder how it would be to kiss you. As you make him wait on that, he will find out how special you are on the inside. It is true, even if he leaves.

HOMEWORK

Homework for this tip is to watch the romantic movie, *An Affair to Remember* with Deborah Kerr and Cary Grant. There is a reason why such classics are actually about falling in love instead of falling into bed. Imagine respecting a person and loving who he really is, as opposed to just how he makes you feel. Imagine having fun with a best friend who actually brings out the best in you. Igniting the fire of lust too soon cannot offer you any of that. Only love can give you love.

You may be thinking, *but I will never find a man that good*. Well, then, what is the alternative; settling for something less than true love? When a woman puts herself in harm's way with the wrong man, it hurts God. Letting a man use you is a *sin*, and sin damages everyone involved—you and God *and* the bad man. Hurting God won't bring happiness. When you don't take care of yourself, it actually grieves the Lord who loves you so. When a woman lets a man use her, it damages her psyche. It hurts God who created her to live life to its fullest in His joy.

The only way to be happy is to learn how to wait on something real. The chances are slim these days when it comes to finding a man good enough for you, especially if you are a Christian in a world of men who are not. It does not mean it won't happen. It could happen tomorrow. But you have to become happy with who you are on the inside first to differentiate between the counterfeit and the real deal. Invest in a happy life for yourself down the road by keeping your standards high—not just for the guy you have yet to meet but for the woman you want to be. It is the only way to know happiness, with or without a man.

Do What It Takes
to Like Who You Are

I was out with my girlfriends recently when we decided to take some photos. One of the women in our group said, "I don't want my photo taken. I'm too fat. I hate how I look." Reluctantly, we agreed to take a snapshot of that fun outing without her in it, as if she were not there. It hurt me to think of my friend ashamed of herself. But there was nothing I could say to relieve her of the weight of her burden, a burden she was carrying *about herself* in that moment. It was her choice not to be in the picture on an otherwise happy day.

Confidence is not about achieving the perfect weight. The ideal weight varies for all of us. Confidence is all about accepting both your body and your soul in keeping with what is best for you as a healthy individual. It is about being fully present. Being comfortable in your own skin is the key to living in the moment. As for meeting a new guy, if you don't like who you are, inside and out, how can you expect anyone else to like you?

When you truly like who you are, another person is unable to give you something you don't already have when it comes to self-esteem. There is a difference between enjoying compliments from men and needing compliments to define you as a woman. You will know that you are at home within your own skin when you can be alone without feeling anxiety manifesting itself in overeating, alcoholism, overspending, gambling, sexual addiction, and so on. When you feel at ease within yourself, you will not have the desire to escape who you are by means of addiction. This includes negative feelings like rejection. The truth is that feelings such as pain, fear, loneliness, and rejection make you who you are as a human being just as much as happiness does. You cannot like the human you are without embracing these negative feelings, too, instead of trying to escape them. Every single feeling makes up who you are as a person. No need to let feelings scare you. They change. One day you can be sad, and the next day you can feel happy. If you were meant to only be happy all of the time, you wouldn't be a human being. The sooner you learn that it is not only natural but permissible to have negative feelings from time to time as a whole person, the quicker the negative feelings will pass. Learn to feel your feelings and let them pass.

Being true to yourself means discovering who God created you to be, not just when you are happy but when you are sad. As a child, if no one was there for you when you felt pain, you learned to self-medicate it away. These thoughts can surface still today in compulsions that keep you feeling badly about yourself overall. Compulsive behaviors can feel like the natural way to handle pain, fear, and rejection until we teach ourselves a healthier response. When healthy reactions to pain become a normal response, that is when a new confidence from within is manifesting itself. As a result, we feel good about ourselves overall instead of ashamed.

There is nothing I love more than working as a health coach to help people free themselves from food addictions. As long as you are addicted to unhealthy food, you will never be able to stay at your healthiest weight due to the cravings, very similar to a drug or alcohol addiction. When you cannot stick to diets, it is not your fault. You are addicted to the preservative-laden foods you crave. Cravings for unhealthy foods disappear as the body gets to the right pH and the palate changes. Unless you have a serious health problem, you can be any weight you want to be.

Just don't give up on overcoming your food addictions and eventually you will get there. It is not about your weight. It is about finding a place to lay your burdens down and be at peace within yourself. Women with anorexia believe they are fat when they are in reality far too thin. Their body image has been distorted in their own eyes to the point of believing they are fat. It just goes to show that we can exercise and diet all day, but it is our soul that has to be in good shape in order for us to be confident.

When it comes to bad habits, if you see something in your character that needs changing, get the accountability required to become a healthier person. No one is above learning from astute counseling. It takes work to break an addiction. Subconsciously, addiction stems from a dethroning of God in your heart and a skewed view of who He created you to be. Have the willingness to become a better steward of all God has given you physically, mentally, and spiritually, even it means talking to a counselor. Defeat keeps us alone in our battles. We are only as sick as our secrets. The healthier we get, the less we will want anyone to think we are better than we know we really are and the less we will try to make people think we are perfect when no one is. Compare yourself only to your own potential, not to anyone else. You owe it to yourself and to the God who made you to aim high when it comes to all that you can be in every area.

Dating a new man is not the answer when it comes to healing. Why would God allow someone else to put your anxiety at ease, when He wants you to learn how to come to Him with it all instead? If you have a habit of yelling in temper tantrums, don't give up on yourself until you learn how to speak calmly as a rule. If you turn to shopping when you are sad, don't give up on yourself until you learn how to feel pain without it costing you a dime. The same goes with gossip, which can also be a huge addiction. It is a waste of your brain to go around in criticism of others all the time when there are far better things to discuss and discover about people. You will never know what you are missing if you keep distracting yourself from you. It all begins with surrendering to God, one day at a time, struggles and all.

Try to objectively see the person you are, inside and out. Ask yourself the following questions: Do I know what it means to deny myself, taking the high road instead of going the easy way when it comes to decision making (including the wrong men and bad food cravings)? Do I handle fear, loneliness, and rejection responsibly or run to escape my feelings in substance abuse (including sugar) as a knee-jerk reaction? Can I say I am sorry when I know I have done wrong, or am I too proud to apologize most of the time? Am I confident enough to distance myself from the wrong crowd? Do I give out of altruism or do I only help others for attention and compliments? Do I discriminate against people, seeing myself as better than others? Am I reliable; do I keep my word? Who am I in secret, when no one sees me but God?

A successful songwriter gave me some advice when I was only eighteen years old in Nashville. She said, "Always be true to yourself." She was referring to my being true to myself as an artist. I did not really know what that meant at the time. Knowing myself artistically came with maturity. The more we know ourselves, the easier decisions come and the less we need to be like everyone else in order to feel acceptance. I know as a Christian that only a life lived according to the Bible is a life where I am true to myself from a standpoint of character. I could never be happy any other way.

A few years ago in NYC I had been referred to a Russian pianist who played in the top rooms around Manhattan. After he heard my recordings with an orchestra from my *Counting Your Blessings* jazz CD, he wanted me to sing with him. He was a famous pianist in Russia with rave reviews in the *New York Times*. I was told he could really help my career. Unfortunately, violins were playing in his mind for an affair behind his wife's back when we met. He not only had the audacity to suggest we have an affair, but he also let me know that it would not mean anything to him or interfere with his marriage at all! He seemed comfortable explaining to me how cheating on his wife meant nothing. I was also comfortable in my response. "I know myself, and we are totally different people," I said nicely. "You have to accept me for who I am just like I have to accept you. You enjoy cheating and sneaking around, and I don't. Such a lifestyle pleases you, but it would never please me. In order for me to be true to myself, I have to live my standards. I would never be happy otherwise." I was proud of myself for keeping a professional demeanor as we spoke to mask how truly appalled I was by his character.

He said, "Please let me know if you ever change your mind." I couldn't help but laugh. I said, "I will let you know if I ever want to be used and feel ashamed of myself." He replied, "I just want to have fun." I said, "I have fun when I live right. I have fun feeling good about myself." When I told him I enjoyed living a *pure* life, he looked as if he had never heard of the word *pure* before. I actually had to define it for him! He lost interest in helping me get gigs around New York City, but that was okay. I remained true to myself, liking the woman I am, keeping that as my main ambition in life. Far from regret, I am thankful to God I never worked with the pianist from Russia who is probably off somewhere today having an affair behind his wife's back. I was created for a much higher purpose and a far grander confidence than any jazz room in NYC or review from the *New York Times* can provide.

HOMEWORK

Homework for this tip is to make sure you are thinking straight. If you have been sexually, emotionally, physically, or verbally abused, your self-esteem has taken a blow. This will help. Start your day by looking in the mirror and saying this out loud: "I accept myself unconditionally, and I do this right now." Say it one more time while still looking at yourself in the mirror.

It is good medicine to help you think clearly, because you do not have to be perfect to accept yourself. If God can love you and accept you today right where you are, you can also accept yourself. If you have been hurt by men, you probably won't mean this little affirmation at first when you begin saying it. Right after a breakup with the wrong guy, it will be especially hard. It is high time to replace the blame you carry and the condemning lies you think about yourself with God's mercy. This exercise will help you accept yourself just as you are today. (Keep in mind that in order for this to work and for you to achieve confidence on your own, you must stay away from any man to whom you are addicted who is not good for you and instead be willing to entrust your heart to God.)

If God wanted every single one of us to be perfect in order to accept ourselves, He would have made everyone *perfect*. Funny thing is, not a person on earth is perfect. There really is no such thing when it comes to body image or character. The irony is that, although no one is perfect, God does not make mistakes. When God created you, He knew what He was doing. Since He loves how He created you, *shortcomings* and all, surely you can learn to begin liking who you are. It is God's desire for you to accept yourself, right where you are today, even though you are not perfect. If you cannot accept yourself, how can you expect any man to accept you?

No matter how silly this may seem, continue for at least twenty-five days to look in the mirror and say, "I accept myself unconditionally, and I do this right now." Keep saying it daily, no matter the doubts you may have about it. If you opt out, thinking instead, "This is stupid. It will not help," you are wrong. It will help. Your perception is your reality. Science has proven that what we believe about ourselves actually changes our brain chemistry.[31] Believe God when He promises that He loves you. Reflect His love in how you begin to view yourself. This affirmation will help. It will take about twenty-five days for it to begin making a difference in how you view yourself, so keep doing it.

Make a list of things you like about yourself and things you don't like, and make becoming your own best friend your top priority. Break

---

31 "Zero Tolerance to Negative Thinking: Goodbye Depression—Hello Positive Mind," by David J. Abbott, M.D. http://positivebutterflies.com/Birdwing%204 .htm

any addiction that needs to be broken and work on your character. If you need a health coach for accountability in breaking addictions (including an addiction to the wrong man), please go to my "Health Coach" page at DwaynaLitzBlog.com. I would love to work with you. Don't settle for anything less than the best person you can be.

"Every good thing bestowed and every perfect gift is from above, coming down from the Father of lights, with whom there is no variation or shifting shadow" (James 1:17).

"There is therefore now no condemnation for those who are in Christ Jesus" (Romans 8:1).

Tip #18

Happiness=Making Someone Happy (Who's Not a Bad Man)

*I*n the summer of 2012 I was sitting on a city bus in Manhattan when the woman beside me began making conversation, which is something most New Yorkers don't do. She was obviously very smart, but she said she was out of work and out of money. She lived in government subsidized housing and said that the plumbing rarely ever worked right in her building. She was on the way to her doctor's office for an eye exam. She felt that life had not been fair to her, and she told me she rarely ever had a happy day.

I asked, "Do you believe in God?" She answered, "Well, I used to, but now I am sort of mad at Him." I replied, "Well, life is not easy. From our pride's perspective, we could all have reason to be mad at God for not giving us our way when the hand we have been dealt seems so unfair. When we start to count our blessings, though, we realize God has been good to us after all, and He is always worthy of our praise." I continued, "As long as you are breathing, you are a human being that has worth in this world and purpose. God can help you in your circumstances and change your life for the better. He wants to be your friend."

We continued chatting, and I felt I should do something I rarely do.

With all the panhandlers in NYC who are shysters, it is rare for me to give money to a stranger. But I felt I should give this woman some cash. I reached in my purse and gave her twenty dollars for food. She said, "Oh, I can't take this." I answered, "Yes, you can. God had us sit together today because He wants you to know that He loves you and will help you." She replied, "I will give it to someone else." I argued, "No, it is for you." She began to cry. She said, "I can't do anything for you." I said, "God will take care of me. You don't have to do anything for me. Besides, it is only twenty dollars." I felt compassion for this woman living in my city with a life of hardship that was foreign to me. Yet our backgrounds did not matter as we sat together talking. It was as if there was no socioeconomic difference between us. She explained, "I need to get in better health so I can work again as a waitress." I told her I was sure she was a hard worker. She kept trying to give me the money back, and I kept telling her it was my pleasure to help her. I asked for her address, because I had some Christian materials to send her about God's love for her. She gave me the address and thanked me in advance for the materials I said I would mail. I got off the bus, and I have never felt better. I love to sing and write songs, but a new song flowing out of me could not have made me happier. Falling in love with a man could not have made me happier. It was a different kind of happiness, which only comes from serving others.

If you want to feel purpose in life, serve someone who has less than you. Befriend someone you might otherwise consider beneath you or unworthy of your time. Humble yourself and love the person and realize we are all the same to a large degree. When you show love to the broken-hearted and the needy, it is so close to God's heart that God will certainly repay you by filling up your heart with His joy. If you know of someone sick in the hospital, go visit that person. Cheering up others will make you happy, too.

When I was living in Nashville years ago, I found myself reading James 1:27 about how it is pure and undefiled religion in God's eyes to visit orphans and widows in their distress. I began praying for God to bring a widow or orphan into my life who needed love. Shortly afterward, I met a little old lady at the grocery store whose husband had died and her only son had just passed away. She had no one and was very sad and lonely. I would visit her and show her love. It made me feel good and certainly took my eyes off of what I did not have and put them on all God had given me. I did not expect to have such a blessing from my visits with her. I thought I would show love to this widow more as a duty unto the Lord, just to let God know how much I loved Him. With all the unbiblical politics I had at times experienced in large churches, I wanted to do something that was "undefiled religion" in God's sight. Something surprising happened. God blessed me as I was blessing Him through my time with her. I would read the Bible to her and pray with her, and God let me feel His pleasure and love for me as I loved this woman. He used such pleasure to sustain me through a very sad period of my life.

Both my mother and father visit the sick in the hospitals and nursing homes on a regular basis and also have sincere hearts to help the poor. I am thankful both of my parents are not the least bit supercilious around anyone anywhere. Too many times to count in my adult life I have sung at nursing homes and assisted-living facilities in compassion for the elderly residents. During the time I lived in Atlanta, some of us from my church went to a government-funded home for troubled teens and led a Bible study there. I loved it! I also enjoy volunteering and singing at soup kitchens. I have never felt more rewarded than when I shared about God's faithfulness in my life at the Bowery Mission's home for battered women on the Upper East Side in NYC a few years back. We will never be greater women than when we are servants to people in need. The only danger for a giving woman who enjoys helping others lies in her propensity to let an emotionally sick man get the best of her as she tries to help him.

I used to be an *overgiver*. A woman can give too much, even to a healthy man, without realizing she is trying to control the relationship through gifts. It could be something simple like sending a card. Back

in 2009 a guy in real estate had been pursuing me, but I felt he was
too young for me. I also knew we were not compatible spiritually or
morally, based on some things he had said. We never went out, though
he called me many times hoping to convince me to change my mind and
date him. His mother passed away, and I asked Marilyn, my counselor,
what she thought about my sending him a sympathy card. She pointed
out that it was too much; it was his place to give to me. She explained
that since he had not bought me gifts or sent me any cards, it was more
than enough for me to just tell him by phone that I was sorry about his
mother passing away. She was right, and I did not send the card. Simply
sending my condolences to him and his family by phone was enough. It
takes practice to break the habit of reaching out in thoughtful gestures
too much with a man. Marilyn called it "giver's control." I am now only
comfortable when I receive and *give back* after the man has been the one
to give to me. For instance, after a guy takes me out on a few dates, only
then do I cook a meal for him. Real men love to give, so I always make
sure I am the one receiving and only giving gifts of appreciation *after* a
man has already given to me.

I had a friend who worked as a model and actress in NYC who said
she "fell in love" in a short amount of time with a sports coach she met
on a Christian dating site. All of a sudden, he totally and completely blew
her off without even a goodbye and just left her life one day without any
explanation. That was that, and he was gone. All along, she thought she
would marry the man. (In hindsight, she was sorry she kissed him too
soon, making her so attached.) He had come to see her in NYC, and she
had been to visit him in Connecticut. One day she called him, and he
never called back. Shocked, she called again. She blamed herself, assuming his abandonment had to somehow be her fault. She kept waiting for
her phone to ring. She continued to pray for him as she cried herself to
sleep at night.

She told me over lunch one day that she bought him a book about
God, which she planned to mail him, along with a nice letter wishing

him the best. She still referred to him as "a good Christian man." I told her that was just the oxytocin at work (as I explained in Tip #7), and her perception of him would become more realistic in time. I said, "Please, do not mail him the book. I will buy the book from you and give it to someone else." She let me do just that and was at peace knowing someone else would get that book through my nonprofit organization. We both rejoiced in the fact that he would not have the opportunity to humiliate her anymore, as she promised she would no longer call him, email, or text, much less send him any gifts in the mail. She felt empowered as she ripped up the letter she had written to him and threw it away. She was ready to let him go, along with all of the pain of trying to have a happy ending with a person so cruel he did not even want to tell her goodbye. Her happy ending was found in God's love for her, even though it hurt. God was obviously protecting her when He let that guy leave her life after just a few months. He was not deserving of her generosity.

Beware of the unhealthy men out there who take advantage of giving women. It can literally be a full-time job trying to make and keep an egotistical man happy. Even if you are dating a good guy and have the desire to buy him a new shirt or whatever, do not let yourself do that unless he has out-given you. Women who give too much to men are women who do not know their worth. As you get more self-confidence, you will realize you are giving him enough when you are in his presence. You are staying in your place as a female when you let him give to you. Only give him gifts to give back. If the man knows he has hurt you, let him be the one trying to make you feel better instead of the other way around. If you are a Christian, save your ministry to those in need who, as the Bible puts it, are the ones blessed by God anyway.

"When Jesus saw the crowds, He went up on the mountain; and after He sat down, His disciples came to Him. He opened His mouth and began to teach them, saying, '*Blessed are the poor in spirit*, for theirs is the kingdom of heaven. *Blessed are those who mourn*, for they shall be comforted. *Blessed are the gentle*, for they shall inherit the earth. *Blessed are those who hunger and thirst for righteousness*, for they shall be satisfied. *Blessed are the merciful*, for they shall receive mercy. *Blessed are the pure in heart*, for they shall see God. *Blessed are the peacemakers*, for they shall be called sons of God. *Blessed are those who have been persecuted for the sake of righteousness*, for theirs is the kingdom of heaven. *Blessed are you when people insult you and persecute you, and falsely say all kinds of evil against you because of Me.* Rejoice and be glad, for your reward in heaven is great'" (Matthew 5:3-12).[32]

HOMEWORK

Homework for this tip is to befriend someone who needs some encouragement, the type of person most people would shun. It will make you a better woman. Ask God to bring someone into your life you can assist who is sincere and lacking in the material gifts you have been granted, so you can encourage and give to her. Do a good deed toward a person without telling anyone else about it. "So that your giving will be in secret, and your Father who sees what is done in secret will reward you" (Matthew 6:4).

---

32 Emphasis added.

Happiness = Compatibility in Character

Years ago, I noticed a really happy couple in church who had been married five years. They seemed so compatible that I decided one day to interview the wife. I asked, "Was it love at first sight?" She answered, "No, we were just friends and went out casually. I really liked him, and we had fun, but it was no big deal. After a few months I thought to myself, 'If he does not kiss me, I think I am going to die!'" They got married, started a family, and have lived happily ever after.

One of my closest friends is a writer and former model in NYC. I have known her for years, and she has never once said anything bad to me about her husband. She truly loves him and respects him. When they first met, they began doing things together as friends. Then she described what happened next as, "He *got* me." She explained she did not really feel that attracted to him initially, but noticed that when they spoke by phone, she never wanted the conversation to end. The chemistry grew from their friendship and compatibility. Having heard stories from me over the years about chemistry blindsiding me with a few men, she wisely warned that nothing good had ever come out of her relationships when they were led by chemistry. She acknowledged, of course, that the chemistry has to hit you at some point; it's just that you have to be compatible enough to truly be friends. About her husband, she put it beautifully like this: "He's not the romance of my life, but he's the love of my life."

It is rare to find true compatibility, along with the chemistry and attraction a healthy relationship requires. Far too many people get themselves into a counterfeit situation, never knowing the real thing even though they are married. How happy I am today that God has helped me avoid such a quagmire when it can be so hard to determine the difference between chemistry and love while dating. True love can only come with true compatibility in character, and that takes *time* to be revealed. I will know I am with the right person when both my heart and brain agree about it.

I gave up trying to change a man (i.e., praying for him to have better character) a long time ago. People are who they are. Too many times I have hoped to influence someone for the better, only for that person to bring me down emotionally by hurting my feelings and taking me for granted. I know myself and am happy with the person I am, and if someone does not fit with me on the inside, it does not matter how physically attracted we are. It will not work. He's not going to change me a bit more than I am going to change him. I like putting in the effort it takes to work on myself to be the best person I can be, inside and out, and I need someone who has that same high standard for himself, too. Without such compatibility, it is really impossible even to be close friends.

A friend is so rare that I have come to see a true friend as a gift only God can give me in both men and women. Think about the attributes you have in common when you have a best girlfriend. For me to want to spend a lot of time with a girlfriend, some things are required: She understands and shares my faith in God. We have mutual respect for one another as people. She does not hurt my feelings but makes me feel good when I am around her. I gravitate toward women as friends who are artistic in some way, since I am a very creative person. She has to have good character. She needs to have a good business sense, assuming wise financial responsibility when it comes to money. She works at taking care of herself. She loves her family. She is reliable and keeps her word. We have fun together. The friendship is mutually supportive and giving. She is intelligent. Having her in my life brings out the best in me. She is someone I want to be like. She has time for me, and I have time for her whenever we need a friend. These are the exact same qualities required in order for me to have a close friendship with a man.

Men of poor character sure know how to ignite the chemistry in us with sweet talk. Chemistry makes us feel loved, even when we are not. Cads only fail at their own game when they target a woman of good character. They won't conquer her if she keeps living her standards, keeping God as her God when temptation comes instead of the new man. Oil and water don't mix. Light and darkness don't match. Maybe you used to have good character before the wrong guy came along to charm you away from being true to who you know you are meant to be. If you are in a relationship now, ask yourself if he brings out the best in you or the worst. Happiness from within frees us to accept a man for who he is without trying to change him to make him right for us. When we get to know a man, we can stay with him if we are compatible and leave him if we are not. We can meet someone, wish he was more compatible with us in character, accept the fact that he is not, and just let it be. This is true even in close working relationships. I don't associate with angry people, and I don't have people with bad character in my inner circle in life. Even when they are some of the most popular, I choose not to work with people in the entertainment business who overtly mock God and mock Christians. I show people respect, and I expect the same. Showing me respect is not too much to ask from people when I am hiring them as musicians to work with me. It is good to have boundaries. We have to take care of ourselves both professionally and personally in life.

If you find yourself being disappointed while dating a guy, stop to think about his character. If he consistently treats you in a way you would not treat him, you two have incompatible characters. It may seem like a bad man wants a good woman, but really he does not. Her standards are too high for him. Water seeks its own level. It is his life and his choice to determine his direction, even if he wants to remain lost. If he is a good man with moral standards, he will only match with a woman who keeps her standards high. Look for your character in another person. When you find it, only then will you have found a match.

When true love is growing platonically, the longer you are with him, the more you will love him. There is no such thing as true love without compatibility in character. Follow these tips and get to know a man in a pure way, and his character will be revealed a whole lot faster. You can't be *one* with a man if your characters don't match.

HOMEWORK

Homework for this tip is to make a list of attributes you need in a friend. Think of your best girlfriend, and ask yourself these questions: Do you pity her as someone who needs saving in order to become whole? Does she try to hold you back, intimidated by your success? Is she jealous? Is she full of rage on the inside? Does she control you so much that it drives you crazy? Is your close friendship with her shameful to you in any way, or is it instead a compliment to your life as a person? Do you find yourself realizing she has such poor self-esteem that you have to build her up emotionally to an exhausting extent? Do you admire the way she lives enough to want her character to rub off on you?

Ask yourself these same questions now about the man you are dating. Compatibility in character is the most determining factor, even coming before communication and chemistry.

"Can two walk together, except they be agreed?" (Amos 3:3).

It's a Trap If You
Are Trying to Save Him

*D*ating a man who does not see his need for God, praying for him, showing him grace, seeing him through eyes of mercy, forgiving *and* forgiving . . . may seem like a noble effort for a Christian woman, but it is not. Just as the Bible teaches us to be merciful toward others, it also gives us boundaries for our protection so our lives will not be brought down. Living by those boundaries certainly makes my life happy today. It is one thing for a Christian woman to meet a man, find out he is not a Christian, tell him about Jesus, pick up on the fact that he is not interested in knowing God, and *let him go*. (Why? Because a woman with a *relationship* with Jesus as her Friend and Savior will never be compatible with a man who does not share in such a relationship; if he cannot understand her faith, he cannot truly understand her. It is far more than just a difference in religion.) It is yet another thing to be jerked around emotionally by a man who appears interested in knowing God but is not and is only out to deceive. It becomes downright manipulative and controlling for a Christian woman to meet a man, realize he is not interested in becoming a Christian, and stay in his life too long, taking him to church, hoping he will get saved. Trust me; it is a trap if you are trying to save him. God never saved you to be in a lonely relationship with the wrong guy. Even if it means staying single, don't miss out on the amazing journey that Jesus died on the cross for, so that you can live as a Christian woman, with or without a man.

Most men without God think they are hot. They are not nearly as hot as they think. One of the most appealing attributes a man can have is humility. It takes humility even to surrender our will to God's. No Christian woman should settle for a man who is incapable of such humility. We all have known men who are atheists and good men when it comes to how they treat their wives. For a Christian, it is more than finding a man who is *good* or *bad*. It is about compatibility. A woman who loves Jesus can certainly leave a man who doesn't in God's hands. No matter how she tries, she won't be compatible with him on the inside.

Affairs of the heart have the power to bring down a child of God like nothing else. I have seen this happen time and time again. We meet a man, begin to pray for him thinking we are being a good influence, when all along he is out to change us. By the time we finally accept this, the guy has emotionally worn us out, and we can see that he was never close to becoming a Christian after all. He was actually hoping to take us away from God. Men who are not saved want us to put pleasing them first, not God. They do not even understand the concept of pleasing God, because they don't believe in God. Too often, these men succeed in totally taking advantage of our willingness to show (too much) mercy on a lost soul.

When I first began counseling with Marilyn Brown, I went to a group session in Culver City when I lived in Los Angeles in 2002. It was only five dollars per group session and priceless to me in all I learned about healthy living. In 2003 I told the group about meeting a man on Match.com who said he was a Christian. By the time I realized he was about as far from Christianity as possible in his beliefs, I had let myself like him way too much too soon. It ended in a relatively short time, despite all of my prayers for the guy. I remained a Christian, and he remained lost in pagan spirituality. Before my relationship with him was over, the girls in the counseling session encouraged me to stay with him too long by saying, "You never know; he may love you enough to convert to Christianity," as if it were that easy.

This particular man turned out to have very strong Hindu beliefs that were 100 percent antagonistic to my faith in Jesus. He did not tell me his true beliefs in the beginning, but by the time the relationship ended, I learned more than I ever wanted to know about chakras and reincarnation. He was convinced that he was good looking due to a *former life*, though I told him science proves it was simply good genes from his mother and dad. Finally, one night (after he had come to church with me several times, and I had given him a Bible, praying every day for him), we attended a Bible study together. On the way home he told me how he used to keep a snake in a cage in his backyard. I asked, "A real, live snake?" The answer was, of course, yes. It was for serpent power and his Kundalini chakras. Worn out with all of this New Age gobbledygook, I had had it. "If you don't renounce this stuff, it is over," I said. Just that quickly, he answered, "Okay, let's end it now."

I went home and cried at the death of another dream. I wrote him a poem, and he sent me beautiful flowers with a note about how we were "once in a lifetime" but hoped we would connect in eternity forever as lovers. What in the world had happened in my two months with this man? What was all of that happiness I felt in the beginning every time the phone rang from him? It had certainly not been true happiness meant to last. It was more like a big misunderstanding, as I had fallen for the man I thought he was initially and who I wanted him to be, instead of who he really was. It was all some sort of fantasy and nothing real.

When I returned to the counseling session, I announced to the group that our relationship had ended, and I can remember Marilyn's response like it was yesterday. I told the group that I wish I had not stayed so long with him, and Marilyn smiled with this canny observation to the girls in the group, "She was trying to save him." Well, yes, I thought to myself, I was. It was a moment of insanity showing itself in all of my missionary efforts with that guy! Marilyn convinced me that although I worked as a missionary in my nonprofit organization, it was not my place to save a man in a relationship. Not all of us get a storybook ending like the *African Queen*.[33] These days when a rebel meets a good woman, he usually stays a rebel and looks for a woman of lesser quality instead of working on himself to become better.

I had a relationship with a well-known author years ago, who told me he loved me. He even said he loved me *because* I am a Christian, and it made him feel good to know I prayed for him. By his own admission, he was miserable on the inside. Though he knew the Bible and had even written a book about its historicity, he did not want to accept God's love for him on God's terms. I decided to buy him a very nice pen. It was a gift for his soul, I explained, as I thoughtfully engraved his name on it with Bible verses about how much God loved him. He didn't want it. He never even thanked me and said it was the craziest thing I could have done. He never cared to look up the verses engraved on the beautiful pen, and I believe my gesture even scared him spiritually. It was too pure for him. I told him he had humiliated me by not even thanking me for the pen or wanting it, and he arrogantly responded, "Well, the root word of humiliate is humility, Dwayna," as if I needed to become more humble. When I bought him the special gift, I thought he loved me. One thing is for certain, he did not love my God, although he had a fascination with fulfilled prophecies from the Old Testament. He had written a book on religion but did not want God in his heart. I buffed out his name on the beautiful pen, put my own name on it, and kept the pen for myself along with the Bible verses for *my* soul. I'll always treasure it. (As a matter of fact, I am pictured with that special pen on the cover of this book.)

You have to let a miserable, lost man go. If God is going to save the

---

33 A classic movie made in 1951, where a rebel played by Humphrey Bogart falls in love with a missionary in Africa played by Katharine Hepburn, adapted from the 1935 novel of the same name by C.S. Forester.

guy, He can do it without you. In all reality, you are too good for a man who does not have faith in your God. You have been "made clean," as the Bible puts it, by the blood Jesus shed on the cross for you. The lost man wants no part of that. He rejects it. Move on. Get happy on your own and stay that way. Remember, you are the apple of God's eye,[34] and He is jealous for all of your heart. God certainly knows how to accomplish His will in your life, and if that includes marriage, God will do it. That means a relationship from God will have spiritual compatibility and will actually make you love the Lord more.

When I was growing up, I naturally assumed that I would get married and have kids. Life was simple growing up in Tennessee. Adults got married. My parents assumed that they would be grandparents to the kids I would have when I married *the right one*. So with this honorable goal in mind, whenever I met someone new I *liked*, I began a routine, which I felt had promise. I took it upon myself to make praying for the new man's salvation my mission. I prayed countless prayers for lost guys, asking the God of miracles to change any of the many wrong ones into the right one for me. If I gave up this routine, I figured, there would probably never be anyone for me. (There was such a scarcity of single men in church circles that I still, to the date of this publication, have never been attracted to any of them as a potentially appropriate mate for me, although I have them as friends in my life and appreciate them as people.)

What I found was that the experience of befriending a man closely who did not understand my love for Jesus would not bring satisfaction to my innermost being. I discovered that such men couldn't even truly *know me* without believing in my God. None of them could offer me lasting happiness, because I found myself feeling lonely when I was with them, realizing how different I was from them on the inside. I knew I would never marry a man *unequally yoked* to me, as the Bible puts it, but I mistakenly thought that spending time with a man who was *fun* but did

---

34 Psalm 17:8

not understand or share my love for Jesus could fulfill me. I was wrong. God's love for me always came between us.

Not only that, but as the years passed, I realized it could very well be the enemy of my soul, Satan, bringing so many deceivers my way to hurt me with the goal of bringing me down. I knew I had to get smarter, but yet I could not give up on my dream of marriage; hence, give up the cycle of praying for some guy who was never compatible with me to become miraculously appropriate for me. I would pray, reminding God that since I did not deserve salvation, perhaps He could show the same mercy to a man of my choosing by saving him and making us compatible. I would forgive guys for way too much, reasoning that I was obligated to go on forgiving them on behalf of all God had forgiven me. It was flawed reasoning. (How different it is now to think of a man who can be there for me when I need rescuing from pain, who is capable of pointing me to turn to God in life when I am the one going through a hard time. It is simply something a lost man cannot do.)

Was I not trying hard enough to find this *right one*? I got on the Internet dating sites to just make sure. I travel quite a bit with my work, always keeping my eyes open to find him when I least expect it. I have gone out looking with my girlfriends, and I have stayed in countless nights being true to myself, married to my work. In all of these years, there has been no one for me. I sang and spoke at Christian conferences thinking, *I may meet the right man for me here.* Though lots of Christian men asked me out and were compatible spiritually, I had zero attraction or chemistry for any of them. It was as if the only thing we had in common was faith in Jesus. Falling in love requires more than that. When it is meant to be, it is mutual. It never was. Maybe it was okay after all. When I woke up one day happy and complete on my own, it actually felt better than having a man.

There are now more single women than married women in

America.[35] I look around to find beautiful, smart women from every background and religion not able to find the *right one*. Not only that, they no longer even need marriage to complete them. I know now my life has turned out just fine after all. God had other things for me to do with my time than deal with the disappointment I would have experienced from marrying the wrong man.

As the years went by and I never got married, some married Christians stumped at my *still single* status would then conclude, "Well, maybe you have the 'gift of singleness' like the Apostle Paul."[36] Was that supposed to make me feel good? They may as well have given me a key to the convent and signed me up to be a nun. How was I supposed to respond to this sermonic *gift of singleness*? How strange sounding, especially since I had never dreamed of the *gift of singleness* for myself as I grew up. I certainly never felt I had it when I was writing songs, caught up in some oxytocin-filled-dream with a guy. I used to pray to God for Him to not let the feeling end every time infatuation swept me away. With all of the flowing creativity, it never crossed my mind that the avalanche of emotion I felt was for the *gift of singleness*. At the end of every relationship, was the *gift of singleness* supposed to hurt so much?

I can make a long list of beautiful and impressive women, Christians and non-Christians, who must also have "the gift of singleness," because there is no man for them either, or at least not yet. We all have our war stories about the guys who turned out to have bad character, who we thought we loved in the beginning, and how, finally, many of us have

---

35 "Why More Women Choose Not To Marry," by Pepper Schwartz, CNN, October 15, 2014, http://www.cnn.com/2014/10/15/opinion/schwartz-single-women/index.html. Also see "Singles Nation: Why So Many Americans Are Unmarried," cover story by Stephanie Hanes, Christian Science Monitor, June 14, 2015, http://www.csmonitor.com/USA/Society/2015/0614/Singles-nation-Why-so-many-Americans-are-unmarried

36 The Bible speaks about some people who never marry having "the gift of singleness" in 1 Corinthians 7:6-9.

become happy on our own. What is the alternative? The alternative to happiness as a single person is self-pity, which is a depowering existence that can only lead to more hurt with more wrong guys.

Call it the gift of singleness if you want. It is simply making the most of every day in a fulfilling life when there is no man compatible. No need to wear a sign reading, *I have the gift of singleness*. At any given time, God can and will bring someone to you whom He has designed for you, *if* He has such a person. It is just that you are not going to put your life on hold in the meantime or make some quest for romance an idol, when trusting in God is simply enough.

When we learn to thank God for whatever He wants and stop feeling sorry for ourselves for not having what we think we want in any area of life, then and only then, will we be happy. When we are feeling sorry for ourselves, we are actually mad at God deep down. He never saved us to be mad at Him. He saved us to praise Him and enjoy Him. If God had given me what I always thought I wanted in a husband and kids, my life would have been totally different. I am sure I would have been very happy if I had married a man I loved and had his children, but I would not have begun a worldwide, nonprofit organization that has helped so many people and worked it to the degree I have. I would not be writing this book. The truth is I have a happy life today, as my fulfillment comes from helping and encouraging others. It is a happiness unlike what any man can offer, and it is not worth throwing away for a man who is wrong for me.

HOMEWORK

Homework for this tip is to read John, chapter 17. Put your own name there as you read it. If you are a Christian, know that Jesus is praying for you as His possession, for you to be kept from "the evil one." Notice that He does not pray for the world but for those who are His because they are "not of the world."

When I read this scripture with my name inserted in those verses and realize that Jesus prays to the Father for *Dwayna*, because *Dwayna* is not of the world, I cannot help but cry. I am amazed at how much my Savior loves me. He is a Good Shepherd and knows how to keep us. Please read this chapter anew as a promise from Jesus to you if you are a Christian. If you are not a Christian and may be confused about what it means to have a personal relationship with God, please read the entire book of John in the Bible and ask God to show you.

Don't ever let yourself feel rejected by a man because you are a Christian. If your heart is in the right place, you will be the one rejecting him with a happiness you already have that he knows nothing about.

Do not be unequally yoked with unbelievers. For what partnership has righteousness with lawlessness? Or what fellowship has light with darkness? What accord has Christ with Belial? Or what portion does a believer share with an unbeliever? What agreement has the temple of God with idols? For we are the temple of the living God; as God said, "I will make my dwelling among them and walk among them, and I will be their God, and they shall be my people." (2 Corinthians 6:14-16)

Beware of Online Dating

*I*n 2003 I was having a happy day in California with a man I had met on Match.com. He owned a gorgeous home in Anaheim, and he had taken me to picturesque places in Laguna Beach in what certainly looked like a beautiful life from any perspective at first glance. We were traveling once again in his new Mercedes on the way to his second home in Arizona. Everything was beautiful, including his swimming pool and boat. We were holding hands in the car, and I was thinking to myself, *This Match.com thing seems to be working out well!* He had begun talking about marriage to me and having kids. He had already told me he loved me after one month. I had purposely never taken a trip with a man before, as I only wanted to take trips with my husband after marriage, but I made this exception to see his second home. He said he respected my values and assured me I would have my own room in his new home in Arizona. He described himself as "Christian" on his Match.com profile.

Driving through the desert to his home in Arizona on a bright, sunny day, he said, "Darling, I need to tell you something." I looked at him and realized he was sounding serious. What was he going to say? He had already told me he loved me. He continued, "Promise me you won't leave." I said, "Well, we are in the desert now, and there is no place for me to go, so tell me. I'm sure there is nothing you could say that would make me want to leave."

He said, "I realize this is going to sound strange to you, because you are a strong Christian." Now I was getting concerned. I repeated, "Go ahead and tell me. What is it?" He said, "Well, I have hesitated to tell you, but we differ a little in our spiritual beliefs," adding, "I just adore your spirituality, though." I could never have imagined what he was going to say. After hesitating nervously, he finally confessed with all sincerity, "I believe there are lost souls in the air, and sometimes I yawn to metaphysically help them find their way."

I swallowed hard and thought, *I knew I shouldn't have gotten on Match.com!*

I asked calmly, "Could you please repeat that?"

He said, "I yawn to help lost souls find their way."

After a pregnant pause I looked at him and said, "Thank you for telling me." I just couldn't keep holding his hand in the car. "Sorry, but that is just a little too weird," I explained, as I began feeling very lonely all of a sudden in the beautiful Mercedes. For the rest of the weekend when he would yawn, I could only think of the *lost souls*, and the yawning scared me to death. With every yawn I would ask him, "What is happening?"

Suddenly my Prince Charming was looking more like a lost soul right there beside me, channeling other "lost souls in the air." I challenged him to read what the Bible says about demons. From a Christian perspective, he was involved in demonic activity. We were no match. No wonder my dad called from Tennessee out of the blue to my apartment in Santa Monica, not knowing what was going on, and asked, "Are you okay?" My dad said he could feel something was wrong as he prayed for me. The poor guy had a satanic spirit. When my mother learned about his occult spirituality, she said, "Oh, honey, he's not the one," with fear in her voice. My entire family urged, "Leave!" Thanks to their prayers and the fact that Jesus keeps me as His own, I left the man, along with all of his lost souls in the air. He was the only man I have ever known who said he was so "highly evolved" that a poltergeist spirit lifted him up off the bed long ago. He said as a child he used to see "dead people" in the air. At first glance, he looked normal and impressive. No doubt he was troubled both mentally and spiritually and nowhere close to right for me. It ended after only two months. The last month we did not see each other very much at all since I was in Santa Monica and his main home was on the other side of Los Angeles. It was over for good all right, for my own good, but it still hurt. The girls in my group counseling session certainly got a kick out of this story back in Los Angeles at the Culver City office with Marilyn Brown. Unfortunately, he came to be referred to in the group as "the yawner." (He is the same man with New Age and Hindu beliefs I referenced in the previous Tip #20.) Needless to say, he was not the one. We were as different as could be on the inside.

Even though we met in person right away, it took a little over a month for the truth to be revealed about who he really was. I am sure it would have taken much longer had we not met in person and just continued *getting to know each other* online. With all of his Hindu spiritual beliefs and practices, I asked him at the end, "Why did you say you were a Christian on your profile?" He answered, "Because I was raised Catholic."[37]

Don't trust anyone you meet online, and this includes Facebook. Don't let yourself start liking men after just viewing profiles. I once connected with a man on Facebook who said he wanted to work with me in ministry via my nonprofit organization, but I am sure now he had ulterior motives. His photos online turned out to be a tad out of date. When we finally met to work together, he was so old I barely recognized him. As we spoke in person, he literally had to pause to fix his teeth from falling out! Don't let yourself feel anything for a mere image online. Stay smart and meet him in the real world before he has a chance to touch your heart in cyberspace.

---

37 For more on the difference between occult spirituality and Christianity, read *Out of India* by Caryl Matrisciana or *Death of a Guru* by Rabi Maharaj.

HOMEWORK

Homework for this tip is to Google "Dangers of Online Dating." When I typed those words into the Internet search engine, I got almost two million results. Most of the dating sites are not free. I also found one site (still in business) charging five thousand dollars to join, and this site was reported on RipOffReport.com for being a fraud. Please go to RipOffReport.com and type in "dating service" to search the site for scams. Be prepared for a lot of reading. When I checked at the time of this publication, there were two hundred and sixty-six reports on match-dating companies exposed as rip-offs. Before you spend your money in hopes of finding the right person on these sites, do yourself a favor and research them. The Internet can be a very dangerous playground.

Some people become literally addicted to online dating, keeping their profile on dating sites for years. If that is the case with you, it may seem too hard at first to stop it altogether. Try taking just a week away from it, then a month, and then hopefully longer. Becoming a friend to yourself and being at ease on the inside is the most important thing. You will never know the life you are missing unless you break free from the false crutch of chronic online searching and emailing. Growing in the strength of walking alone until you meet someone for you in the real world can be a much more enriching life.

On the other hand, I have known people who have gotten married after being introduced online. It is just nice to remember that men and women have been meeting and getting married long before the computer age. As for me personally, I have gotten to the place where I have lost all desire for online dating. I simply have better things to do with my time than perusing hundreds of profiles and emailing strangers online. Remember, God has a way of bringing two people together if He has someone for you, and He does not need the Internet.

"Do Not Give the Devil an Opportunity"

I went back to Internet dating in 2003 on all the Christian dating sites, hoping to speed up the process of finding the right match for me. After my experience with the man I just described in the previous two tips, I was ready to meet someone new. After all, doesn't it take my meeting someone new to get over the last guy? The answer is, of course, no, but at the time it seemed like the only way to ease my loneliness. I found that there was always another man waiting online, and another and another—all different varieties of *wrong*.

It did not take long for a guy to begin emailing me from the Los Angeles area who had an impressive *Christian* profile. He had his own plane, according to the online description, and he had posted many photos of himself in *his plane*. I noticed right away that we were compatible politically, and I found myself getting very excited from the first *wink* online. He called, and we set up our first date.

When he came knocking on my door with flowers, he was much taller than I thought he would be. You would think I could have picked the right height for me on this made-to-order match, but men often lie about their height on the profiles. At least he was not shorter than I ever imagined, as an overabundance of the guys online had turned out to be.

He was about 6'4", and I am 5'3", so I definitely chose to wear my heels. He was still really cute, so we were off to dinner.

I could tell from the conversation during our two hour dinner that he was looking for a woman to help raise his little girl, although he said that he and his wife were still best friends and went to many functions together. On that first date, I found out the plane was actually not his. "It used to be," he explained. The picture was getting clearer. We spoke more about his little girl and ex-wife than about me. I listened as he was challenged to describe his jobs in real estate, fumbling for words to articulate more about his being an entrepreneur. By the end of the night, I realized he was the type to spend far more time digitally winking at women online than working in real estate.

He valet-parked his car on our date, and guess who had to pay? He did not have any cash, so he asked me to pay! I thought, *So much for this entrepreneur with his own plane*, as I handed him twenty dollars for parking. We spoke some about Christianity, as I told him about the work of my nonprofit organization. I could tell my Christian work was something he had no desire to understand. Though he said going to church on Sunday was an important part of his life, I knew on the first date we were no match made in heaven.

As he drove me back to Ocean Boulevard in Santa Monica where I lived, I was thinking, *This guy is not it*. He walked me to the door and gave me a kiss. (This was way before I had learned to date without kissing.) Then something very strange happened with this man who was not at all right for me. He gave me the best kiss of my life! The kiss was like we were destined to be together forever. All of a sudden, I felt like I was never meant to stop kissing him.

He left my apartment, and I hit my knees in prayer, asking God to help me. I knew I was in trouble, because suddenly I *liked* this guy with whom I was not compatible. I asked God to help me leave him, because there was a very strong attraction between us. The next day when he called, I conveyed that it was best for us not to see each other again. I explained, "I know your daughter means a lot to you, as she should, but I am not her mother and never will be. I am glad she has a close relationship with her mother, and all three of you do many things together, but this does not seem like a smart situation for me. I want a man who can be emotionally monogamous with me. It seems there would be no real place for me in the triangle of your child, the mother of your child, and you." He replied simply, "You are a smart girl." We said goodbye. Although he promised previously to pay me back for parking, I had to add, "You do owe me twenty dollars for the valet parking." He said he would leave it with my doorman. I wished him the best, and we hung up. I thought that was that.

The next day, after our goodbye, he emailed to let me know he had left the money with my doorman and then had the audacity to write, "Dwayna, I just wanted to say that I find myself extremely attracted to you. If you ever want to get together to just have sex let me know."

"How could you ask me such a thing? Even if I were not a Christian, I wouldn't want an arrangement like that," I replied. "I have a nonprofit organization supported by Christians who give to my work because they trust me to live it. I fit only with a *real* Christian, a man who shares my same standards." I ended cordially, "Thanks for the dinner and for paying me back the twenty dollars."

He wrote back to apologize and gave me many compliments. Then he asked again, "Don't you want to have sex?" I realized nothing good would ever come of keeping him in my life for any reason. I answered, "No, I don't want to be used, and please don't ever be in touch with me again."

What a jerk! Though we both professed to be Christians, our morals were about as compatible as oil and water. I can remember it all like it was yesterday because it was such a disappointment. If I had been wiser, I would not have been so disappointed because I would have known better than to get my hopes up about a person even before the first date.

Can you imagine how much it would have hurt me if I had not stuck to my standards? Do you think I could have dated that man in a pure way? Absolutely not, not after that kiss and all of those fireworks that came with it! The only thing I could do was leave.

The Bible has a definition for immorality.[38] I choose to believe it. As a result, I never have to worry about getting sexually transmitted diseases or getting pregnant outside of marriage. It feels good to live my standards. I have never regretted living in authenticity, no matter what it has cost me. Sin only brings regret and pain. God does not want us even flirting and toying with immorality, so close to sin that we are in a dangerous place, all the while asking God for strength. God does not want us so consumed by lust that we cannot even think straight, while at the same time praying for God to help us resist it. He wants us far, far away from danger in a very safe place. As I have previously explained, when we feel a lot of lust for someone, this does not necessarily mean it is love or that love will follow. The Bible says there are spirits at work—the Holy Spirit draws us to Jesus, and evil spirits draw us away from Him . . . People have a soul and a spirit, and not all spirits are the same.[39]

Lest you call this battle between good and evil some sort of fantastic fiction, consider that if Satan did not exist, Jesus would have had no reason to die on the cross for our sins. Satan does exist as the spiritual enemy of mankind, and he is immoral. It is not by accident that some of the worst people on earth always do what "seems right in their own eyes,"[40] sleeping with whomever they want, whenever they want.

God does not say to fight temptation; He says to flee it.[41] There *is* such a thing as *sin*, though the Hollywood mainstream denies it.[42] We see that when we are *tempted* (something that could not exist without the existence of sin) that temptation has the power to hurt us and even

38   1 Corinthians 6:18; 1 Thessalonians 4:3-4
39   Matthew 12:43-45; Acts 19:1-20; 1 John 4:1
40   Judges 21:25; Deuteronomy 12:8-9; Proverbs 21:2
41   1 Corinthians 6:18-20; 2 Timothy 2:22
42   Romans 3:23; Romans 6:22-23

ruin our lives.[43] We must take it very seriously. If we *don't* know what the Bible teaches about how to live, that is not God's fault. He gave us His Word, which is a blueprint for how we are to protect ourselves in this world with confidence as we rely on God. He gave us His Word because He loves us.[44]

When you find yourself attracted to a married man, for instance, the only way to win is to leave. Stay away from him. Remember that seduction *feels* good, but Satan is "the spirit at work in the sons of disobedience."[45] Satan seduces with lies to hurt people as an assault on God. Satan knows that God created us to know and walk in His love—love that is pure and honest. The only way to find love for your soul and peace is to choose to live in obedience to the Bible. "Beside the still waters" is where God wants to keep us to restore our soul, as Psalm 23 teaches, not in immoral danger.

A wise life is nowhere close to the illustration in the Bible of the prodigal son's "pig pen."[46] The story of the prodigal son is about a son who squandered his inheritance. He ended up literally feeding pigs in a dirty hog pen when his father was missing him all along in a royal palace where he could have remained, had he not run away. He finally humbled himself to go back home, expecting his father to be angry. But much to his surprise, his father greeted him with open arms and threw a homecoming party in celebration when he returned. The father had been missing his son all along. He was not satisfied living in his father's beautiful home where clean living seemed boring, so he left. It was the son's fault he had squandered his inheritance from his wealthy father. Yet the father was there missing him and loving him the whole time he was off wandering around, even when the son ended up slopping with hogs in the mud without a penny to his name. All he had to do was find his way back home for his father to mercifully take him back with open arms.

---

43 James 1:14-15
44 John 3:16
45 Ephesians 2:2-5
46 Luke 15:11-32

That is how it is with us if we are God's children. God offers us happiness, peace, sobriety, honesty, and all the gifts money cannot buy if we stay close to Him. Our Father is rich in houses and lands and owns the whole world.[47] We just have to wait on Him when it comes to our rewards.[48] Sin can offer us nothing, yet we sometimes think that we are missing out on what the world's immoral party has to offer, so off we go to squander our inheritance. But the world's drunken playground will always be dirty and uncomfortable to a child of the King,[49] because Jesus never redeemed us for the hog pen. Christians are called lambs in the Bible, with Jesus as our Shepherd to lead us.[50] If you are a little lamb, get out of the dirty hog pen. You don't belong there. Come back to the clean, green paths of righteousness the Father has for you far away from the filth of sin.

Did you know the core theme of Satanism is to do whatever you want (in rebellion from God's law), as long as you do not hurt anyone?[51] Is this what you believe, too? Consider this quote from Altreligion.about. com on Satanism: *"To the LaVeyan Satanist, Satan is a myth, just like God and other deities. Satan is also, however, incredibly symbolic, representing all of those things within our natures that outsiders might tell us is dirty and unacceptable."*

Decide today, for your own protection, to agree with God about not only who He is, but who Satan is. The Bible teaches that God created us in His image to be *pure*, like Him. The heart of the Christian message is self-denial.[52] Satanism is all about self-indulgence and rebellion— rebellion from God's commandments, rebellion from Jesus and why He came to die on the cross for our sins. We have two enemies: the devil and

---

47 Isaiah 40; Psalm 95; Psalm 50:10-12
48 Isaiah 40:31
49 Revelation 19:16
50 Isaiah 40:11; Luke 15:1-7; John 10
51 See *The Book of the Law*, Aleister Crowley, 1904 and *The Satanic Bible*, Anton LaVey, 1969.
52 Matthew 16:24

our flesh.[53] It is because of God's love that He gives us rules for living, because He wants to protect us from the bondage of sin. Satan sets you free *to* sin. Jesus sets you free *from* it. Choose the freedom that brings no shame.

HOMEWORK

Homework is to read the story of the prodigal son in Luke 15 in the Bible. If you have roamed far away, know that your heavenly Father is waiting for you with His arms wide open to welcome you back. Even before you tell Him you are sorry, His mercy waits for you. If you would like to become born again into God's family, there is a Savior death could not hold just waiting to redeem you . . .

Download on Kindle *The Awesome Wonder of God's Word*, by Warren B. Smith.[54]

Follow these tips, and you can stay far away from the road of self-destruction. Even if it means remaining single, it is worth it, as you will have gifts within your being no sexual immorality can give you. You will experience how it feels to be happy and at peace within yourself, with or without a man.

"Everyone who commits sin is the slave to sin" (John 8:34).

"Do not give the devil an opportunity" (Ephesians 4:27).

---

53 Galatians 5:13-25
54 Published by Lighthouse Trails.

Don't Date Your Neighbor in Your Apartment Building

I've made this mistake twice, and I think I have finally learned my lesson. Don't date your neighbor in your apartment building. There is no place like home, so keep it as a place free from anxiety. If you feel you must date your neighbor, by all means, follow my advice in Tip #16, and don't kiss him for at least three months. If it is not meant to be, you will probably know it within a month of no kissing, and you will be so thankful you never kissed your neighbor when you see him coming and going with other women *where you live*.

In 2002 I had just moved to my apartment in Santa Monica. I was checking my mail when a guy behind me said, "Hey, Babe." (Yes, this is the same guy I wrote about in Tip #9.) Unfortunately, I was too naive at the time to know that when a guy calls you *Babe* at first glance that is a bad sign. He introduced himself and explained he was my neighbor. He lived on my floor, and he invited me over to watch the sunset in his apartment with his ocean view. He was very handsome and was never at a loss for words. I remember thinking I had never met anyone like him. That was right, because I had never in my life met a womanizer to the degree he was, and at that point in my life, I had never known a man who was supported financially by women. As it turned out, he conned women to give him their money and was not able to support himself financially as the entrepreneur he claimed to be, despite his Ivy League education in finance. Life for him was one big party. But with all his smooth talking, time exposed him to be emotionally unavailable when he began to truly care.

We never officially dated. It was as if he had some sort of fear of my relationship with God. That certainly did not keep him from mocking the same faith that intimidated him. It was the first time anyone ever called me a "Bible Thumper." Once again, my relationship with God was my protection. I would find out in due time that he saved his dates for the women with whom he had (group) sex. And women there were. The elevator was like a revolving door, as I would see all the women coming and going living on the same floor with him. I got to know a few of his girlfriends by first name, and we would speak when they passed me in the hall on their way to see him. His sex addiction was more about his ability to control women than anything else. He would go out to a bar at night with the challenge of whether or not he could convince a woman to come home with him. It was all about the challenge. He was one lost man, and I felt the need to pray for him. I had not yet found happiness apart from such a mission, so I prayed for him every day. I would find out soon enough that when the Bible says, "Love thy neighbor," God did not mean this one!

His family was from Nashville, like mine, and I ended up befriending his sister and mother when they would visit to the point that I saw them in Nashville when I visited my family. They were hoping and praying he would get saved. They figured I was the perfect girl for the job. His sister and mother called me "a good influence." I guess they did not stop to think about whether or not it would be good for *me* to be around him as a so-called friend. On this mission to soften his hard heart, it was my heart that got broken. No one is perfect, but I will say this: we were not on the same level in character there on the same floor.

After I had bonded with his family, I could tell his heart had been touched. He stuttered so much around me that this gregarious womanizer was at a loss for words. I am thankful for the moment because God taught me it was not just that he did not *want* to settle down; but he *could* not. He didn't know how to be his true self. He didn't even know how to talk to a woman if he felt sincere emotion for her. The forty-five-year-old man regressed to a nervous third grader. He could barely finish a sentence that day when his heart had been touched toward me. That was as close as we ever got to anything real. If I had only been street-smarter, I would have kept my distance from him initially. But we don't know what we don't know. It takes our missteps sometimes to keep us on the right path in the long run.

I said goodbye to him many times, but it seemed nearly impossible to stay gone living on the same floor. No matter how I tried, I could not stay away longer than a month. I would see him in the elevator, and we would begin talking about his family or whatever subject he wanted to bring up to manipulate his way back into my life. I will give him one thing—he did not want to lose me as a *friend* in his life. He even went so far as to take photos of me doing my Christian nonprofit work at Venice Beach for newsletters. He also helped me get all of the paperwork done for the official 501c3 to be registered. As we were walking along Ocean Avenue one day after lunch, out of nowhere, he told me he loved me. I am not sure what he meant by that. I guess we had both come to rely on each other to an extent. He gave me a key to his place, asking me to water his plants while he was out of town. He would come back, and we would be talking when a woman would call. He would say, "You need to go now, because I have a date. You have to leave now, because one of my girlfriends is coming over." I would go back to my apartment, cry, and pour out my heart to God in prayer. Trying to be a good influence on him sure was hurting me. It was a lonely experience, being his friend.

One day after saying goodbye several times to him over the course of six months, and for whatever reason returning to try once again to be *friends*, I gave him back his key to his apartment. I had had it. I had grown to care for him way too much. He did not keep his word half of the time, and it hurt me to see the other women coming and going. I knocked on his door and said, "Here are your keys. You don't really care about me. I'm done." Without any warning, he lashed out at me like never before and raged, "I care about you! I care about you! Get out!" Fuming right up in my face, he cursed and pointed out the door for me to leave. There he was, telling me he cared about me while ordering me to leave at the same time. I headed back to my apartment in tears, promising myself that this time I would never return. He yelled down the hallway, as I walked away, "See you next month! You'll be back!" This relationship had reached an all-time low.

My codependent efforts to help him had been to no avail. But my prayers were paying off, because I then took a big step to help myself. I began getting professional counseling for the first time in my life. I never went back to the man. His sister even asked me to go back to befriend him and continue to try to "witness to him" to tell him more about my relationship with Jesus for him to get saved. I refused. I ended up losing touch with the family. From the terrible day when he ripped me apart verbally, right up in my face commanding me to leave, I never returned. When I would see him in the elevator, I kept looking up and did not respond ever again when he spoke to me. When the day came for me to move out of the apartment building, I never told him goodbye. I began getting private counseling with Dr. Sherrie Zander in Los Angeles and then Marilyn Brown in group counseling, and I really needed them both. When a woman is with a man with so many problems, she has problems, too. I learned that if you don't want to get sick, you have to stay away from sick people. Disease is contagious. I shook the dust off my feet there in Santa Monica at my apartment next to the ocean. Much to his surprise, I kept on walking away.

His family apologized, and his parents said, "We don't know what happened to our son." When we first met, he did not introduce himself as a sex-addicted atheist who was an alcoholic, financially supported by the women he dated. He didn't tell me that his ocean-front apartment was under rent control, and he was getting it for about half of what I was paying for my smaller place. I had to find out all of that on my own, as well as waste a lot of my days in sadness wishing he would give me something that he could not even give himself, much less any woman—sincerity.

Years later I was living in Atlanta when a cute guy got in the elevator with me in my condominium building. He flirted, "You look great. Where are you going?" I answered that I was simply running errands, and as he got out of the elevator he said he hoped to see me again. We lived in a high rise with secure parking. He followed me out of the parking garage in his nice car. When we stopped at the light to get on Peachtree Road, he got out of his car, walked over to mine, and knocked on my window. I rolled it down, and he said, "Have dinner with me tonight." I was flattered and amused by this in the middle of traffic. It was charming. I hesitated, and he said, "Come on, give me an answer. The light is changing. We can meet in the lobby and go to dinner." I hesitated again, but I figured one dinner could not hurt, so I said, "Well, okay." We had a nice time over dinner. I could tell though, through conversation, that this man was not right for me. He seemed like a party guy, and I have never been a party girl. I told him I did not kiss on the first date, but he kissed me anyway. That night on his balcony, I made the mistake of kissing him back.

The next night when he came to take me out again, I said, "I am a Christian, and I know you are not a Christian. Let's not go out anymore, because this is not going anywhere." He looked sad and replied, "I just don't feel I need saving. I don't need Jesus as my Savior." I said, "Well, I do, so we are too different." He left, and how I wish that could have been the end of the story. Unfortunately, we both had inexplicable chemistry for each other. It was unfortunate because the chemistry, once again, had not come to offer me love.

It was a gift from God that the man was planning to move out in a matter of weeks. (I was well on my way to happiness without a man, but I had just not arrived yet.) This man ended up calling me so much *as friends*, even after he moved out, that I had to block his number from my phone. When the blocking time expired from Verizon, my cell phone would ring again from him. After I had told him goodbye, he would call and say on my voice mail, "I am driving past your building missing you. Don't ever say I do not care." The saga continued. I had become a challenge for the man, and he was not about to give up. Marilyn, my counselor, told me that she thought he had a personality disorder. Though he would pursue me, it was as if he was out to hurt my feelings overall, jesting about my faith as a Christian with derogatory comments here and there. Yet, he would not leave me alone. How I wished I had not had that first dinner with him!

The guy turned out to be a compulsive liar, lying about minor things even when the truth would have been better. He did not have a good enough memory to keep all the lies straight, and the immaturity became too predictable and shallow for me over time, thank God. At one point, I asked him to pray with me. I reached over to hold his hand, and he jerked it away like the thought of praying with me terrified him. He said that he was afraid of reading the Bible. I told him such a fear was abnormal and alarming. I tried to explain to him the meaning of spiritual warfare. He did not excel at conversations with depth. He couldn't be real, even with himself, and once again, a lost soul remained lost in spite of all my prayers. I can only praise God for the fact that the whole thing got very old to me, and I moved on, literally. The calls finally stopped when I moved to New York City in 2011 and changed my cell number. If that had not happened, I believe the man would still be calling!

Another man living right above my unit in Atlanta went to church with me and said he wanted to date me. He probably was a genuine Christian, because he went to church with or without me, but he was going through a divorce with two children, and I did not feel it was a situation for me to enter. By his own admission, his ex-wife was a fine woman, and I was sorry for their broken home. Though we never dated, he could see when I was out on my balcony and would call and leave a message saying, "I know you are there. I just saw you out on your balcony. Please pick up the phone." It was hard to have privacy. When I told him I did not feel it was meant for us to date, he said, "Well, let's just do things as friends." I'm thankful I did not agree to that, realizing that unless I wanted to date him, it would not be fair to do things *as friends*. He obviously wanted more. It was harmless except for the frustrating months it took for him to finally get the point. He was a nice man but not right for me. He ended up moving out, and I was able to enjoy my balcony again in privacy.

It was there in Atlanta when one morning I woke up with the best gift God could give my soul. I did not feel lonely. After years and years of journaling, praying, counseling, memorizing Scripture, obeying the Bible, fleeing temptation, dating wrong men too long, *falling in love* and loving too much, my happiness had come. I was back to the girl I used to be as a child. God was enough. I was enough. I could feel myself as being whole, finally. God had been at work to give me something better all along, every single time I had prayed so desperately for a man.

HOMEWORK

Homework for this tip is to look up the definition of *home* in a dictionary. When I moved to NYC in 2011, I was shocked to find how many people living in my apartment building were hooking up and sleeping with each other. A neighbor of mine in Manhattan began having an affair with a guy who lived in our building on the penthouse level. She wanted to move when the relationship began spiraling down. Protect your home as a haven of peace for yourself away from the troubles of this world.

Have what I call a prayer spot in your home, a place to get down on your knees and talk to God. He is the only one who knows your every weakness and fear, and He is the only one who can heal you, not a man. If you believe yoga meditations are the same as prayer to God, please order the booklet *Be Still and Know That You Are Not God* by my friend, Warren B. Smith, on Kindle. Or you can read the text for free on the website for Lighthouse Trails Publishing.[55]

---

55   http://www.lighthousetrailsresearch.com/blog/?p=17572

It Doesn't Matter What a Bad Man Thinks of You

In 2014 I led the only free support group for battered women outside of a hospital in NYC. (I gave more details about how that came about in Tip #10.) A woman would speak about crazy-making mind games and horrific verbal and physical abuse she endured before leaving her abuser. Then she would ask, "Do you think he will miss me? Do you think he will ever be sorry for how he treated me?" She still wanted her abuser to think well of her. I would answer that because he is a person of bad character, his opinion does not matter. He is an abuser. Instead of worrying about him, it is her job to learn how to think clearly about herself.

If you leave a bad man, and he does not *like you anymore* (essentially because he has lost control), you have to remember that his opinion of you never mattered in the first place, not when it comes to defining who you are as a person. Even on his most complimentary day, his opinion of you was only his opinion. The truth about you is still the truth, no matter what he thinks.

Dating as my tips suggest is the best litmus test to show a man's true character. If a jerk cannot take advantage of you, he probably won't *like* you, and that is just fine. Don't worry. Hidden beneath his inflamed narcissism, he will admire your tenaciousness as the one who got away *after* you cherish yourself enough to move on. Bad men are choosy when picking their victims. Love is conditional depending on how much a woman can be manipulated.

Though it is a harsh parallel, abusive men pick needy women much like pedophiles pick needy children to molest. In the perpetrator's abuse of power, he makes the child feel very special in order to gain control. The perpetrator hides his true self like an actor. Only when he is told, "No," and the victim's sense of worth becomes more legitimized, is it revealed that the same friend who made the child feel so loved was all along the child's greatest foe. It is a perverted cycle of praises and insults, *and it has nothing to do with the victim*. The perpetrator is just being the deceiver he is. The fact that he has no respect for the child is out of the child's control.

When Jerry Sandusky chose underprivileged children to sexually abuse at Penn State, it was not because he was insane.[56] Don't be fooled; a predatory man knows exactly what he is doing. He knew the vulnerable victim was in need of his acceptance from the first *caring* conversation. The jig is up before it even begins with a woman who is happy and confident already.

I want to reiterate a point I made in Tip #9 about the dynamic at play in abusive relationships. The reason a woman returns to her abuser to be hurt over and over is because the same man who abuses her is also the same man who makes her feel better than she has ever felt. As bad as he makes her feel, he makes her feel that good again. Who is she without him? She must keep in his good graces because her sense of worth is contingent on his opinion of her.

The *father of lies*[57] wants you to doubt what you already know to be true about yourself and about God. Why would he change his methods when they have been working since the Garden of Eden? If he can make you doubt that the Bible is true and doubt sin will have consequences, you will probably succumb to any old sinister scheme at work. Sweet talk can be evil, coming from a bad man. God wants you in a more confident

56 https://en.wikipedia.org/wiki/Jerry_Sandusky
57 John 8:44

place where charm has no dominion over your brain.[58] It is a gift the good Lord will give you, if you will just pray it through.

Imagine Satan incarnate disguised as very handsome, telling you the most compliments you have ever received in your life. You feel so good. You like him! Not much more time passes until you are sure you also love him. There is one small problem. This *nice* man is only out to offer you hell on earth. You just don't know it yet. He is motivated by the art of the con. He thrives on selfishness. He has nothing good to offer you, and his spirit is out to take you away from the only God in existence with victory for your life. The old devil moves fast in lust to rob you of your fortitude. By the time you see him for who he really is, he is hoping you will be drained from all courage to leave. But Jesus is there interceding for you, giving you His strength in the midst of your weakness. Jesus destroyed Satan's power at the Cross, and Satan is already your defeated foe. You see now you were caught up in a delusion. This egotistical being was never even capable of love. He was just a deceiver all along. Far from romance, there was an invisible war going on for your soul.[59]

If you have just left a man with bad character, ask yourself why it matters to you what he thinks of you? It is your pride that makes you feel as if everyone needs to like you in the first place. As you get healthier, you will realize that God's opinion of you alone is enough to measure your worth. Besides, when you stop to think about it, the truth is that bad people usually don't like good people. Birds of a feather flock together. It can be a compliment to your good character when a bad person does not think well of you.

If I sense someone does not like me for some unknown reason, I stop to consider why. If I have done something to offend, I apologize and try to make it right. That being said, I don't idolize my friendships or my reputation. I give a lot, sometimes to a fault. When I am hurt by a *friend*, I often find myself thinking, *I would have never treated him (or her) that*

---

58 Romans 6:14
59 2 Corinthians 10:4

way. That is what happens every time I have tried to be close friends with a person of incompatible character. It does not work. I can think of times I have given way too much and stayed way too long in relationships, sometimes in hopes of vindicating myself in the eyes of a person who has shown too often not to appreciate me overall. In order to move on, you have to get to the point where it just does not matter.

I promise, if you will just give yourself enough time away, a jerk's cruelty and lack of appreciation will be totally irrelevant to your new-found life. You will know you are over him when you can leave him and his opinion of you in God's hands. If you have just had a breakup and are wondering whether or not your ex-boyfriend still thinks well of you, ask yourself whether or not you think well of him. If you don't like him, based on his character, why does it matter what he thinks of you?

Homework

For homework, Google *Oprah's Conversation with Child Molesters* to view the video on Oprah.com. Watch how they admit to telling the child everything they feel the child needs to hear in order for the child to feel loved. The molesters say they do this to gain control. They also admit in the video clip to never caring at all about the child.

If the underprivileged, innocent children could testify against Jerry Sandusky and, as a result, learn to live without his compliments in life, you can live without the compliments of a bad man, too. You can graciously leave a man who has hurt you with a strength he cannot steal away by trusting in God.

If you want to prove an abuser wrong and exonerate yourself against his insults, just go be happy. Make wise choices and live right. Build a great future for yourself where people of bad character don't belong. Wish any man well who has hurt you, and let your happiness be the best revenge.

Many Children
for You to Love

I always thought I would be a mother, and like my mother and grandmother, I have a love for children. I never wanted to have kids, though, without the right man. It was a big surprise as the years passed and the right man never came along to marry. God has given me peace about it. If I had had kids, I wouldn't have been able to accomplish all that I have in helping strangers via my nonprofit organization. With the world as it is today, I am sure I would have wanted to raise my children giving them my full attention to protect them from bad influences. I don't think I could have settled for a nanny raising them. Since I have poured my heart into other achievements, with a career that continues to be fulfilling, I can't complain about never having kids.

If you don't have children of your own and have a love for children, there are many ways for you to reach out to make a difference in a child's life: adopt an orphan; babysit children; volunteer as a teacher's aide or work as a substitute teacher in schools; become a nanny; teach kids at church; volunteer at a home for troubled teens; visit a sick child in the hospital; call Cancer Research Foundation or St. Jude's and find out how you can help children with cancer; work with children at a youth camp, and the list goes on and on.

A more unique opportunity would be to log on to my organization's website at Lighting the Way Worldwide[60] or directly at Rescue Ministries[61] and read about rescuing orphans in the Philippines. Find out more about how you can support an orphan, rescuing children from a literal trash dump in Cebu, to place them in a Christian children's home. Join Christians on a trip there, and you might even look into adopting a child to bring to America. Another special outreach is Harvest Home, a ministry that provides housing for pregnant women, helping homeless mothers and their babies. For opportunities to volunteer visit the website.[62] Or check out a crisis pregnancy center near you to help unwed mothers with child care after their baby is born.

Perhaps there is a hospital in your area with a Child Life Director who organizes crafts and other involvement with sick children, including holding sick or terminally ill infants while their parents are away. The hospitals allow volunteers to hold sick babies to help them recover, since the parents cannot be there around the clock. For instance, New York Methodist Hospital has a "Cuddler Program." Here is the description from their website: *A Cuddler is a trained volunteer who is able to hold and comfort fussy babies in the Neonatal Intensive Care Unit (NICU). Research has shown that the care Cuddlers give to babies helps lead to shorter stays in the Hospital, faster weight gain and improvements in development.*[63]

If you don't have kids and have always wanted them, be thankful you have not had children with the wrong man. Bad men sometimes get diagnosed as having personality disorders, and these disorders are genetic.[64] Raising a personality-disordered child would not be easy. If you are dating someone new and are thinking about marrying him and starting a family,

60   www.LightingTheWayWorldwide.org
61   www.TheRescueMinistries.org
62   www.TheHarvestHome.net
63   http://www.nym.org/Get-Involved/Volunteer-Opportunities/Cuddler-Volunteer.aspx
64   Personality disorders often go misdiagnosed in youth as hyperactivity, manifesting itself in behavior problems and the inability to stay focused. See "Personality Disorders" for a list with descriptions at http://psychcentral.com/disorders/

ask yourself if you would like for his personality traits to be inherited in your children. Sometimes a woman may think that having kids with a man of bad character will make him better, but it does not work that way. She already has a child on her hands with him!

HOMEWORK

If you've always dreamed of having children but do not have them, homework is to mark your calendar for volunteer work with kids. Children are close to God's heart, and there is no gift more precious than a wide-eyed child full of imagination and wonder, born with a need for pure love. Save the money you make to donate to charities for children. Let God meet the maternal needs of your heart by using you to meet the needs of needy kids all around you by investing in their lives.

"Be fair to the poor and to orphans. Defend the helpless and everyone in need. Rescue the weak and homeless" (Psalm 82:3-4).

"But Jesus said, 'Let the little children alone, and do not hinder them from coming to Me, for the kingdom of heaven belongs to such as these'" (Matthew 19:14).

"Put on the New"

God never tells us to give up a relationship, only to leave us feeling abandoned without it. When we ask God to give us something or someone, He never says, "No," if we belong to Him. He either says, "Yes," "Wait," or "I've got something better."

In keeping the faith, we have to be vigilant when it comes to taking care of ourselves. After determining to leave a bad relationship, stay on guard by making a list of all of the reasons you left. When the good memories come to make you want to go back, read the list out loud to yourself at least once per day. You will only continue to hurt yourself with the same old thing if you return. Something strange will happen while you are missing him with zero contact. As you continue to stay gone, new life will come your way! The Bible calls it putting off the old and putting on the new.

"Put off, concerning your former conduct, the old man which grows corrupt according to the deceitful lusts, and be renewed in the spirit of your mind, and that you put on the new man, which was created according to God, in true righteousness and holiness" (Ephesians 4:22-24).

If the days seem too boring apart from being in love, you are falling in line with the thinking of a love addict. If you do not believe it is possible to be happy on your own, a surprise beckons you. The first thing you have to do is get back to the child you used to be where the simple moments of life were enough. In giving up any addiction, including addictive relationships, you have to replace the time you spend engaging in a self-destructive habit with something new. Drugs offer *immediate gratification*; when you get high, it makes you feel good immediately. The only problem with such intoxication is that addiction thrives on emptiness, as the addict needs another fix to fill her up again. Growing up requires learning to feel pain temporarily for *delayed gratification*, which means, essentially, an honorable happiness in the future without shame where you are confident and whole. Happiness apart from addiction gives us the priceless gift of self-control.

To "put off the old" requires a state of mind to trust God and be content in obedience to the Bible with all God has to offer you every single moment of the day. Don't try to escape from loneliness or other negative feelings in addictive behaviors that are hurtful to you. Staying connected to the pain means staying connected to yourself and God. The Lord will not leave you miserable if you stay connected to Him. He's got something better in store. Remember the Don Juan from Tip #2? After that relationship ended, I "put on the new," only to become happier than I could have ever been if I had stayed with him. As a result of my desire to live an honest life, God opened a door that would have never opened if I had been off on a tangent with that man who turned out to be so terrible. Let me explain:

Still living in Atlanta back in 2011, I was on another pre-planned trip to NYC for work. This guy was living in Manhattan (after his second marriage had ended), and he had been trying to convince me that he was seriously thinking about marrying me, that he had changed, and so on. I can't help but laugh now as I think about how he tried to get me to stay with him in his one-bedroom apartment while I was there. I refused and booked a hotel room for myself. That is when, as I later found out, he got back on his Internet dating site to find himself someone much easier to use. The night I arrived in the city, he set a time to meet me in a beautiful place. Much to my surprise, it was to tell me goodbye. He had found someone new to "meet his needs," as he put it. That was that. Without one bit of empathy, he said he was sleeping with someone else. This was the same weekend he had begged me to stay with him in his apartment, as if he had been serious about a relationship me! He was so cold when he said goodbye that it was unbelievable. This man for whom I had prayed daily had evidently never cared for me one bit, despite the long emails he had sent me signing them with *love*. He did not show one bit of emotion when he said goodbye. He had an icy stare with satisfaction in his eyes as he watched me cry.

The next day in Manhattan, after a recording session, I sneaked into a church I had attended previously. I just wanted to get somewhere by myself and pray. I sat in the back of the empty auditorium and thanked God as the tears fell. I knew God had let that guy tell me goodbye for my good. God understood more than I why it hurt so much. (I realize now that I had become traumatically bonded to this bad man. Traumatic bonding feels like love, but it is not.)[65] I could feel God's love for my soul as I prayed. By faith, not knowing what tomorrow held, I thanked the Lord for His faithfulness. The guy was gone. He had found someone new to "meet his needs." God was proving once again His faithfulness to meet the needs of my heart, over and beyond my dreams.

I called my pianist to ask about going to one of his gigs around NYC. I explained how a relationship had just ended, and I did not want to be in my hotel room sad every night. I jotted down the places where my pianist said he would be playing and was determined to take myself out nightly. As it turned out, he was playing with a big band orchestra one night, and I had the time of my life there. I smiled the whole evening. As I was listening to the music, I realized I was there because I was not off somewhere else, in a much less fulfilling place, with that wrong man.

Because of my night with the big band orchestra, I ended up recording my jazz album "Counting Your Blessings" with those same musicians.

---

65 Lundy Bancroft teaches about traumatic bonding in his excellent book on abusive men, *Why Does He Do That?* (New York: Berkley Books, 2003).

Look at how God rewarded me! Not only did God do all of this on the outside that weekend in NYC, but He healed me on the inside, too. I lost all desire for this man in just one day after our last communication. While in NYC, I bought an extra copy of *Why Does He Do That?* by Lundy Bancroft, a book on abusive men. My eyes were opened. I could see how intentional all of his sadistic games had been the whole time. I did not even have an inkling of desire to have anything to do with him again.

I was right where I was supposed to be, away from him. As a result of my recording with the orchestra, I ended up moving back to NYC at the end of that year. It all happened because I made the *little* decision to get my own hotel room instead of staying with that man in his apartment. It was because I got my own room that the bad guy left my life, and it was because he left my life that much more exciting doors opened for me in music. I "put on the new!"

"Putting on the new," as the Bible teaches (by deciding to take care of yourself and live God's way), will work for any woman. It doesn't matter whether you are a prostitute or a virgin. If you want Jesus, He wants you. There's a new day waiting for you, if only you will take it. God wants to fulfill His plan for you more than you could want it, but here's the catch. His plan is pure. Your job is to enjoy your relationship with God, and that means staying where He saves us to be, far away from sin and harm. We can't do that if we are wasting time with the wrong men.

Don't give up on your pursuit of God, as He is after all of you. Read the Bible to find out about a Love that is waiting as you "put off the old" and "put on the new." If you can't be content in a pure life, with or without a man, ask God to heal you. Begin reading the New Testament in the books of Matthew, Luke, or John. Get to know this God who loves you so. You will never know the satisfaction you will be missing if you keep going back to the wrong man. Experience a better way, a more rewarding happiness, in a new life God has already prepared for you.

HOMEWORK

Homework is to ask God to help you leave your old way of living and thinking behind for something new. Ask God to help you get out of the rut you are in if you have lost your sense of identity after staying with a wrong man too long.

"Put on the new" by volunteering at a nonprofit organization to serve others with your time; take up a new hobby; take a long walk; work out; give up food addictions; start to save your money; travel; set goals and reward yourself when you meet them; spend time with people who make you feel good; and, whatever you do, keep walking away from self-destructive sin. Don't just sit around feeling lonely. Seize the day, and let the day seize you!

Don't run away from the pain of obedience to God. Be patient as God is at work in you to "put off the old" and "put on the new." Give yourself time. Happiness is on the way as you abide in Jesus, even if it takes a lot of tears to get there.

"If anyone is in Christ, he is a new creature. The old things passed away; behold, new things have come" (2 Corinthians 5:17).

Tip #27

He Has to Live with Himself, but You Don't

*D*on't let it fool you when you meet a bad man who is full of himself. He's empty on the inside. At the end of the day, it's all an act. In the Bible, God swears that certain people will not experience His *rest* and will never be at ease within themselves as a consequence of their disobedience to Him. Bogus personalities extinguish themselves in due time without rest. The price of rebellion from God and living in sin comes with the worst imaginable result—no rest within. "I swore in My heart, they shall not enter My rest."[66]

I have all I need abiding in Jesus. I have *His rest*. It is available to me in Jesus, with or without a man. It is from His rest that I am enabled to truly live! Jesus was not lying when He said, "I have come that they may have life and have it more abundantly."[67] On the other hand, the Bible teaches " 'There is no peace,' says my God, 'For the wicked.' "[68]

There are gifts only God can give that bad men do not have. Gifts only God can give are not for sale; money cannot buy them. Fame has nothing to do with these great gifts from God. Praise from Christians at church cannot compare. Education won't produce them within someone's heart. Talent and looks are irrelevant. No amount of therapy alone will suffice.

---

66 Psalm 95:11; see also Hebrews 2-3; Revelation 14:11
67 See John 10:10; 15:5-7, 10-11
68 Isaiah 57:21

Nobody on earth can offer anything close to the gifts only God can give to His own.

Bad men sometimes mimic these gifts through a counterfeit kindness called "love bombing." Love bombing is when a man overwhelms a woman with so many compliments that it keeps her from thinking clearly. He seems like the nicest, most caring man on earth, as he uses the love bombing to sweep her off her feet in the beginning. It is intense seduction, almost impossible for any woman to resist who is not privy to this dangerous ploy. He love bombs her every time she turns around. The smoothest psychopaths and abusive men use love bombing in the beginning of a relationship to ignite lust. They know that women fall in love with their ears. (See Tip #9.) If you will resist the love bombing without kissing, the bomb he turns out to be on the inside will surface a whole lot sooner.

Here is how one Internet site explains love bombing:

> *Love bombing is . . . the constant bombardment of communication from the sociopath. This can take many forms. Excessive texting, constant comments on your social network page, emails, telephone calls, or just literally bombarding you verbally in face to face communication. He might overwhelm you with gifts and will constantly flatter you. It feels overwhelming [as] you are swept off your feet. At first you will not perceive this as bombardment. You will initially be flattered that he is paying so much attention to you . . . It is like something from a movie. That's because it is like that; it's more fiction than reality. Already he has assessed you, and he is now mirroring you, so he is reflecting back to you exactly what you want to hear . . . This is an important manipulation tool for a sociopath; love bombing does the following things: It doesn't give you time to think about what is really happening . . . It gives a false impression of the sociopath, within a short space of time. It*

*moves the relationship forward very quickly (often before you are
ready).*[69]

There is a world of difference between the darkness of love bombing
and the light of love, and it all has to do with motive. Of all the gifts from
God that bad men can counterfeit initially, they cannot counterfeit God's
peace. The love bombing won't be enough to give you peace when you
stop to pray about it, and that will be your warning signal that something
is amiss and the man may be a phony. In all of his *kindness*, you will know
instinctively that something is off if you can just have the wherewithal to
keep your head on your shoulders.

There are people the Bible calls "accursed," who never experience the
gifts only God can give.[70] Only abiding in Jesus can give us the fruits of
the Holy Spirit as defining characteristics of who we are on the inside.[71]
Jesus promises to give peace to those who abide in Him: "My peace I
give to you, *not as the world gives* do I give to you. Do not let your heart
be troubled, nor let it be fearful."[72] The world gives a kind of peace, but
not the peace only Jesus can give. We, as Christians, have peace that our
sins are forgiven, and we have peace about eternity. Karma cannot offer
us assurance about our eternity and neither can reincarnation. The peace
we have through Jesus is predicated on His death and resurrection, not
based on our works. Everlasting life in heaven is as certain as His empty
grave for those who believe in Him.

Bad men live lives characteristic of "immorality, impurity, sensuality,
idolatry, sorcery, enmities, strife, jealousy, outbursts of anger, disputes,
dissensions, factions, envying, drunkenness, and carousing." The Bible
goes on to explain "that those who practice such things will not inherit

---

69 http://datingasociopath.com/sociopath-character-traits/cunning-and
    -manipulative/i-love-you/seducing-and-love-bombing/
70 Revelation 22:15
71 Galatians 5:22-23
72 John 14:27

the kingdom of God." [73] They are their own worst enemies. "His own iniquities will capture the wicked, and he will be held with the cords of his sin." [74] Just as God gives people who walk with Him enriching gifts that money cannot buy, He allows con artists to have a misery that no amount of love bombing can deplete.

"For God is opposed to the proud and gives grace to the humble" (1 Peter 5:5).

"He stores up sound wisdom for the upright; He is a shield to those who walk uprightly; He guards the paths of justice, and preserves the way of His saints" (Proverbs 2:7-8).

"And My people will never be put to shame" (Joel 2:27).

HOMEWORK

Homework for this tip is to Google "love bombing." Learn the signs. Beware of men who seem so smitten they are ready to marry you on the first date.

Read the NY Times bestseller *His Way* by Kitty Kelley on the life of Frank Sinatra.[75] With his choice of any woman he wanted to take to bed, he couldn't sleep at night. He abused women physically, emotionally, and sexually. All the while, he was filled with rage. Life in the fast lane served to distract him from his conscience. A quiet, normal life was too challenging for him, because he had no rest within. He was a basket case of obsessive-compulsive phobias. He had to always surround himself with people, due to how he could not live with himself alone. Though he was known for singing beautiful songs about love, he could never be sexually or emotionally monogamous with any woman until the end of his life

---

73 Galatians 5:19-21
74 Proverbs 5:22
75 Kitty Kelley, *His Way: The Unauthorized Biography of Frank Sinatra* (New York: Bantam Books, 1986).

when he was in poor health. He was an alcoholic diagnosed as manic depressive and tried to commit suicide more than once. Mia Farrow, one of his wives, arrived on a movie set black and blue after he beat her. When he hurt a woman, he never apologized. He was sometimes referred to as a "monster" with his frightening outbursts of anger.

His Way: The Unauthorized Biography of Frank Sinatra is a great study on how the "Godfather of Hollywood" was so very unimpressive and bland on the inside. The same romantic crooner, who made women swoon and was a master at love bombing to sleep with any woman of his choosing, bombed at love. In the very front of the book, before the Author's Note, Kelley quotes Thomas Paine with these words of wisdom: "Reputation is what men and women think of us. Character is what God and angels know of us."

Healing=Life Free from Addictions (Including Food and Men)

When I was thirteen years old, I was traveling as a soloist in revival meetings affiliated with the Southern Baptist denomination and went to India with an evangelistic crusade team to sing hymns during the meetings. When we arrived, I was informed that there was not a room for me. It had been decided for me that I would sleep with the evangelist in his room. He sexually abused me.

There were only three of us in the crusade team—the preacher, the pianist, and myself. Despite the fact that this evangelist was lauded in so many circles that he was awarded an honorary doctor's degree and received accolades from Christian organizations and churches, as far as I know, he never showed one bit of repentance. It was said he preached with fire, but only God knows if he escaped the fires of hell himself for all eternity after he died of cancer just a few years after I stopped traveling with him. His crusades were built on pretense, though the true gospel message he preached proved to transform the lives of others. If only it could have transformed his own life, but he sinned like a charlatan.

I was on the other side of the world from my parents, who had just gotten a divorce, and I had no power in the situation when it was decided

I would sleep with the preacher, due to the *mistake* that had been made in the reservations with no other room available for me. The pianist told me that he would rather I sleep in the bed with this man than himself, with only two rooms for the three of us, so he got his own room, and I slept with the preacher. No doubt, Satan had come to ruin my life through that pedophile preacher. People looked up to him like he was God. When I told the pianist what happened, the first words out of his mouth were, "The board members cannot find out about this," as if my innermost being did not matter. I was called the "13-Year-Old Singing Sensation," but, obviously, neither of these men as leaders of the organization cared about the girl at the core of the singing sensation.

I developed an eating disorder shortly after the abuse. Since there was no intercourse, it took years for me to realize I had been sexually abused. The shame, however, was palpable immediately. I was not the same on the inside. The twelve-year-old I had been just the year before, who had just become cheerleader in the seventh grade, was no longer free, and this new me had been robbed of peace within. I had never kissed a boy before, and I certainly was not prepared for an old evangelist to kiss me while sleeping with me. I remember the ceiling fan, the color of the walls, the entire look of the room . . . and details I would rather not think about. He called me *Lover* once, bought me secret jewelry, and insisted on my calling him at his office every day at a certain time. I loathed calling him every day at five o'clock at the age of thirteen, but that is how he wanted it. Being raised with respect for church leaders, my mother could not wrap her mind around the fact that this guy was a pervert. She has since cried tears of remorse too many days and nights to count, feeling so guilty for letting this happen to me. My dad blames himself because he was not there. I realize if my parents could have handled it differently at the time, they would have, and no one in my family is to blame. We were all doing the best we knew how. I don't blame anyone but Satan, as well as the fake people on the crusade team who did not care one thing about me.

The attitude of the team behind the scenes was to remain silent about slips from the preacher's display, such as his cursing every now and then (once I recall from the pulpit) and his lapses of flirtation with other women on the crusade team, even before I came along. I was told that one time he reached out and grabbed a woman's "boobs," as the story was told to me behind his back after a revival meeting. A joke was made of it, as if that was funny. Everyone was supposed to let him always have his way in order to "bring God glory" in the evangelistic crusades. In the name of Jesus, it was all about the evangelist. I never saw any conviction from him over his hypocrisy.

The preacher totally controlled my life, making me leave my school with all of my friends, beginning in the eighth grade, and go to a Christian school of his choosing, which I never liked. What I liked did not matter. He said he was afraid the boys would lust after me as a cheerleader in the short skirts, so I had to exit my school with all my friends and leave the cheerleading I loved. In reality, all the boys my age had treated me just fine, and he was the only one lusting after me. Thank God, shortly after, I went to Nashville to record my third album, and the preacher was losing control. He did not like my new songs recorded in Nashville, and he only worked with people he could control. I stopped traveling with him.

Behind the scenes and cameras at the area-wide crusade meetings and television shows, it was all about manipulation, secrets, fame, and money. But we did not realize that when my family and I used to watch him on television every Sunday morning before church, long before I ever met him. His preaching, evangelistic tracts, and books were very popular, and I heard that he has been inducted in some hall of fame for evangelists with a Baptist mission board. God used him, in spite of himself, to bring people sincerely to salvation. I can still see people walking down the aisle to get saved after he preached a wonderful message from the Bible about salvation, even though he had himself lost the way.

This man's act was rather bewitching as he seemed to have no fear of God in all of his double life. My family and I only regret not contacting the board members and reporting him to child services when I was thirteen and the sexual abuse happened. It took place long before Anita Hill brought more attention to sexual harassment through the Clarence Thomas case, and the public was not as educated on sexual abuse and pedophilia as we are today. My mother had never met any preacher so mendacious. She is the most sincere Christian I could ever know, and I am thankful to have her as my best friend. She was raised very active in the Baptist church with respect for her pastors and sincere love for the Lord. As an outgoing honor student in school, I had never been around something as reprehensible in my whole life, much less a victim of it.

Jesus was still there in my heart, loving me through it all. He was just as pure as ever. And He was not going to give me up to perversion. As a child soloist, every time I sang a hymn about Jesus I meant it, and He knew my heart was in it as I sang His praises. People in the congregation felt the Holy Spirit so much when I sang the hymns, that they would cry. I remember thinking I had not done well unless I could see practically the whole church crying as I sang. That is how much the Holy Spirit used me to touch people with God's love as I sang His praises from age two and up through my teens. Satan hated it. I meant every word I sang about Jesus and love Him even more today. My mother had always had a heart for missions, and she was so thankful that God could use her daughter in the Baptist revival meetings all around the world as I sang solos of the hymns. All she ever wanted was for my brother and me to glorify God with our lives. She was doing the best she knew how to do at the time as a single mother, and God could have never given me a better mother or a mother who loved me more. How could this internationally renowned evangelist who was drawn to her daughter singing hymns about the Lord be sent to us from hell? How could the flourishing evangelist known for "winning souls" not have one himself?

For many years to come, I would not know how to be comfortable within my own skin alone. I found myself challenged as to how to be happy again on the inside, especially without a man's validation. Calories became a chief concern, whereas I had been raised never knowing a thing about them. I had never heard of the concept of food addictions before. Being from the south, we would eat homemade, delicious food together on any fun day. I wanted fun days like my childhood before the sexual abuse, so I ate a little more. Then I had to work out a lot or starve myself for many more days to come, until more and more was never enough. I did not know how to stop the cycle. I had always been slim, competing at baton competitions from age five to age twelve. I was disciplined with my eating growing up, very much in control. I remember being conscientious about carbohydrates and living without bread and potatoes in order to stay a "10 Slim" at age ten. When I began counting calories, staring at *Vogue* magazine, wanting to look like the skinny models and working out too much, it all seemed like the natural next phase as a teen. The denial within myself began at age thirteen, because I never stopped to cry about the abuse. I learned to live with two secrets: the sexual abuse and the eating. No matter how I fought it, I gained weight to become a little chubby at age sixteen. After the sexual abuse, it was the first time in my whole life that I remember viewing myself with disapprobation. I lost that weight by the time I was eighteen, but eating right and staying the best size for me continued to be a challenge until I learned how to stop the habit of emotional eating.

Because I knew nothing about an eating disorder, I just assumed that I was lacking in willpower when I was hurting and turned to food. I did not know that certain foods are chemically addictive for anyone, though enjoying foods of all kinds had never been a problem for me before. What happened to the girl at the baton competitions who could only have one cookie with no desire to eat a whole batch? How about the child I was who ate a bowl of cereal in the mornings as opposed to wanting to eat the whole box, while hiding out alone in my room as a teenager? How could I get *me* back? I prayed to God for help. Surely He would send the right guy to save me and let me live happily ever after, married (the sooner, the better) with kids and a career to bring me joy. Perhaps, my salvation would come in fame and fortune as a singer. If the world loved me, wouldn't I? I moved to Nashville at age seventeen with the country music industry setting the stage for my happiness.

It was not at all difficult for me to get the attention of men on Music Row. Much like the evangelist, the songwriters and music executives were ready and waiting for the next pretty singer who needed acceptance. Sadly, I recall having about as much true love for me on Music Row as there was for Jesus—not much true love at all to be found, and what sincere love for my soul I did experience only came from the few Christians I met. It was practically an oxymoron to be a true Christian in the country music scene with the Bible so antagonistic to the degenerate games people play for power in the entertainment industry. I was so unhappy in the midst of it all, and the eating and overexercising was spinning out of control.

I memorized Bible verses to help me get through the day, but I still wanted to eat when I felt lonely, which was most of the time. I needed acceptance. I knew God loved me, but I did not know why. At least I did not feel worthy of love without achieving success in music with fame and fortune. I figured such an accomplishment would make me worthy of love, but who was I without it? The cycle of an eating disorder had come to enslave me since the sexual abuse, as well as confusion about what love was supposed to look like from a man. I wondered how a man could fall in love with me without sex. Music Row certainly reinforced that premise as I worked in Nashville. The answers seemed much more clear-cut in my childhood, before the evangelist came to proselytize my innocence away.

I bought every self-help book Christian bookstores offered, and none of them helped. I became addicted to diet bars filled with sugar, as I would overeat on them and then do crazy things like jog in one hundred degree weather in a fleece sweat suit or take about four aerobics classes in a day. I bought a treadmill and spent hours on it. I needed it, since I was always hungry without a man to make me happy. Like magic, when a man would come along to love me, I felt satisfied on the inside and full. The problem was that the feeling was too short lived with all the womanizers I met in country music, and I was challenged once again to figure out why I wanted to eat so much when I was all alone.

My mother was living in Florida, and I decided to take some time away from Nashville and stay with her there for a few months. I took the daring step, which felt so humiliating at the time, of attending my first Overeaters Anonymous meeting there in Boca Raton. I quickly experienced abstinence from overeating by attending the meetings and making daily phone calls, and I made friends with women who understood my struggles with food. I wanted God to heal me before returning to Nashville to work on Music Row as a singer again. If only I could meet Mr. Right soon (since I never felt hungry when I felt loved) to put an end to my eating disorder forever, but my healing was not that simple. I kept praying to get my big break, when all the while God was breaking me. God loved me too much to let me go in any direction but to Him. God was teaching me how to die to all I had felt I needed externally to be happy. This was excruciatingly painful. But the new me that God was shaping would be wiser and more indebted to Him than ever before—this was the greatest blessing God could give me because of the joy He gave my heart as I learned to lean more heavily on Him.

The fact that I was willing to do whatever it took to get well was in and of itself an answer to prayer. I did not agree with everything I heard in the twelve-step meetings about spirituality, but God gave me the humility to listen to people when they spoke about their abstinence from binging on food. I made getting free from the shameful cycle of compulsive overeating my number one priority. I have never been a drinker, but I attended Alcoholics Anonymous meetings just to listen to people speak about *how to feel*. I wanted to learn from them, and I did. Since I had never cried for the first few years after the sexual abuse, I had to allow myself to feel the pain I had been trying to stuff away. I had been entirely too hard on myself in my early teens, as if it were a sin for me to feel sad. When I began to cry around age nineteen, I felt I would never stop. I cried an ocean down on my knees through my twenties. God met me in my pain and loved me enough to teach me *how* to leave the idols of my heart and run to Him every moment of the day. All it felt like at the time was pain, but now I see how much He was healing me with every tear. I would come to realize that when the Bible teaches "the joy of the Lord is my strength," it means He gives me *His joy* in my heart from His love for me as I lean on Him in my sadness; it is His joy that is my strength from day to day through times of struggle, not my own.[76]

I was in and out of twelve-step meetings for years. I learned to stay off sugar but was held captive living according to the strict measuring of food suggested by the OA members. Counting exchanges was much like counting calories. I went from attending the physical meetings to the phone meetings for accountability, until shortly after I began professional counseling when I could feel myself turning the corner on understanding more about the connection my eating disorder had with men. These meetings, of course, were only a tool for me, not the answer. God is the only one I can entirely thank for "working all things together for my good" to get me where I am today.[77]

When I began eating raw foods, steamed vegetables, and whole grains, I could feel my entire pH changing in my body. The raw foods made me lose my craving for refined sugar. I gave up diet foods like fat-free frozen yogurt filled with sugar. I can't even recall the last time I had a glass of milk, and my allergies have gotten much better since giving up dairy. I educated myself on health vs. the diet-food industry. I bought a juicer and began juicing fresh vegetables and fruit. After a short while, I was craving spinach instead of sugar! Refined carbohydrates looked terribly unhealthy and unappealing to me.

Most every night now I have steamed organic vegetables and tofu

---

76 Nehemiah 8:10
77 Romans 8:28

with either organic brown rice, black rice, or quinoa. I make delicious buckwheat muffins with unsweetened applesauce and no sugar, and I no longer miss junk food at all. I practice fasting from time to time, which is excellent for digestion and the whole body, and I learned to give up eating late at night.[78] I work as a health coach to help others free themselves from food addictions with testimonials of success. I never dreamed life could be so sweet working out a moderate amount every morning, eating right, and staying away from the wrong men.

When I was growing up on my grandmother's southern, delicious desserts, she used to say, "A little bit won't hurt you." Well, a little bit can addict me now all over again, so I do my best to stay off sugar altogether. Raw almonds and walnuts are delicious, but I only eat them raw with no oil and no salt and have about a handful per day. I used to never touch them, thinking they were too fattening. I enjoy healthy oils such as coconut and avocado. I am sorry I missed out on so much delicious food God gave us from the ground to heal our bodies all of those years I was eating manufactured diet *food*. Now when I eat fruits and vegetables, I find myself in awe of God's creation with every bite, though I rarely have fruit due to its sugar content. Eating a plant-based diet gives me so much energy, and my skin is perfectly clear. The most delicious food to me now is the healthiest. When people tell me I can eat whatever I want, I tell them I do! It is just that my palate has changed, and I no longer desire junk. Nowadays, I am eating what I want when I eat what is good for me.

By reading books by Dr. Joel Fuhrman,[79] I began to learn about phytonutrients, which heal the body. Animal protein has no phytonutrients, so I get my protein mostly from juicing kale drinks and eating nuts, beans, and tofu. Though I never touch red meat and seldom have fish or chicken, I do not require the same standard for my clients with whom I work as a health coach. I work with people on an individual basis

78 Matthew 6:5-18 teaches us to fast as Christians; also see Dr. Joel Fuhrman's book, *Fasting and Eating for Health* (New York: St. Martin's Griffin, 1995).
79 www.drfuhrman.com

to help them break food addictions in a way that works best for them. For instance, I'd recommend a piece of chicken any day before grabbing a sugary protein bar. Many of my clients have been successful without giving up animal protein. I have just gotten to the point where I literally crave and prefer vegetables.

I have not exercised as a compensation for overeating in years. I work out now in the mornings, but not to lose weight. I keep my weight down from eating right and only exercise for energy and enjoyment. I love walking, biking, swimming, and hiking. Sometimes when I can feel myself under stress, I call a health-conscious friend to whom I can be accountable with my eating to stay on track. God finally answered my prayer when I kept asking Him why I overate all of those years. I was running from my feelings, *and* I had become addicted physically to refined sugar. The chocolate chip brownie diet bars kept the cravings alive and well. The raw foods are far more delicious. I savor every bite these days and remain the right size, which is best for me. It is all by God's grace, and it is worth all of the work it takes. I have never felt better about myself.

Living in victory over addiction requires dependency on God with all of your heart, which is exactly how He wants us to live. I realize many Christians criticize twelve-step meetings. People who know Jesus as Savior already have a Higher Power, and He is far higher than a god of our own understanding. The purpose of the twelve-step meetings for me, as a Christian, was accountability and to learn from others on how they have found abstinence from sugar and other toxins. The people there who were serious about recovery helped me. I met two of my best girlfriends in the meetings years ago, and we have been living in recovery together as friends ever since. We are still there for one another, to encourage each other to stay on track when it comes to eating right. The Bible teaches clearly about how we are not meant to be enslaved to any addiction. God honors it when we humble ourselves enough to do what it takes to heal.

I have not gone to an OA twelve-step meeting since 2008. I now seldom ever eat anything that is bad for me. When struggling with food addiction, I don't fault a Christian for *not* wanting to attend the meetings since the twelve-step meetings don't require a spirituality exclusive to what the Bible teaches about God, but at the same time, I don't fault a Christian for calling in to the phone meetings or attending in person. Before criticizing such accountability meetings, be sure that you have arrived at a place of health yourself, which includes living abstinent from food addiction. Yes, I am talking about the gluttony the Bible calls sin.[80] I do believe that we must take the log out of our own eye, as Jesus put it, before condemning others.[81] It is only by God's grace that I am now living in abstinence, and I thank God every single day for it. I realize now I am no better than an alcoholic or cocaine addict running from feelings, apart from God's mercy. That realization has made me a better woman. God has ordered my steps, and there have been many more than twelve steps for me to take. Life is hard, but it is okay, when Jesus is walking with me.

I want to reiterate that there is no perfect size. We are all different body types and meant to be different sizes. This tip is to empower you as a woman to get to the place of being happy with yourself. For me, I feel my physical best as a size 2, because I am only five feet, three inches. *Whatever size makes you happy and confident,* be that size and stay there. Unless you have a chronic health problem, you actually *can* lose the weight and live at the size you want. Your weight does not have to drastically fluctuate through sad times. Emotions were never given by God to make people overeat.

When Satan came to tempt Jesus *through food* to turn the stones into bread, Jesus answered, "Man shall not live by bread alone but by every word that proceeds from the mouth of God."[82] I would not be the person

---

80 "Whoever keeps the law is a discerning son, but a companion of gluttons shames his father" (Proverbs 28:7).
81 Matthew 7:5; Luke 6:42
82 Matthew 4:4

I am today, had it not been for my sexual abuse at the age of thirteen and for the eating disorder that followed. It is a blessing to be healing from it for the rest of my life, as God won't be finished teaching me how to depend on Him for everything until I get to Heaven. The vulnerability I feel as a person who lives in recovery keeps me needing God intensely, which is such a gift. I don't take for granted the happiness I feel today, and it is worth running to God with all of my heart, soul, mind, and strength as the Bread of life for my heart. My reward is feeling good about myself. It's a glorious life, too healthy for an unhealthy man!

"Do not mix with winebibbers or with gluttonous eaters of meat. For the drunkard and the glutton will come to poverty and drowsiness will clothe a man with rags" (Proverbs 23:20-21).

HOMEWORK

Homework for this tip is to order books by Dr. Joel Fuhrman[83] to learn about health. Dr. Fuhrman teaches that if we all lived on a desert island, we would all be skinny because there would be no preservatives. I recommend reading all of his books.

Watch documentaries on breaking food addictions, such as *Forks Over Knives*,[84] *Food Matters*,[85] and *Fat, Sick and Nearly Dead*.[86] Educate yourself on food addiction. Don't expect anyone else to do it, including the government with a vested interest in selling us propaganda on behalf of food corporations. The hormones now found in most chicken are carcinogens, and the GMOs in corn and soy are killing us, so only eat non-GMO, organic food. Studies show that the cancer rate is far higher in people who consume a lot of animal protein. Preservatives also cause cancer and weight gain. If you can't pronounce an ingredient, even in

83   www.drfuhrman.com
84   www.forksoverknives.com
85   www.foodmatters.tv
86   www.fatsickandnearlydead.com

bread, rest assured it is probably toxic. Drink water all day. Your goal is to get your body more alkaline vs. acidic, which, you will be glad to know, will obliterate sugar cravings. The more water, the better; I normally drink three to four liters per day.

Here is a recipe for cleansing water that will help cleanse the colon and liver, curb your appetite, and get your body to a more alkaline state. Mix 1 gallon of distilled water, 3 tablespoons of apple cider vinegar, 1 lemon juiced, and 2 ounces of Aloe Vera juice. Shake it all up and drink it cold. I love it and drink it as often as possible, sometimes even drinking the whole gallon in a day. *Cut back of Dairy*

I dare you to juice this recipe every day for a week to experience a change in your body's pH balance: 2 apples, 2 lemons, handfuls of spinach and kale, and a few slices of fresh pineapple. Say goodbye to sinus problems, and throw away the cold medicine, because you won't need it if you drink fresh juices like this and eat a plant-based diet.

If you are not the size you want to be, the first step is to get off the sugary, artery-clogging junk food. Get an accountability friend or hire me as a health coach to help you change your lifestyle at DwaynaLitzBlog.com. Stick to an eating plan, and keep a diary of your progress as you begin to feel happier and more confident. If you love toxic food too much to give it up, then at least admit you are an addict. You may think you have freedom to eat whatever you want, but there is no true freedom for anyone enslaved to cravings. Remember, many so-called foods are created by the food corporations for the purpose of addicting you.

Make a salad your main meal tonight, and thank God for every unique flavor of the vegetables in it. Let God bring healing to your body from the foods He made for you. Remember, abstinence from overeating *feels* far better than any junk food tastes. Get ready to feel good about yourself and fit in whatever size of clothing you wish. It is not about working out more. It is about breaking addiction. The only way you will fail to break your food addiction is if you give up trying, so don't give up!

If you are a Christian, God explains in the Bible that your body is a temple where the Holy Spirit dwells. Romans 12:1 is one of my favorite verses: "I beseech you therefore brethren by the mercies of God to present your bodies a living and holy sacrifice, pleasing to God, which is our spiritual form of worship." We have a responsibility to take care of ourselves.

"Jesus said to them, 'I am the Bread of Life. He who comes to Me shall never hunger'" (John 6:35).

Go to the Safest Place
to Feel Pain

Life is hard. It is scary to let ourselves be vulnerable in this world. But everyone needs someone. Events for singles can leave us lonely. Dating services can cost thousands of dollars without any man to show for it in the end. You can be left with a bank account empty of money by the time Scientology is finished "increasing your spiritual awareness," leaving you more messed up than when you began.[87] Yoga meditations may be relaxing, but we are still left with our mere selves. As much as a good counselor can help, therapists are only human and do not know everything. Not even a close friend can understand us completely. Church is not always the best place to pour out our hearts. Where in the world can we go to be totally understood, cherished, and healed? The safest place to feel pain is down on your knees before God.

These days we hear a lot about "bad energy" or "good energy," as if impersonal energies are our only hope. It is true that spirits can be good or bad, but Jesus reigns supreme over all the other spirit energies.[88] (See Tip # 14.) There is a God who wants to "direct your path,"[89] always for

---

87 Scientology-Lies.com; the 2015 documentary *Going Clear: Scientology and the Prison of Belief*; and Scientology.org
88 Romans 8:39; James 2:9
89 Proverbs 3:6

your good. He reigns over luck; your future is not left to chance.[90] He promises you are not here by accident. He knew you in your mother's womb.[91] God has a personality and cares about how we live. He sent His Son so we can know who God is. Though Jesus died, He rose again and promises to His own, "Lo, I am with you *always.*"[92] Jesus will *always* listen when you pray to Him, no matter how often you need Him day or night. You see, God does not want us to just be good. He wants to draw us near so that His loving and pure Spirit indwelling us *enables* us to be good. Spending time *with* Him in prayer means more to Him than anything we could ever do *for* Him, because Jesus wants our hearts.

I suggested to a Christian girlfriend who was going through a hard time last year that she simply turn off the television at night and get down on her knees to pray. She had been raised in the church, but she could not bring herself to slow down enough to simply go to God with her pain. Barely able to pay her bills, she felt she was missing out on life if she wasn't going out at night and spending more money every weekend. Finally, she realized the nights out on the town were not really making her happy. Months later, she stopped running from God and at last got down on her knees to pray. She began to cry and cry as she could feel God touching her heart to turn her life around. He was there all the time. My friend realized that all she needed in life was not out there somewhere else to be found but right inside her heart with her relationship with Jesus.

If you are someone who has never prayed to God before, it is easy. God wants us to need Him as a little child needs a father. Because God knows our thoughts, we can pray to Him silently. There is certainly no script necessary in order for God to hear. He just wants us to talk to Him as we would talk to a best friend, realizing by faith that He already knows us intimately. Many a day or night when I have felt at the end of my

---

90   Isaiah 46:10
91   Psalm 139
92   Matthew 28:20

rope, I have gone off by myself to get down on my knees and pray. The Lord's Spirit has always met me there to let me feel His love. I usually start off singing a song in praise to Him, and then I just begin to pray about situations in my life that only God can change. I pray for loved ones and pray for myself, for God to keep me where I am meant to be in a life for His glory. It is through those times of prayer that God has strengthened and changed me. He has opened doors and closed doors for my good, as He has worked through my prayers.

Before I could talk plainly, my mother began teaching me to sing the precious old hymns about Jesus. Oh, how the hymns have blessed my life. It is said that the Bible will keep us from sin. So will the hymns. I can't sing a hymn to God and remain the same if I am heading in the wrong direction. I am reminded of how Jesus suffered for me on Calvary when I sing those hymns, and I can feel Him with me to keep me living for Him.

Here is one beautiful hymn I have often sung to God in times of prayer alone with Him: *Have thine own way, Lord. Have thine own way. Thou art the Potter. I am the clay. Mold me and make me after thy will, while I am waiting yielded and still.*[93] It may seem too simple, but getting down on my knees in prayer and singing praises to God when no one can hear but Him has rescued me from many a snare.

Within my lifetime it has become cool in America to sit for hours in the lotus position emptying out the mind in yoga meditations but uncool to pray with cognizance to our heavenly Father down on our knees. Both disciplines are very spiritual, though coming to God His way requires self-denial in order for Him to make us better. Unlike yoga meditations, Jesus taught us to pray, "Not my will, but Thine be done."[94] Throughout history, kneeling in prayer has been a prayer position for God's people. I share in my quote book on American history, *America Come Home*, how Isaac Potts, a Valley Forge resident, recorded in his

---

93   "Have Thine Own Way, Lord" by Adelaide A. Pollard, public domain.
94   Luke 22:42

Diary of Remembrances hearing America's first president, George Washington, pray down on his knees.[95]

In this submissive, reverent position before God, we admit He is higher than we are, and His will is far better than our own. He honors it when we bow before Him as Lord. We can fight every battle and win it when we learn to fight our battles down on our knees.

"For this reason also, God highly exalted Him, and bestowed on Him the name which is above every name, so that at the name of Jesus every knee will bow, of those who are in heaven and on earth and under the earth, and that every tongue will confess that Jesus Christ is Lord, to the glory of God the Father" (Philippians 2:9-11).

HOMEWORK

Homework for this tip is to watch the documentary *Going Clear: Scientology and the Prison of Belief.* It just goes to show how much money people are willing to spend while still believing the oldest lie in the Bible—that man can become like God. Since L. Ron Hubbard's death, former members of Scientology have been exposing all of the lies they were taught about Hubbard and this psychology cult. For research I toured the Scientology Center in Los Angeles back in 2004. In one room I saw people sitting across from one another literally barking out loud like dogs. In another room I saw people staring at each other in total silence. As I witnessed all of this, I thought of the great lengths people will go to be healed, instead of simply getting down on their knees to pray to the God above all powers and dominions for cleansing from sin and newness of life.

If you are tired of trying everything else, get down on your knees and pray. Tell God that you want to know Him, even if that means the God of all is different from whom you have assumed Him to be. After all, if

---

95 Dwayna Litz, *America, Come Home*, (Lighting the Way International, 2013), 33. Available on Amazon and Barnes and Noble websites.

you are not willing to know who God really is, there is no way to have a relationship with Him. Get to know Him by reading the Bible. If you are a Christian and have a hymn memorized, sing it to God. If you mean the lyrics you sing, God will use it to convict you of sin and give you the strength to live His way, which is the best for your soul and well-being. You can sing a simple song like "Jesus Loves Me" or "Amazing Grace." Sing it from your heart, and think about the words. I cannot sing a hymn to God like "Jesus Keep Me Near the Cross"[96] or "'Tis So Sweet to Trust in Jesus"[97] without God meeting me there in worship and letting me feel His love.

We have a God whose name is called Wonderful, Counselor, and Prince of Peace (Isaiah 9:6). Pour your heart out to Him down on your knees, and He will meet you there. All that it will cost you is your pride.

---

96   "Jesus Keep Me Near the Cross" by Fanny Crosby, William Bradbury, and Howard Doane; public domain.
97   "'Tis So Sweet to Trust in Jesus," words by Louisa M.R. Stead and music by William Kirkpatrick, public domain. Lyrics were said to have been written after Stead saw her husband drown, choosing to trust in Jesus in the midst of her pain.

Tip #30

"If Life Doesn't Get
Any Better ..."

I know what it is like to have to take life one moment at a time, one day at a time. You may be going through something so difficult that you think, *If life doesn't get any better than this, I'm going to die!* Take a deep breath. Even if your circumstances do not change, your life can get better. God can change *you.* Never underestimate the power of happiness. It can hit you in unexpected ways through simple things like holding a child or taking a walk in nature. Just as flowers need the rain to grow, God uses pain in our lives to make us stronger and wiser. In God's plan for your life, the pain is not there to defeat you.

I remember wishing at one point that I could push a fast-forward button to move ahead quickly toward the happiness I felt *I deserved,* which I assumed was off somewhere waiting for me. Even though I was a Christian, I wished for some sort of immediate relief that could transport me far away from fears, disappointments, and loneliness deep within. There was no fast-forward button. It was only when I learned to welcome the process and ask God to teach me what I am supposed to learn from pain, that I could accept what I was going through for my good. Had I been God, I would have given myself a much easier time. God loved me too much for that.

When I was working in Nashville in my early twenties, people in the music industry would assure me that I would *make it* to a successful career in music and just had to "pay my dues." I kept hanging in there making the rounds through the hardest time of my life, outside of the popular clique of award winners. These people were not exactly the picture of happiness themselves, but they had fame and fortune I did not have. Hardly anyone in the crowd acknowledged someone's character and worth apart from their talent. I was so sad through those years. All I ever wanted was a happy life. I did not want to have to *die* to my dreams and live only to please God, whatever that meant, like some stoic weirdo. All I knew was I wanted escape from all of my unplanned pain! I could not bear the thought of who I would be apart from being a famous singer and songwriter. God would have to teach me my worth, and He did.

Paying my dues during those years was actually God's mercy at work in my life to change me inside out. The happiness God had waiting for me would be far more satisfying than what I had imagined for myself. He was drawing me closer to Him.[98] Through every long day I spent miserably broke, God was at work to take my eyes off my circumstances and pride and put them on Him instead, where there is fullness of joy.[99] He had already paid my dues at the Cross, and He cared more about the perfect plan for my life than I, because He created me for it. With every part-time job I hated during those years, in and out of production and publishing deals, God was teaching me to lean on Him. It was not a waste of time after all.

A very wise person gave me a challenge during those Music Row years. He said, "Think about what you feel you have to have in order to be happy." That was a no-brainer. I answered to myself immediately, *Record deal.* He continued, "That is an idol of your heart." I never forgot it. God arrested me right there on the spot in that moment with His love. Though it felt like I was wasting my time with my talent on a shelf, that

98 Hebrews 7:25
99 Psalm 16:11

was not the case in all reality. God was changing my heart and preparing me for what He planned for me to do in the future, including even writing this book.

God was there walking with me through the *boring* valleys when there was no one else and sometimes carrying me when I could walk no further. Now God has taken me to a place of victory! The same victory is offered to any woman reading this, too. I no longer fear being *wherever* God wants me to be, doing whatever He wants me to do. Some tasks that may seem menial to us have great significance to God. We just have to pray to see our circumstances through God's eyes. God has proven, no matter what, that He will keep me at rest within myself when I am where He wants me to be.

God brought me to the point of finally saying in the midst of my pain, "If life doesn't get any better, I will still praise You. If You bring someone my way who needs to hear about the love of Jesus, that will be enough to make me happy today." Well, right after I could bring myself to say that, something strange began to happen. I started getting happier. As I began finding my life's purpose from sharing with people in need about the love of Jesus, one person at a time, God let me feel His love for *me*.

After years of praying for God to bring me a *husband* (more like an emotional caretaker for me at that time) and other external desires to heal my hurts, He's given me something better. He has enabled me to truly enjoy my life as a single person and see it as a gift. He has healed me to the point where I feel good about myself and am at peace within when I am alone. I do not need a man to affirm me. If God gives me a companion in the future who could actually be a compliment to me in life, it will be a blessing, but I no longer need that to make me happy. I have enough already.

John Bunyan, author of my favorite book other than the Bible, *Pilgrim's Progress*, was put in prison for telling people about Jesus. He got to the point where he was thankful for the prison walls that drew him closer to God.[100] Recently I heard a pastor from China tell about the persecution of Christians in China. Dr. Wei said that their favorite verse in the midst of persecution is "Rejoice always. In everything, give thanks."[101] He pointed out that this is the key to a successful life. Even in the midst of persecution, we can rejoice. Praise is a heavenly characteristic. Praising Jesus in the midst of trials will make us overcomers.[102]

If you are rebelling against God, that alone is the cause of your pain. God always leads us through obedience to His Word. Just like talking with a friend, you can tell God you are sorry and stop resisting whatever He is trying to do in your life for your good. In the Bible, Paul was thrown in jail for telling people about Jesus; yet, he teaches in the book of Philippians, "Rejoice in the Lord always. Again, I will say, rejoice! Let your forebearing spirit be known to all men, the Lord is near. Be anxious for nothing, but in everything by prayer and supplication with thanksgiving let your requests be made known to God, and the peace of God which surpasses all comprehension shall guard your hearts and your minds in Christ Jesus."[103]

Finding true happiness and peace within is worth its struggle. Tell the Lord today, "If life doesn't get any better, change *me*." And, I promise, Jesus will start changing your life for the better as He answers that prayer. You see, happiness is not some far off place. Yes, you can find it in the arms of a man, but that is not the only place. Men are not here to be used like a god to *make you happy*. God created you to have a relationship with Him for happiness. A good man comes as a gift from God in your life for you to enjoy but not worship. Happiness is when you can trust God enough to count your blessings and be content. Happiness requires growing up. Happiness means healing for your soul. Jesus is alive and hears you when you pray. Make a date to spend time with Him in Bible

---

100 John Bunyan, "Prison Meditations," a poem written in 1665, from *The Complete Works of John Bunyan*, 1876.
101 1 Thessalonians 5:16, 18
102 Revelation 7; 14
103 Philippians 4:4-7

study; go serve someone in need who is sick in the hospital or a widow who is a shut-in; help the underprivileged. For any true Christian, when you serve others in the name of Jesus, happiness is a place where, *if life doesn't get any better*, you are fine.

Helen Keller said, "True happiness . . . is not attained through self-gratification but through fidelity to a worthy purpose."[104] Make your purpose and success in life contingent on knowing God. He is much more reliable than karma. (Karma is an *it*; God is a *He*.) Stay far away from sin to guard your childlike freedom and self-confidence, so no one can steal it away.

"But as for me, the nearness of God is my good" (Psalm 73:28).

HOMEWORK

Homework for this tip is to offer up what the Bible calls *a sacrifice of praise*[105] in the midst of your pain. Make the choice by faith to thank God for what He is doing in your life, even when He is not giving you your way. Determine within yourself that you only want to be happy by living God's moral way, and decide right now to trust Him. Stop trying to relieve pain within through sin.[106]

Ask God to heal your pain. Meeting the needs of your heart does not exhaust God at all. As a matter of fact, He delights in it.[107] But you must come to Him believing He is who He says He is. If you don't know Him, spend some time getting to know God by reading the Bible.

"Consider it all joy . . . knowing that the testing of your faith produces endurance, and let endurance have its perfect result, that you may be perfect and complete, lacking in nothing" (James 1:2-4).

Schedule an hour on your calendar to spend time with God one

104 http://www.brainyquote.com/quotes/quotes/h/helenkelle386922.html
105 Hebrews 13:15
106 Romans 6:23; Proverbs 14:12
107 Psalm 147:11

night to read the Bible and ask Him to meet you where you are. He will! No need to feel all alone, because Jesus is alive and cares for you. If you tell Him you are sorry for your sin, He will forgive you and draw you near. The God who created you wants your heart. Happiness does not have to be so hard to find.

Ask yourself these questions: If you believe in God, how does your life show it? Ask yourself if you consider your belief in God to be based on a *relationship* with Him or mere religion? How can you know God is more than a figment of your own imagination? If Jesus did die on the cross for you, do you really think living for Him should cost you nothing? If there is a Supreme Being who loves you, are you willing to risk never having the pleasure of loving Him back? It is worth slowing down to think about.

Here is an excerpt from a beautiful poem by Alice Hansche Mortenson, which I discovered in J. Vernon McGhee's book, *Why Do God's Children Suffer?*[108]

> *I needed the quiet so He drew me aside*
> *Into the shadows where we could confide*
> *A place to grow richer in Jesus to hide*
> *I needed the quiet, so He drew me aside . . .*

Ask God to help you get to know who He is as you read the Bible. It is up to you whether or not you will let Jesus lead you as your Shepherd in life, like the twenty-third Psalm or John, chapter 10, explains. If so, you will find you have nothing to lose—and no man to lose—worth having.

---

108 Dr. J. Vernon McGee © Thru the Bible Radio Network, http://www.ttb.org/ contentpages/21793/ecac65f6-d183-45d5-b6da-75662d98e6ca/ ElectronicBooklets.aspx

There Are Two Kinds of Broken

The definitions of *broken*, according to the Webster's Dictionary, are: "Being irregular, interrupted or full of obstacles; having undergone or been subjected to fracture; violated by transgression; subdued completely; reduced in rank; not complete or full."

No doubt life can break us. Where is God in the midst of our pain and brokenness? He is ready and waiting for us to come to Him, if only we will. He'll turn our sadness into joy, if we will only stop trying to mend our brokenness in our own strength. It is our choice. We can be broken over our sin to make a change for the better and turn our life around or broken because we choose to settle for less than our best in a life far away from God. In other words, we can be broken because of our obedience to God or broken because of our rebellion resulting in never knowing the pleasure of feeling whole within.

Awhile back I met a man who was a well-known speaker. He lectured at universities, churches (though he had never been a pastor), and TED conferences. I was naive enough to think well of him based on his positive speeches on morals. That was before I got to know his immoral character. When I first met him and complimented his work, he replied, "I'm a broken man." I didn't hold that against him when he said that, realizing God had certainly *broken* me for the better over the years. Though we both considered ourselves to be broken, I would soon find that we were two totally different kinds of broken.

He wanted to begin a relationship with me. As I got to know him, I discovered that he was quite a case study on hypocrisy. This gregarious man, who spoke to large crowds all over the world, was as hollow as could be on the inside. He admitted to having a pain deep inside that no one could take away. Though he had seen an array of therapists, therapy had never helped him. In the drama of his own instability, his life was a wreck. It was true. He did not have it all together. The man was indeed broken. He had terrible character behind the scenes. His failed philosophies had left him without any answers for his past, present, or future. He even showed disdain for my desire to live a life in obedience to the Bible. It did not take long to see that we were not at all compatible in our brokenness.

There are two kinds of broken people: those who are broken because they live in sin, and those who are broken because they don't. This man was broken because he lived a life of immorality. I was broken because I didn't. He was broken because he didn't want God. I was broken because I do. He was broken because he was living for himself. I am broken because I am living for Jesus. Neither existence is complete on its own. Brokenness apart from Jesus and apart from repentance of sin brings shame. Brokenness as a result of loving a Savior that this world hates gives us depth of character. Choosing to live in obedience to Him leaves us going against the flow in a greedy world. Yet it is this very painful brokenness that is healing to our soul.

Falling in love is a mystery. There is no greater blessing than a true companion in life. A little child running into your arms is a joy like no other. That being said, the fact still remains that no one can complete us but God. There are two kinds of broken. We can be broken and complete in Jesus,[109] or we can be broken far away from Jesus with no one else to make us truly whole.

---

109 Colossians 2:10

By God's grace, He makes His own broken in dependence on Him. We become broken in a way that makes us better when we live in obedience to the Bible, no matter the cost. This is a brokenness that brings glory to God and honor to our life, because in our weakness He is strong.[110] In this powerful brokenness, we have victory through a Savior who was pierced for our transgressions and crushed for our iniquities.[111] Sin no longer controls us in such beautiful brokenness before God, thanks to Jesus giving us freedom from it. Such brokenness is a reward from God, as opposed to the brokenness God allows as the consequence of rebellion from Him.

In God's prophecy against Moab, we see brokenness as a denouement of Moab's disobedience to God: "Moab is broken . . . 'For I have broken Moab like an undesirable vessel,' declares the Lord" (Jeremiah 48:4, 38).

When people live in hostility to God's will,[112] their momentary *happiness* is always followed by a heavy heart and a broken spirit: "Behold My servants shall shout joyfully with a glad heart, but you shall cry out with a heavy heart, and you shall wail with a broken spirit" (Isaiah 65:14).

The brokenness, which God blesses as a result of submission to His *pure* and loving will, is promised to us in the Bible. Not only does He bless this brokenness, but He is the one who produces it in our hearts as He draws us nearer to Him. Just as wild horses have to be broken to become calmer, obedient and no longer dangerous, in much the same way, God breaks us to make us obey Him. He breaks us to fear sin's backlash enough to stay away from it. When we are broken to love God more, we see how much our pride separates us from God and how the tantalizing lusts of this world really don't fare so well in the end.[113]

I have known people who pride themselves on being wild as a buck and stubborn as a mule. Though wild living has its moments of euphoria, it cannot offer peace. The good news is that no one is so wild and stubborn

---

110 2 Corinthians 12:9
111 Isaiah 53:5
112 1 Corinthians 6:9-10; Revelation 22:15
113 Proverbs 1:7; Proverbs 1:9

that he or she cannot be broken by God. It is actually by God's mercy and love that He breaks us. He teaches us through His justice that we were not created for sin.[114] We still reap what we sow,[115] no matter how sorry we are. It is a universal principle. This is because God is not just a God of love but a God of justice.[116] It is only through the blood Jesus shed on the cross that we can be forgiven.[117] What a blessing it is to be broken enough even to want that forgiveness through Jesus Christ our Lord![118]

"For he who does wrong will receive the consequences of the wrong which he has done" (Colossians 3:25).

"The sacrifices of God are a broken spirit; a broken and a contrite heart, O God, Thou wilt not despise" (Psalm 51:17).

I have spoken and sung at Angola Prison (Louisiana State Penitentiary) to criminals portrayed as the meanest people on earth. Through rehabilitation, some men there have newfound reputations since their incarceration. I have personally met a few of these men, who have been through Bible classes and seminary while in prison and are now teaching Bible studies to other inmates. I'm sorry to say that a few of them may be more contrite over their sins than some of the men I have dated! Not that I plan to start a relationship with a man in prison, but I believe some of them could be an improvement over the psychopaths I've met out here in the *free* world, where such troubled men live in a prison within themselves. No doubt, God has rewards stored up in heaven for His own, even though some may be in prison today; whereas, He has a prison in store for eternity for some who seem convinced their day of judgment will never come.[119]

A few years ago I was given a book I cherish, *The Valley of Vision*.[120]

---

114 Romans 6:1-2
115 Galatians 6:7-8
116 Isaiah 30:18; Psalms 9:7-8; Revelation 20:12-13
117 John 3:16
118 Colossians 2:8-10
119 Matthew 10:28

120 *The Valley of Vision*, Arthur Bennett, ed. (Edinburgh: Banner of Truth Trust, 1975; print edition 2006).

It is a touching compilation of Puritan prayers and devotions from the sixteenth and seventeenth centuries.[121] Here is an excerpt from it to remind us that the first and greatest commandment in the Bible—to love the Lord our God with all of our heart, soul, mind and strength—is only for our good.[122]

"Thou incomprehensible, but prayer-hearing God, known but beyond knowledge, revealed but unrevealed, my wants and welfare draw me to thee, for thou hast never said, 'Seek ye me in vain.' To thee I come in my difficulties, necessities, distresses; possess me with thyself, with a spirit of grace and supplication, with a prayerful attitude of mind, with access into warmth of fellowship, so that in the ordinary concerns of life my thoughts and desires may rise to thee, and in habitual devotion, I may find a resource that might soothe my sorrows, sanctify my successes, and qualify me in all ways for dealings with my fellow man. I bless thee that thou hast made me capable of knowing thee, the author of all being, of resembling thee, the perfection of all excellency, of enjoying thee, the source of all happiness."[123]

To pray such a prayer is to know what the Bible promises!

"Rejoice, be made complete . . . and the God of love and peace shall be with you" (2 Corinthians 13:11).

"Now may the God of peace Himself sanctify you entirely, and may your spirit and soul and body be preserved complete, without blame at the coming of our Lord Jesus Christ. Faithful is He who calls you, and He also will bring it to pass" (1 Thessalonians 5:23-24).

Here is another excellent devotion from *The Valley of Vision*[124] to show the brokenness God blesses. It reminds us that our feelings can deceive us. When our feelings veer to take us in a direction contrary to God's Word, trusting in the Lord is always safer.

---

121 Its influence continued throughout the nineteenth century. Arthur Bennett explains in the preface of *The Valley of Vision* that the British preacher Charles Haddon Spurgeon (1834–1892) is regarded as the last of the Puritans.
122 Matthew 22:36-40
123 *The Valley of Vision*, "God Enjoyed," 18-19.
124 *The Valley of Vision*, "The Divine Will," 14.

"Oh, Lord, I hang on to thee. I see, believe, live, when thy will, not mine, is done; I can plead nothing in myself in regard of any worthiness and grace, in regard of thy providence and promises, but only thy good pleasure. If thy mercy make me poor and vile, blessed be thou! Prayers arising from my needs are preparations for future mercies. Help me to honor thee by believing before I feel, for great is the sin if I make feeling the cause of faith. Show me what sins hide thee from me and eclipse thy love. Help me to humble myself for past evils, to be resolved to walk with more care, for if I do not walk holily before thee, how can I be assured of my salvation?"

"He heals the brokenhearted" (Psalm 147:3).

HOMEWORK

Homework for this tip is to order *The Valley of Vision, A Collection of Puritan Prayers and Devotions* on Amazon. It is not a book of prayers to teach you how to pray—only your own prayers can teach you how to pray. Pray to God in your own words. These prayers show a maturity our present culture lacks. It is a good reminder of what the Bible teaches about the rewards of living life in submission to God. These days we are taught too often, even in churches, that if you come to God it will all be fun and games like some genie-in-a-bottle type of thing, where prayer and meditation are obliged to always give you your way. That is not biblical. God has a will for your life that is higher than your own. The greatest life is one of sacrifice.[125] Ironically, such a broken life is the only way to true and lasting happiness with no shame. [126]

Stay away from broken men who need fixing. The longer you are with them, the more they will bring you down. Leave a broken man with personality problems in God's hands, especially if you have been hurt by one. God knows how to deal with him. Stop trying to fix him or in any way vindicate yourself in his eyes. All you need to care about is

---

125 Luke 9:23; Matthew 16:24
126 Psalm 34:18

God healing your life to make your brokenness complete in Jesus. Date only men who can complement your relationship with Jesus. If there is no man around who meets that standard, realize you have all you need today to be happy alone. It won't work otherwise. If you are a Christian, trying to have relationships with men who are not saved will only keep hurting you. If God has someone compatible, He knows how to bring that man to you. Meanwhile, God wants you in a brokenness that draws you closer to Him.

"And let endurance have its perfect result, that you may be perfect and complete, lacking in nothing" (James 1:4).

> *Lord, high and holy, meek and lowly, thou has brought me to the valley of vision, where I live in the depths but see thee in the heights; hemmed in by the mountains of sin I behold thy glory. Let me learn by paradox that the way down is the way up, that to be low is to be high, that the broken heart is the healed heart, that the contrite spirit is the rejoicing spirit, that the repenting soul is the victorious soul, that to have nothing is to possess all, that to bear the cross is to wear the crown, that to give is to receive, that the valley is the place of vision. Lord, in the daytime stars can be seen from the deepest wells, and the deeper the wells, the brighter thy stars shine; let me find thy light in my darkness, thy life in my death, thy joy in my sorrow, thy grace in my sin, thy riches in my poverty, thy glory in my valley.*
>
> *—The Valley of Vision*[127]

---

127 *The Valley of Vision*, Introduction, xxiv-xxv.

Degrees Don't Make a Man

I am not against education. I am against the worship of it. It is a little known fact that nine of our American presidents never went to college: Harry S. Truman, Grover Cleveland, Andrew Johnson, Abraham Lincoln, Millard Fillmore, Zachary Taylor, Martin Van Buren, Andrew Jackson, and George Washington. Andrew Johnson never even went to school and was taught to read and write by his wife.[128] It took my getting to know some men who were graduates from Yale, Harvard, Princeton, and Dartmouth to no longer be impressed with the crowd as a whole. They are no better than the rest of us. People are born with a certain IQ level. Education cannot make someone smarter, only more educated.

I had the chance to work with a musician in NYC who is actually a graduate of the Massachusetts Institute of Technology, but he had no snobbish air about him. It was my pleasure to work with him. The enjoyment I got from our recording session had nothing to do with his engineering degree from MIT. As a successful musician, he has ended up not even using his degree in engineering. It has been shocking to me how messed up some highly educated people are emotionally, many lacking in common sense, unable to hold down jobs. I don't really care to spend my time in general with the elites. I would rather be around ordinary

---

128 See my quote book on American history, *America, Come Home*, 34.

people who are authentic. I thank God for allowing me to be born into a family of hardworking people, both educated and not, who measure their success by how much they love their neighbor and live according to their morals with no need for the Harvard Room to make them happy.

People who work hard to get a college education and graduate degrees deserve respect for academic accomplishment, but that is all it is. It is not nearly enough for respecting someone overall as a person. Many professions require a certain level of education, and I applaud the achievement of a good education. I appreciate sincere pastors who have gone to seminary to learn the original Greek and Hebrew of the Bible to better teach us. Education is like talent or looks or money—we can bring God glory from it or bring glory to ourselves, and we should never solely judge a person by it.

Some people get degrees just because they want more respect. I once met a man as I was doing my nonprofit work at Columbus Circle in NYC who, by his own admission, had gotten several graduate degrees in hopes of respecting *himself* more. He said no matter how many degrees he acquired, he never felt it was enough. (I explained to him that Jesus wants us to get our worth in what He has done for us on the cross, and that is the only way for any of us to really *be* enough.) It is one thing to get a degree for a profession or honorable purpose, and it is another to simply attain a degree for the praise of others in hopes of finding our own worth in it. Degrees don't make a man. When we stand before God, He is not going to say, "Let's see here. Before I let you in heaven I have to ask you a question. How many degrees do you have?"

God does not judge according to appearance. God's *righteous judgment* goes straight to the heart.[129] The Bible teaches that we judge no man *according to the flesh*.[130] This includes whether or not a person has a degree from a certain school. Furthermore, God teaches that the worth of a person is not at all contingent on whether he or she is known

129 John 7:24
130 2 Corinthians 5:16

as an intellectual. The attribute of being smart is supposed to be for God's glory, especially in the life of a Christian. We are taught to *put no confidence in the flesh*,[131] instead of boasting in it. God wants us to experience our worth in our relationship with Him. If education had been so important to God, Jesus would have been highly educated. Yet the Bible teaches that everyone was amazed by the knowledge of Jesus, because he was not a "learned man."[132] No wonder, it also warns, "Let him who boasts, boast in the Lord." [133]

Billionaires who never finished college include people like Bill Gates, founder of Microsoft, and Steve Jobs, founder of Apple. Having a college education is not always the impetus for financial security. I know one man in NYC who has a degree from Princeton, and he works on and off as a taxi driver and has never been able to hold down a stable job. It is not the education or lack of education that matters as much as *how* we use our God-given intellect and the choices we all have to make in life.

As I referenced previously in Tip #30, John Bunyan penned what used to be the most popular book in America, second only to the Bible, *Pilgrim's Progress*. He was a genius. He received very little education. He wrote *Pilgrim's Progress* from his jail cell, incarcerated for preaching about Jesus. He had such passion for God that he said, "I will stay in jail to the end of my days before I make a butchery of my conscience . . . ," continuing to believe, "What God says is best, is best, though all the men in the world are against it."[134] He didn't get that relentless devotion from college. His wisdom came from God.

Education cannot cure personality disorders, neither can it turn an abusive man into a caring one. It cannot make a man great. Through my singing and speaking at support groups and shelters for battered women, I have had women tell me specifically about men charged with domestic

131 Philippians 3:3
132 John 7:15
133 1 Corinthians 1:31
134 http://www.quotesy.org/quotes/author/john-bunyan/; see also James Kiernan, *Hudson Taylor, John Bunyan and William Carey and Why Their Lives Matter.*

violence who are heart surgeons, dentists, scientists, congressmen, investment bankers, lawyers, executives in technology, and even pastors with doctorates from seminary. Anyone educated on domestic violence knows that abuse is no respecter of persons.

Degrees don't matter when it comes to the making of a wise person. Growing in *the wisdom and knowledge of God* is what matters,[135] as manifested in a man's loyalty to his wife and family and character in general. The wisdom of the world is not the same as God's wisdom. God promises that He will make foolish the wisdom of this world.[136] As I explained previously in Tip #18, God describes pure and undefiled religion as loving widows and orphans and keeping ourselves unstained by the world,[137] not getting degrees from a certain university or seminary.

I once knew a seminary professor who was totally enamored with his intellect. A few fellow pastors and seminary professors who knew him seemed enamored with it, too. He would brag about how many books he read, and the fellow pastors and seminary professors would brag on how many books this man read. At just the mention of his name, they would comment, "He is really smart," with no mention of whether or not he had attributes like honesty and humility. The core problem with all of the adulation was that the man was getting more glory than God; plus, the seminary professor had terrible character. With all of his education and the books he had written *about* God, he was not living for Him. He was such a flirt with his female seminary students that he almost lost his job as a *Christian* seminary professor. He was reported and had to take a sabbatical to get counseling. He was actually a very silly man. Education alone does not make someone a great man in God's eyes. It shouldn't in ours either.

A man is either smart or not, education or no education. Many people are far smarter than those with Ivy League degrees; they just did not have the money, opportunity *or* desire to attend an Ivy League university.

135 Romans 11:33
136 1 Corinthians 1:20
137 James 1:27

God will not share his glory with *education* when it comes to greatness in a person. It is stupid of anyone to judge themselves or others based on external qualities, such as degrees from prestigious schools. Begin to define success from God's perspective, including success in your own life. Are you living a life in obedience to the Bible? Are you treating people with kindness? Are you forgiving your enemies (with boundaries)? Are you living according to your morals? All that really matters is what God thinks of you, and He sees the heart and our motives behind every action.

God's standard requires far more than worldly education can ever give a person. Leave your reputation in a life *hidden with Christ*,[138] and praise Him with His pleasure over you when you live your life close to Him. No one is perfect, but God sure has a way of turning a lot of mistakes around when we make it our heart's ambition to begin living in humility and love toward God and others, especially when our faith is tested. The smartest people on earth are not those who know they ought to live right, but those who do.

HOMEWORK

Homework for this tip is to watch the television show *Shark Tank*. Notice how an education is not required when it comes to making money. Hard work is the key.

I hesitate to recommend my own book, but I have an easy-read quote book on American history called *America, Come Home* available on Amazon and Barnes and Noble. It really shows the depth of wisdom our American culture used to exhibit as a model of greatness for the world. My book features color photos I took of today's culture, which contrast the quotes from America's founders and past presidents to illustrate how much our culture has shifted. It is a coffee table art book of quotes. As you read through the quotes, you will see that the faith that built

---

138 Colossians 3:3

America was not attained through formal education.

Maybe you are a woman reading this feeling as though you are lacking because you did not go to college. My prayer for you is that you will know your worth in Jesus. Obedience to the Bible and faith in God are what the good life is all about. "The God of heaven will give us success."[139] Don't ever underestimate what Jesus can do through you if you make Him your Lord. With God, any ordinary person can have the most extraordinary life, down in the valley or high on a mountaintop with Him.

"Beloved, I pray that in all respects you may prosper and be in good health, just as your soul prospers" (3 John 1:2).

---

139 Nehemiah 2:20

Tip #33

You Can Have Chemistry for a Man You Don't Like

*I*f you are feeling chemistry for a man with bad character, there is only one thing to do. Even though it's sure to leave you in tears, break all ties if possible. Though the chemistry you share can make having no contact with him excruciatingly painful, you are playing with fire if you keep in touch. (See Tip #7.) If you stop engaging with him on any level, in any way, you won't regret it. When a rush for the wrong man feels overwhelming, you are only putting yourself in harm's way by having anything to do with him. If his bad character makes you pity him, realize he does not need you as a *friend*. Leave him in God's hands. The only way to truly help anyone is to first take care of yourself, so the best thing you can do for a bad man is stay away. If you will take my advice, you can get through such a test unscathed before the chemistry backfires. Reach for a Bible to help you gain wisdom enough to take care of yourself, even when it's your own compulsive feelings that are working against your good.

Chemistry is powerful, but this mysterious magnetism that draws us as women to certain men is not the same as love. When the man's character is not good, it sets us up for addiction. Sheer chemistry is often mistaken for love, producing songs, poetry, long letters, euphoria and millions of tears. It certainly makes an otherwise casual acquaintance a serious one. Here are two stories based on my own experience as a reminder that chemistry is only chemistry and not necessarily the same as love at first sight.

In between publishing and production deals as a singer in Nashville, I got a job as a receptionist at a law firm. I felt immediate chemistry when I was introduced to one of the partners. I had done absolutely nothing to invite such an attraction. It hit me as an unwelcome surprise. It was obvious that he felt it, too, and he hired me on the spot. As I came into the office every day, I never knew what to expect with his mood swings. He yelled quite a bit. During one of his anger sprees, a secretary leaned over and whispered to me that he had been diagnosed as "bipolar." This was during the late nineties, and I hadn't heard of anyone being bipolar before. Everyone knew he had problems. The arrogant outbursts continued on a regular basis, followed by a rote apology. When he was not yelling at me, he would flirt with me. Despite his crazy flights of anger, the chemistry I felt for the man would not yield. I began praying about it from my very first day of working for him. It was scary, especially because he was my employer.

He had a reputation around town for being one of the best attorneys in Nashville. He had a reputation inside the firm for sleeping with his office staff. It did not take long for me to figure out he was having an affair with one of his married clients. They would head off for afternoon trysts, and he would come back to the office and stand around my receptionist desk to flirt with me afterward. It became sickening. On slow afternoons I would be sitting there at the desk, reading my Bible in between phone calls. (I needed all of the protection I could get with that guy!) Well, within just a few days, something strange began happening when this slick attorney came around me. He could barely speak. His nervousness rose to a freakish degree the more he tried talking to me. One time he had to put his hand over his mouth, because his lips were quivering so much as he was trying to play me in his little game of deception. At first I thought it was because he liked me so much, but now I truly believe it was spiritual. I believe he got nervous because I was a Christian with Jesus in my heart.

The Bible says that demons tremble with fear at Jesus. Yes, even the demons believe that Jesus is God. Because Jesus lives inside my heart, demonic spirits cannot harm me. No wonder that attorney was so scared when he tried to get close to me! It is written in James 2:19, "You say you have faith, for you believe that there is one God. Good for you! Even the demons believe this, and they tremble in terror."[140]

After I left the firm, his paralegal told me she had never seen him nervous like that and had worked with him for years. I also learned from her that he had to drink a whole bottle of vodka nightly to get to sleep, and that the married woman with whom he was having the affair, drank the vodka with him. He could not start his day without reading his astrological chart, though he considered himself to be an atheist. His first wife ended up in an insane asylum before getting over him, because, "He drove her crazy," the paralegal explained.

Why in the world had I felt chemistry for a man so repulsive? He was unethical by any standard, and I did not respect how he treated his employees or his clients, for that matter. Within three months of my nightly prayers to God for help, my time at that firm was over. The attorney yelled at me one too many times, and I told him I knew about his affair with his client and added that he did not have to ask me to forgive him for yelling at me *again*, because I already had learned to forgive him for his mistreatment of me from the very first day on the job. After I left the firm, he stalked me for an entire year. I really believe the man had an evil spirit. After I got a new job, I would see him jogging around Music Row at lunch. When he spotted me, he would stare at me with total hatred seething from his eyes. I began getting scary phone calls from him.

The Bible teaches no temptation has *overtaken* me,[141] and that was

140 New Living Translation of the Bible
141 1 Corinthians 10:13

proven once again in my life through my time at that law firm. I knew that God had protected me by never letting that attorney touch me. I ended up speaking to another attorney about how this man was stalking me with phone calls, but I realized it was not worth the trouble and expense to do anything about it legally. (This was long before we had cell phones with blocking features.) I thank God for keeping me safe. Greater is He that is in me, than he that is in the world.[142] It finally stopped, but not until I left the state of Tennessee and moved to California.

Right before I moved to Los Angeles, I got a job working as a makeup artist at a department store in Nashville. We had been advised that the regional head of all of that chain's stores in the South was transferring to our location as our new store manager. I remember working on cosmetic inventory in a drawer at my counter when someone said, "Dwayna, meet our new store manager." I looked up and shook his hand and immediately felt a wave of chemistry from head to toe. I could hardly look him in the eyes because there was so much chemistry.

I began praying for God to keep me away from the new store manager. One of the women in my department had known him for years in the retail industry, and she had nothing good to say about him. She informed me that he had what he called an open marriage and was known for having girlfriends on the side. I tried my best to avoid him. Every time I looked his way, he was staring at me. I was a top seller, and he had offered to give me a promotion. Four long months later, I left and moved to Los Angeles. As we said goodbye in the witness of others, he shook my hand and said, "I don't know why you are leaving," with an intense look in his eyes. With God's help, I had managed to successfully dodge the married store manager day in and day out. The chemistry did not get the best of me. I will be eternally grateful to the Lord for protecting me from it. Every single time I have triumphed over "chemistry" has been "by the spirit," as the Bible teaches, not "the flesh."[143]

142 1 John 4:4
143 Galatians 5:17

In both of these true incidents, the way I won was *simple*. I kept my distance from the bad men, spent time in prayer down on my knees, and forced myself to read the Bible. Believe me, it does not come naturally to read the Bible or sing a hymn about Jesus when lust strikes. This is because sin keeps us from the Bible, just as the Bible keeps us from sin. God's Word enables us to see things more realistically and gives us the desire to flee immorality.

In the midst of such a "fiery trial" brought about for my testing,[144] I knew it would do no good to fight the battle in my own strength. I would have lost. Every time I could get to the Bible and open it to my favorite passages, such as John 10, the book of Ephesians or Galatians, or the book of Psalms . . . *God would change me.* He gave me the strength to stay away as I renewed my mind to the truth in the Bible. The Bible is called a sword, because reading it empowers us to win any spiritual battle.

"For the word of God is living and active and sharper than any two-edged sword, and piercing as far as the division of soul and spirit, of both joints and marrow, and able to judge the thoughts and intentions of the heart" (Hebrews 4:12).

If you are feeling chemistry for a man you do not like, your responsibility is to stay away from him. Open the Bible, read it, and pray to God for help. That, along with a sincere desire to do what is right, is all it takes for God to do the rest. He will draw you to Himself, where you are safe, and give you the strength to stay away from sin. As I have written previously, I've also found I cannot harbor sin in my heart when I get down on my knees alone before God and sing a hymn. The words of the hymns touch me so much that the Holy Spirit meets me there and purifies my desires. He changes the direction I would otherwise go. I can't have such a prayer time of worship and remain the same. God gets the credit for keeping me. Without Him, I do not know where I would be, especially in the grip of devil-may-care, wayward chemistry that feels like love.

---

144 1 Peter 4:12

Instead of judging the Bible, let the Bible judge you. It is the key to a happy life. You'll stand amazed at how the power of God is stronger than all other powers, even when chemistry for the wrong man is stronger than you could ever fight alone.

"Do not fear, for I have redeemed you. I have called you by name; you are Mine! When you pass through the waters, I will be with you; and through the rivers, they will not overflow you. *When you walk through the fire you will not be scorched, nor will the flame burn you*; for I am the Lord your God, the Holy One of Israel, your Savior" (Isaiah 43:1-3).

HOMEWORK

Homework is to pray a prayer for victory, especially if you are currently being drawn by lust to a bad man. The first step is to realize your feelings can be deceiving. Get a Bible and look up Proverbs 28:26: "He who trusts in his own heart is a fool." The second step is to understand *how* to stay out of trouble. Believers in Jesus are called the "bride of Christ" in the Bible.[145] This may come as a surprise, but the Bible teaches that you cannot be a stainless, pure *bride* in His eyes by doing any amount of good works.[146] It is only possible by the blood Jesus shed on the cross.

This is because Jesus died on the cross to pay the penalty for our sin.[147] The blood He shed on Calvary is our only means of being cleansed from sin today. Jesus destroyed the power that sin has over us when He died on the cross and destroyed the power of death when He rose again. This is why our victory is in Jesus alone.

"But God raised Him up again, putting an end to the agony of death, since it was impossible for Him to be held in its power" (Acts 2:24).

You see, your battles have already been won, but only if you will surrender to Jesus and give Him your heart by something the Bible

---

145 Ephesians 5:25-27; Revelation 21:2
146 Ephesians 2:8-9; Galatians 5:4
147 1 John 1:7

calls *repentance*. It means, basically, to turn around and go God's way: "Therefore, having overlooked the times of ignorance, God is now declaring to men that all people everywhere should repent, because He has fixed a day in which He will judge the world in righteousness through a Man whom He has appointed, having furnished proof to all men by raising Him from the dead" (Acts 17:30-31).

Turning away from sin, as God defines sin in the Bible, and turning to God, is how we win. It is the means by which we find strength in the midst of our weakness. It is the almighty power that raised Jesus from the dead at work within us that saves us from these snares in life, not ourselves.

Morals are only morals. None of us is perfect. If morals could save us, Jesus died in vain. He called the most moral people of His day "whitewashed tombs" and "snakes" because of their self-righteous pride.[148] We need mercy and forgiveness when we fail. We are all sinners in need of a Savior whom death could not hold. Only Jesus defeated sin.

"He saved us, not on the basis of deeds which we have done in righteousness, but according to His mercy, by the washing of regeneration and renewing by the Holy Spirit" (Titus 3:5).

Isaiah 30:15 warns, "This is what the Sovereign Lord, the Holy One of Israel, says: 'In repentance and rest is your salvation, in quietness and trust is your strength, but you would have none of it.'"

Make today the day you stop running from God. Tell God you are sorry for all of your sin, which includes all of the time you have spent in life going your own way. You know you are not perfect. Why not go to God His way? Ask Him to forgive you, and He will. Jesus is the only way to victory over deceiving spirits, including cunning chemistry you feel that could very well be out to destroy your soul. Jesus died on the cross so that chemistry cannot conquer you, if only you'll believe in Him as the *only* Savior above all other powers and dominions and let Him be the Master of your life.

---

148 Matthew 23:27; Matthew 23:33

"Jesus said to him, 'I am the way, and the truth, and the life; no one comes to the Father but through Me'" (John 14:6).

"For there is one God, and one mediator also between God and men, the man Christ Jesus" (1 Timothy 2:5).

"For I am convinced that neither death, nor life, nor angels, nor principalities, nor things present, nor things to come, nor powers, nor height, nor depth, nor any other created thing, shall be able to separate us from the love of God, which is in Christ Jesus our Lord" (Romans 8:38-39).

If you really want to get well, praying the following prayer for salvation is more powerful than the most expensive therapy, especially when you consider that therapy cannot offer eternal redemption for your soul. Salvation is free to you today because of the blood Jesus shed on Calvary. He paid the price. Knowing Jesus as your Savior will never cost you anything worth having. There is just one way to eternal life and only one escape from hell. Trust in the only God who destroyed death and the power of sin. If you want to belong to God and have God belong to you, pray a little prayer like this:

"Dear God, please forgive me for my sin. I believe that Jesus paid for my sin on the cross, and I need You to come and help me today. Save me from myself. Help me to understand the Bible when I read it, and help me to follow You—not Christians who may disappoint me or man-made "religion," but You, Jesus. Thank You for Your love for me. Thank You for dying on the cross for me. Come and live inside my heart to never leave. Meet me where I am today as I read Your Word, the Bible. I need a Friend, and I want You to be my God. Save me and never let me go. Guide me, and help me to live for You. In Jesus' name I pray, amen."

Praying a prayer like that is all it takes to be saved. Choosing to accept Jesus as your Savior is how you can be forgiven for every single bit of your sin. Aren't you glad the God who made you does not require you to say some long, religious prayer you don't even understand or sit in some strange position for hours? He simply wants you to come to Him like a little child, believing He is who He says He is. He wants to be your

Lord. He wants to be your friend. He has more love than any man on earth can offer you, but you have to want it enough to let Him turn your life around for His glory.

Praying a prayer for salvation does not mean that God will take away all of your desires for a bad guy when lust is involved. It means you are giving yourself to God; your body is now His property. He will see you through if you will lean on Him and flee immorality.[149] Acting on lust can destroy you. God's way will leave you with respect for yourself.

I have been saved from a slew of wolves because of Jesus, my Good Shepherd, and His love for me. I take no credit for it. It is because the *chemistry* I've felt for the wrong men was conquered for me at Calvary. Your victory is not in your own strength but in a Person death and sin could not hold.

"If you confess with your mouth Jesus as Lord, and believe in your heart that God raised Him from the dead, you will be saved" (Romans 10:9).

"There is salvation in no one else; for there is no other name under heaven that has been given among men by which we must be saved" (Acts 4:12).

---

149 1 Corinthians 6:18

Tip #34

A Con Artist Will Con
Your Therapist, Too

*I*f you are in a relationship suffering ongoing verbal, emotional, or physical abuse, you may think, "Maybe he would change if he could speak to the pastor of our church." I have come to believe that very few pastors, deacons, and elders are equipped to understand a church-going abusive man's propensity for guile. You may spend a lot of your energy researching top therapists who charge anywhere from one hundred to four hundred dollars an hour, hoping he will agree to talk with one of them. You might as well save your money. Even if he consents to the meeting, which is a big if, he's bound to use the same trickery he used in the beginning with you to strong-arm the therapist against you. The meanest of abusive men are usually the nicest con artists who feel totally justified in their mistreatment toward a woman *in private*. If he does not have the gumption inside himself to tell you he is sorry, repent before God, and begin to show signs of change on his own, he will not benefit from counseling. It will more than likely empower him even more to continue his abuse toward you by the time he finishes conning the counselor.

Very few counselors are wise enough to know not to take the abusive man's word for anything without also talking to the woman involved in order for the truth to be confirmed. Couples counseling usually attempts to level the ground, pointing out what the victim is doing wrong as well as the abuser, as if they are both to blame. Often, it is presented that simple communication skills can solve all of the problems. As I explain in Tip #40, most counselors do not understand that an abusive man is abusive by character. Even when a woman is perfect, an abusive man will still be abusive. He doggedly resists assuming responsibility for his scary temper tantrums. Many counselors do not understand that abuse toward another person is never contingent on the victim's behavior. It is not the victim's fault.

I hesitate to mention this because of how much good counseling has helped me. You must keep in mind, however, that not all therapists are good. I do not mean to stop you in any way from getting individual counseling but only to make you cautious about choosing the right therapist. Some therapists are more than happy just to take your money without helping you get any better. If you have been seeing a therapist for years, do yourself a favor and think about how you can notice your character improving. Make a list of the positive changes you have made since you began the therapy. If you are not getting any better, maybe it is time to realize this and stop wasting money by the hour. Counseling will only help someone who is willing to do the work it takes to change. A good counselor will not want someone to become addicted to therapy, but, rather, want to see his or her client get better.

The counselors who have helped me improve my life have been those who have already learned how to live themselves. It is your prerogative to interview therapists. After all, it is your money you are spending. Why not get to know them a little before letting them get to know you? If the counselor is not living a healthy life, more than likely he or she will become defensive and not want to answer any questions you ask. You would be surprised at how unhealthy some therapists are. Try to find out if the counselor's life makes sense before trusting him or her with yours. If you are battling abuse and only want to go to a Christian counselor, be sure to ask how much he or she knows about abuse. When asked that question, I have heard some pastors simply reply, "Well, I know the Bible," as if that is all it takes to understand domestic violence. There is a difference between offering wisdom pertaining to the character of God when making judgments vs. counsel that grieves the Holy Spirit by taking scripture out of context and lording over a woman by means of spiritual abuse.

I once heard a pastor from a large church in California say publicly that because the Bible does not address domestic violence, a woman suffering under physical abuse must stay married. I guess he thought, in such a case, it could be God's will for the woman to be beaten to death. His advice revealed his misogynistic view of women. To counter that, another pastor from a large church in the South told a friend of mine that unless there was physical violence, she had no grounds for divorce. She silenced the pastor by replying wisely, "The Bible does not say that. You have made that exception based on your own reasoning, not giving me, as a Christian, the freedom to do the same. You don't know what it is like to live under emotional and verbal abuse every day. It can be even worse than physical violence."

At least he was nice enough to empathize and agreed with her about the pain of nonphysical abuse. The pastor went on to explain that the woman's husband had been in to see him recently, insinuating in their meeting that she had been the one mistreating him. He had presented himself to the pastor as the pitiful victim, as the loving husband who never wanted a divorce. She answered, "Well, let me tell you what he did this week," as she went on to detail his recent mistreatment of her emotionally and verbally, unmasking her husband's false self. The pastor just listened without reply. After she explained her husband's abuse, she added, "If you keep pressuring women to stay in abusive relationships, you will have a woman in your church commit suicide. God never saved a woman to be abused. You all are going to keep on until a woman kills herself." The couple divorced. My friend, who stayed with this abusive man as long as she did because she wanted to be pleasing to God, had to leave the church. It became too awkward when her crafty ex-husband quickly found a new woman within the church to remarry.

I have a friend who is a Christian and married a man who sexually abused her children. There is no specific verse in the Bible that gave her reason to divorce him, yet no one in his or her right mind would agree that it is God's will for her to stay with the pedophile. Like sexual abuse, domestic violence affects the whole home. This includes ongoing violent outbursts of verbal abuse that leaves emotional scars. There are many things the Bible does not address. The Bible cannot tell you how to bake a cake or get a driver's license, for instance. God gives us principles of wisdom and freedom to make our own decisions based upon those principles. Yes, God hates divorce, but He also hates sexual, physical, emotional, and spiritual abuse. We cannot please the Lord and bring God glory with our lives without first knowing the difference between wise counsel and spiritual abuse.

It is hard to believe these stories are true, but I promise they are. It can be so disheartening to hear about men in Christian leadership positions who do not support women. We have to balance the negative stories with all of the extraordinary men who are making a difference for the better in the lives of women. Here are some examples: I have a friend who is a pastor in California who does outreach to AIDS victims. I have worked with him in ministry, and it is a delight just to know him. He reaches out in love with no condemnation toward anyone with AIDS. I also have a friend who leads an organization against sex-trafficking, and he is an all-around great Christian guy, including being a dedicated husband and father. A retired pastor with a foundation for biblical counseling was the one who taught me that if a woman is being abused, she should care about Jesus to the point of taking herself out of the abusive situation. He explained that when a man hurts a woman, it hurts God. Sometimes it is not about a woman having enough self-confidence but more about a woman loving Jesus enough to leave a bad guy and stop allowing the

Holy Spirit within her to be grieved. I have never heard better sermons or felt the Lord's love more than when I recently worshiped at a church in Charleston, SC. I noticed that the women were certainly not treated like second-class citizens. I was told that the African Methodist Episcopal Church was famous for their support of women. I found myself wanting to move to Charleston just to go to that church every Sunday!

After sharing these heartwarming examples, as much as I would like to continue on the respite of positivity, the fact remains that it is not always safe to let down our guard with men, even when we meet them in church. Right after I moved to Southern California and became active in a church there, I met a woman at Bible study who quickly became my best friend. We enjoyed meeting before church and sitting together during the services then going out afterward. We were both artistic, had a lot of fun together, and we planned on always being close friends. It was not long before she *fell in love* with a man going to the seminary there. They sought out premarital counseling from an elder at the church. After *getting to know them* better through counseling, this church elder was convinced the two were a match made in heaven. She made a beautiful bride dressed in white, married there at the church.

Right after the wedding, her husband's control over her began escalating. He would not allow her to have a television and would monitor even the time she spent listening to the radio. Much like a cult leader, he reminded her often, "I'm the head over you," as she lost her own opinion about anything that differed from his. Though they had more chemistry than they knew what to do with while dating, after a few months into the marriage, he refused to touch her to punish her for anything she may have said or done that was, in his estimation, *disrespectful* toward him. One night they began arguing, and he almost killed her. She had internal bruises on her throat. The neighbors called the police, and he was thrown into jail. Shockingly, the same church elder who counseled them before marriage told her to tell her husband she was sorry for showing him disrespect that night and convinced her that she had provoked the abuse. She had the nerve to have an opinion of her own when he almost strangled her to death.

I advised her to get out from under the control of the church counselor. The elder's advice was obviously contradicting God's will for any victim of domestic violence. I explained that she had been abused twice—once by her husband, and then by her church. I pleaded with her to start thinking for herself and reminded her that elders are sinners saved by grace like the rest of us. They are not gods. Her own dad, who was a devout Christian, said, "This elder is not prepared to counsel you. He is wrong," and begged her to leave with the kids and return home with them until the divorce was final. Sadly, the last I heard from her, she was back with her abusive husband. She wrote me a letter back in 2005 bemoaning the semblance of strength she had previously shown, when at least she was willing to have me in her life as a voice of reason. She was probably forced by her husband to write the letter to me asking, "Please forgive me for telling you anything negative about my husband. The argument was my fault that night when the neighbors reported it to the police. I am praying God will help me show my husband more respect and make me a godly wife." I can only hope she is alive today. As smart as she was, that man had brainwashed her. Thanks to him and the church counseling, she could no longer think for herself.

When I was only eighteen years old, I crept in to see a counselor at my church, ashamed to admit I needed help with what I knew had become an eating disorder. It was clear to me that he could not relate to what I was going through with food addiction, though he encouraged me to stay out of twelve-step meetings (where I eventually found people who could in fact understand). He gave me some Bible verses to read, which I had already read. I still did not know why I wanted to eat so much when I was hurting. I was just as perplexed when I left the counselor's office as when I came. He meant well, but the meeting was a waste of time for both of us.

Find a counselor who is a living testament of health, who has worked to overcome some of the specific struggles you are facing. Don't be afraid to leave any counselor if he or she has no understanding *based on experience* when it comes to what you are going through. We have to remember, the best Counselor is God.[150] Let the Holy Spirit guide you through wisdom as you spend time in prayer and Bible study. Be patient with yourself when it comes to the Lord's timing for deliverance. He can certainly use a wise counselor to help you, as I finally experienced in my own life. Just don't waste money with anyone whose advice would be contrary to the abundant life Jesus died for you to have.[151]

HOMEWORK

Homework for this tip is to learn more about the severe wounds caused by verbal abuse by visiting VerbalAbuse.com. Take some time, especially if you are a Christian, to also research spiritual abuse and spiritual addiction. I recommend the book, *The Subtle Power of Spiritual Abuse: Recognizing and Escaping Spiritual Manipulation and False Spiritual Authority*, by David Johnson and Jeff VanVonderen.[152] Read "When Religion Goes Bad" at SpiritualAbuse.com. Of course, there is nothing wrong with church on Sunday and Bible studies throughout the week, as long as Jesus is glorified and people are not treated like gods. As Dale Ryan puts it, *If your god is not God, fire him.*[153]

A sincere pastor once gave me some great advice, which I never forgot. Not only does Satan not want you to know what the Bible teaches, he doesn't want you to know what it means. When we know what the Bible verses mean in application to our lives, we can discern the difference between religious addiction and a real relationship with God as a loving Father.

---

150 Isaiah 9:6
151 John 10:10
152 Bethany House Publishers, 2005, available in paperback and on Kindle
153 Dale Ryan, "If your god is not God, fire him," posted at http://www.spiritualabuse
   .com/?page_id=4. Dale Ryan is the CEO of Christian Recovery International.

If you are looking for a good counselor and would like to speak with Marilyn Brown, the therapist to whom I dedicate this book, just write me via my blog at DwaynaLitzBlog.com, and I will give you her contact information. Specializing in addiction, she is an overcomer. She has battled far more than I in her life and now has a healthy marriage, so compatible with her husband that they never even argue. Thanks to her help, I now live in recovery from my eating disorder and understand addictions with men and how the two used to work together in my life. She was the only one who ever told me she wanted to see me get happy on my own, rather than to continue dating men who are wrong for me. It was one happy day for both of us when I finally began taking her advice and stopped wasting my time with all of the wrong men.[154]

154 I also recommend my friends Keri Newell and Dr. Sherie Zander as experts at communication with men: http://communicationmagicwithmen.com/meet-the -experts/. I thank Sherie Zander for all she has taught me as my first counselor when I lived in California. Lundy Bancroft is a leading therapist when it comes to the wiles of abusive men, and I am thankful for all his books have taught me. He holds counseling retreats for abused women. Visit his website at http://www .lundybancroft.com/.

Leave a Man Who Cannot Be Emotionally Monogamous

*Y*ears ago, I went out a few times with a guy who talked incessantly about his ex-girlfriend. My dates with him were filled with anecdotes about her. He viewed it all as very innocuous. He said she simply needed his opinion on things as friends, which was why she called him daily. He had no intention of ever losing touch with her and saw no need of distancing himself from her. He knew she was not over him, and he felt too sorry for her to cut off the communication. After all, he explained, he had broken her heart when they stopped dating.

The more I dated him, the more I realized that if I wanted him, it was a package deal that came with her, too. Not meaning to overreact or come off as unjustifiably jealous, I mentioned his strong emotional connection with this *ex-girlfriend* to Marilyn Brown, my newfound counselor, in our group counseling session in Century City. Marilyn replied, "Leave him. He cannot be emotionally monogamous." She said it emphatically, as if she knew it had everything to do with his character and nothing to do with me.

By the time my relationship with him was over, I had heard so much about the woman that I could have written a book about her. If I had married the guy, I would have felt like I was part of some emotionally polygamous marriage. It would have been as if he had two wives calling him and needing him. When it ended, I told him to have a wonderful life with her. I truly hope they are still together *as friends* to last a lifetime. It did not take long for me to leave that guy with his quest for an emotional threesome.

There are two kinds of men in this world. There are those who need attention from more than one woman and those who are one-woman-men. A good man is a one-woman-man, where just one woman needing him and loving him is more than enough. Some married men are too narcissistic for that. They need attention and affirmation from as many women as they can get. Some married men assume that flirting with women behind their wife's back will draw a whole world of other women to them. They are wrong. It only draws the ones with bad character. Smart women of quality see it as a red flag, as a sign of bad character.

Back in 1952, Hank Thompson had a country hit, "The Wild Side of Life," which stayed number one on the Billboard country charts for fifteen weeks.[155] It was about a woman who went "to the places where the wine and liquor flow . . . to be anybody's baby," as if she preferred that lifestyle over being married to a good man and remaining true to him always. Thompson's lyrics beckoned a response from Kitty Wells in her following hit song that same year:[156]

> *It wasn't God who made honky tonk angels*
> *As you said in the words of your song.*
> *Too many times married men think they're still single*
> *That has caused many a good girl to go wrong.*

---

155 Written by Arlie A. Carter and William Warren. Copyright EMI Music Publishing. For more background, see https://en.wikipedia.org/wiki/The_Wild_Side_of_Life.

156 "Honky Tonk Angels," written by J. D. Miller, was first recorded in 1952 by Kitty Wells as an answer to the Hank Thompson hit, "The Wild Side of Life." Copyright Peermusic Publishing, Universal Music Group. Dolly Parton, Loretta Lynn, and Tammy Wynette also recorded it in 1993 as the cover tune for their *Honky Tonk Angels* album.

It is not fair to a single woman when a married man comes on to her. He is attempting to exploit her vulnerability as a single person looking for love. He is hoping she will be stupid enough to drift off into some *If-Only-He-Was-Single* dreamland about him. Well, whether she is that obtuse or not, he is to blame in the first place for not being emotionally monogamous to his wife. An emotional affair with a married man cannot be real because he is not single. It does not matter how much he tries to justify it. She is available. He is not. He wants to have his cake and eat it too.

I have certainly met way too many married men who act like they are single, and this includes so-called Christian men in leadership positions. It is as if, with all of their knowledge of the Bible, they have somehow forgotten the Bible verses about how God sees the heart. Each wanted to strike up a friendship with me behind his wife's back that was inappropriate, so I ended up having to lose touch with them altogether. Fostering a connection with a bent toward immorality is actually not innocent at all. An emotional affair with a married man is wrong on so many levels, and the one hurt most is God.

Statistics show that an emotional affair means more to most women than a physical one.[157] The next time some married man comes on to you, ask yourself, *Would I want my husband flirting like this behind my back?* Before the married sweet-talker means too much to you as a single woman, ask yourself, *How would it feel to be married to a man like that?* Come back to reality. Remind yourself that you will always win as a woman when you think with your brain.

When a good man is unhappy in his marriage, he knows he has one of two choices: either stay to make the marriage better or get a divorce. Cheating is not an option, because it does not fit the lifestyle of a man with good character. When a married man pursues a single woman to

---

157 "Is an Emotional Affair Worse Than a Sexual One? Men and Women
     Disagree," posted on *Huff Post*. Feb. 7, 2014 at http://www.huffingtonpost
     .com/2014/02/07/sexual-affairs_n_4747121.html.

begin an emotional affair, who is he kidding? Of course, he knows it could easily develop into a physical one. Yet many married men pursue an emotional relationship with an attractive woman on the side just like it is fine and dandy. The married man is looking for a little ego boost. God help the woman who thinks she can find love with such a man. If he was really capable of true love, would he be cheating on his wife? Sometimes you cannot help it when you click with a person. You can help what you do about it.

When I work with a man who is married, the first thing I try to do is befriend his wife. It is just smart for everyone. Talking about his wife and including her in my relationship with him protects us both from any compatible dynamic that could otherwise be misconstrued. As a rule, when a married man wants me as a "special friend" to "hang out with him" on a regular basis without his wife's knowledge of my existence, I either become friends with her or lose touch with him. When the married guy is overtly acting like a single man around me—my, my, how befriending the wife changes things. It is funny how the inappropriate, flirtatious emails and phone calls stop as soon as I become friends with his wife.

Remember, as much as he may seem like some dream come true for you, he is not. He's his wife's dream (or nightmare). It is only real when two people are single and dating out in the open with nothing in secret. If he happens to be an exceptionally good man who is in a bad marriage, you can trust God enough with the entire situation to lose any connection with him and not get back in touch as long as he is married. No woman needs to be so desperate for love that she settles for a married man who belongs to another woman. Not only is it cheating, but it is stealing.

Put it to the test if you find yourself attracted to a married man. Leave the situation completely. God always honors it when we decide to live right. Odds are that he is on your mind in the first place, because he is not an emotionally monogamous man in general. You were not the first woman to be hurt by him behind his wife's back and will not be the last. It is true that there are some nice men out there with bad marriages, but it is also true that many jerks have bad marriages. If his marriage ends, let it end without your having anything to do with it. Players do not make good husbands. If he would easily cheat on his wife with you emotionally, he would do the same thing behind your back if you end up marrying him. Cheaters cheat. Know your worth. You deserve to come in first place in a man's life, both emotionally and physically, just as any married woman deserves with her husband.

You are far better off staying single and confident than fostering an emotional attachment with a married man that will only bring you down. Sin hurts everyone involved. There is no honor in cheating and a whole lot of heartache in store for him, his wife, his kids, and you, so wise up. Do yourself a favor and get away from the pain of *him* altogether. Let the rover move on to hurt someone else behind his wife's back. Keep your life clean. Don't let such a selfish person waste your time. God will reward you for it, most certainly in ways no married man can.

"Man looks at the outward appearance, but the LORD looks at the heart" (1 Samuel 16:7).

HOMEWORK

Homework is to read *Chatting or Cheating* by Dr. Sheri Meyers.[158] Check out the website at ChattingOrCheating.com.

Read "The Truth About Emotional Affairs," by Michelle Weiner-Davis, published Sept. 29, 2015, in the *Huff Post* section on Divorce online.[159]

Stay away from men who don't understand that an emotional affair is still cheating. There is no married man on earth you need for a special

158 Published by From the Heart Media, Inc., 2012.
159 http://www.huffingtonpost.com/michele-weinerdavis/the-truth-about-emotional _b_1958709.html

friend—he has his wife for that. Trust God to bring you a special friend in a man who can belong to you if it is His will. If that does not happen, you have enough anyway to be happy today on your own. Immorality is not an option for anyone searching for true happiness.

People with good character don't lead secretive lives. Dishonest people do. There is really no lasting happiness apart from an honest life. Any emotional connection you feel for a married man is a test you can win by fleeing it altogether with no regrets looking back. You have the rest of your life ahead of you. If you spend it crying over a married man who acts like he is single, one thing is for sure. You won't be the only woman crying over him.

A Crazy Man
Will Make You Crazy

The Academy Award–winning actor Heath Ledger was an adorable little boy with a winsome smile. He had a bright future ahead of him. When he set off for Hollywood with his remarkable raw talent, he never dreamed he would die at age twenty-eight of an accidental drug overdose.[160] Losing himself inside the mind of a clown-faced villain in *The Dark Knight* earned him much critical acclaim, though he didn't live to see the movie released. In an online article about Ledger, "Batman's Burden: A Director Confronts Darkness and Death," the *New York Times* reports:

> *Mr. Pfister, the cinematographer, said Mr. Ledger seemed "like he was busting blood vessels in his head," he was so intense. "It was like a séance, where the medium takes on another person and then is so completely drained."*[161]

---

160 Associated Press, "Heath Ledger died of accidental overdose," Feb. 6, 2008. http://www.today.com/id/23029566/ns/today-today_entertainment/t/heath-ledger-died-accidental-overdose/#.Vg3ZJPlViko

161 David M. Halbfinger, "Batman's Burden: A Director Confronts Darkness and Death," *New York Times*, March 9, 2008. http://www.nytimes.com/2008/03/09/movies/09halb.html?_r=2&oref=slogin&ref=movies&pagewanted=all&

As Ledger put his soul into the demonic character, it was as if he could not take it back again for his own sake.[162] Right after his death, the *New York Daily News* reported:

> *Ledger recently told reporters he "slept an average of two hours a night" while playing "a psychopathic, mass-murdering, schizophrenic clown with zero empathy . . . I couldn't stop thinking. My body was exhausted, and my mind was still going." Prescription drugs didn't help, he said.*[163]

Just as Heath Ledger spent day and night comprehending the psyche of evil when he inhabited *The Joker*, we can also underestimate the power of becoming spellbound by an aura of wickedness when it comes to letting ourselves get too close to an ominous person. A smart woman can easily stay too long with an abusive man in her efforts to make sense out of her own confusion, fascinated by his contradictions. Play it safe, and leave while you still can. The only way the mystification will ever end is to move on far away from the craziness. Let the next poor girl take on the role of trying to figure out the baffling, dark personality that consumes him at times and steals away the light. If you are finding yourself in a relationship where you are trying to discern the lies from the truth, remember, the spirit at work confusing you is not of God.

"For God is not the author of confusion but of peace" (1 Corinthians 14:33).

"Walk while you have the light, lest darkness overtake you. The one who walks in the darkness does not know where he is going" (John 12:35).

---

162 JayBird, "Friends Say They Saw Heath Ledger's Death Coming, Celebitchy, January 23, 2008. http://www.celebitchy.com/8836/friends_say_they_saw _heath_ledgers_death_coming/
163 Joe Neumaier, "Jack Nicholson Warned Heath Ledger on 'Joker' Role," January 24, 2008, Daily News. http://www.nydailynews.com/news/jack -nicholson-warned-heath-ledger-joker-role-article-1.340786

The challenge of trying to regulate his emotional swings, so as not to make him crazy, can prove to be a crazy-making process intrinsically for any sane woman. Are you eating right and sleeping well at night? Do you like the person you are? Are you proud of how you communicate in general with people? All of this can change if you let yourself get carried away with a toxic person. There is no worse consequence than not being able to recognize the person you become as a result of a bad influence in your life affecting your entire personality.

If you are involved in a relationship now with a man, ask yourself the following questions about your *connection*: Does being around him make you a better person? Does the thought of becoming like him appeal to you? Is the chemistry drawing you to him bringing out the best in you? Heed the warning—the longer you stay with him, the more you are apt to become like him. If you are someone who is honest, break it off if he is a liar. If not, you may end up stretching the truth yourself in areas you never dreamed you would, as his shenanigans may seem more justified over time and not as shocking as they were in the beginning. If you are not one to lose your temper in general, just keep walking on eggshells in between his temper tantrums, and before long you will probably be flying off the handle at every little thing, too. Before you know it, his anxiety will become yours.

If you are determined to do whatever it takes to make it last forever with an unhealthy man, the roller coaster ride of codependency can be enough to get the best of you. One day you may realize you can no longer think for yourself, and you have lost all sense of individuality. Living in denial could drive you to the edge where he actually looks like the stable one compared to the person you become. When he, seemingly at ease, calls you demeaning names like "psycho," you might get to the point of believing he is right. Good women can spiral down by assuming too much responsibility, especially when it comes to changing a man. Stay long enough, and you will hear him blame you for your erratic behavior as if he had absolutely nothing to do with it. Without him assuming any responsibility for how much his sick behavior has made you sick, you will more than likely agree with him and blame yourself for your embarrassing outbursts. His opinion will become yours *about yourself* as you lose your own sense of identity.

When a man is inconsistent, his inconsistency addicts a woman. Whether he realizes what he is doing or not is irrelevant. He is just being who he is. Even *trying* to be consistent can wear out such an unstable guy. It is hoping for too much from him. Addiction hinges on drama. You have to accept who he is and move on at the first signs of addiction, before it drives you up the wall. After all, a leopard cannot change his spots. Addiction can lead to a woman calling too much, following the guy around town, and all sorts of crazy things. If any of this sounds familiar, it is because you are addicted. This is not the picture of love.

It takes two to tango in the land of crazy. When it comes to staying away from the wrong men, we owe a debt to the Russian psychologist Ivan Pavlov for all he discovered about conditioned responses to stimuli. He studied salivation in dogs upon being fed. The dogs began salivating as a normal response to the food he gave them. When he would feed the dogs, he would sound a bell until Pavlov's dogs salivated at the sound of the bell. Dogs do not naturally salivate at the sound of a bell, of course. It was learned behavior based on their appetite for the food they associated with the bell. Pavlov also noticed the dogs would salivate whenever he entered the room, even when he entered with no food. The dogs did not have to see food; they only had to associate an event or person with food. If the dogs could associate a person with the event of being fed, they would salivate as a conditioned response to the person, even when the person had no reward for what they craved. Hence, when Pavlov fed the dogs and used a bell, the dogs later began to salivate at the sound of the bell, even when there was no food. He addicted the dogs to the bell, apart from food, by association. The dogs never wanted the bell. They only wanted the food. Pavlov had conditioned them through inconsistency to react the same to the bell as they did to being fed.[164] Women become addicted to bad men in much the same way. It is not the abuse we want. It is the association to love that the charming abusers represent to us when they are not being abusive. The dogs would have never become addicted to salivation at the mere sound of a bell if Pavlov had not fed them as he rang the bell half of the time.

I have known some good men for over ten years in working relationships, both in music and via my nonprofit organization. It is has been only smooth sailing because they are reliable and consistent. There is no reason not to get along with them. They have great character. If you are going through the beginning stages of a relationship, look for consistency. If you do not see it, be consistent within your own present, moral fiber enough to leave.

HOMEWORK

Homework for this tip is to read chapter 1 in the Psalms in the Bible. Learn that God does not want us befriending everyone in this world. Because He loves us, God warns us to stay away from certain people in order to guard our lives.

Keep your distance from people who are unstable. If you are dating a guy who does not have it together, the best thing you can do for him is to let him go and let God get his attention when he is too far away from you to hurt you. Trying to help him could be enough to cause your own personality breakdown. Attend an Al-Anon meeting,[165] especially if the thought of leaving him scares you, as if you do not know who you would be apart from him. You do not have to speak at the meeting. Just

---

164 "Pavlov's Dogs," Saul McLeod, Simply Psychology, 2007, updated 2013. http://www.simplypsychology.org/pavlov.html

165 Al-Anon is a twelve-step meeting formed for family members of alcoholics, but it also addresses areas of codependency in general and the dynamics of relationship addiction. http://www.al-anon.alateen.org/

listen and hear as others tell firsthand about the extent to which toxicity is contagious.

If you are dating a man who is emotionally, verbally, or physically abusive, attend a support group for battered women to find the strength to leave him. Women who have been with abusive men often say, looking back, "But I wasn't perfect either. I also said things I shouldn't have said . . ." Well, of course, you were not the same together person you were before he came along. When a man demeans a woman on a regular basis, she cannot be expected to say and do nothing as a perfect response day in and day out without going crazy.

One of the best reasons to make the most of your life, with or without a man, is coming to the realization that settling for a man with bad character will contaminate yours. I sang my song "Honest Life"[166] in a women's prison a few years back. The warden told me as I was leaving that it was a blessing for the women to hear my testimony in song about God's love and faithfulness. She went on to explain, "Most of the women are in here because of men."

---

166 "Honest Life," written and recorded by Dwayna Litz; Litz Music (ASCAP), on the album *Still*, available on iTunes and CD Baby

How to Have a Happy Valentine's Day Without a Man

Valentine's Day is one of my favorite days of the year, with or without a man. I mark my calendar every year and plan to do something special on February 14. Of course, it is fun with a guy you really like. I can remember exciting times over the years, getting all dressed up and going out that night for dinner with whomever I was dating at the time. That being said, there is no candlelight dinner, flower delivery, or chocolates I have received that can compare to the memories I cherish in my heart of helping others on this holiday. It really is true—it is more blessed to give than to receive.[167]

One year I bought a card and some candy for a neighbor whose husband had just passed away, and we went out and had fun together in NYC. I can remember singing at an assisted-living home in Florida on Valentine's Day and feeling so good afterward, knowing I had made a difference in the lives of the people there. It had not been a wasted day. Other favorite ways I have spent that holiday without a man include volunteering at a NYC food bank or doing outreach to troubled

---

167 Acts 20:35

youth when I lived in Atlanta, giving them candy hearts and cards after praying with some teenagers that night to receive Jesus as their Savior. As I shared with those teens about God's love for them, I felt His love so much for me that I could not help but cry. As I was leading a support group in Manhattan in 2014 for women who left abusive men, we set a time to meet on Valentine's night. I bought a box of pretty cards that we exchanged. After each woman shared about what she had been through, we passed out the cards to one another and took the time to write one another notes of encouragement with sincere compliments. It was meaningful and rewarding. (For more on these stories, read Tip #10 and Tip #18.)

I have to think long and hard to remember a Valentine's Day where I have felt lonely. I begin by being grateful to God that I am not one of the many women who let men sexually use them on February 14, only because they do not know how to be alone. If you are alone on Valentine's night, just be glad you will not be waking up on February 15 with regret. You can rejoice knowing you are not with the wrong man, who could leave you very sad on an otherwise fine day in February. When someone in a relationship tells you something like, "I am so sorry you are alone on Valentine's Day," you can reply, "I'm not sorry. I'm happy and making the most of this day, thankful I'm not involved with a man who is hurting me. I am enjoying my freedom as a single person."

No one up with the times would pity you in the first place. Statistics tell it all. Marriage is on the decline in America, and the trend does not look as if it is anywhere close to changing.[168] Jon Birger, a former writer for *Fortune* and *Money* magazines, has written a book on the lack of single men in this country actually looking for a serious, monogamous relationship, especially in some of the bigger cities. Here's more evidence supporting the rise of good women remaining single from a

---

168 Sarah Jacoby, "Here's How Many People Your Age Are Still Single," Refinery 29, June 9, 2015. http://www.refinery29.com/2015/06/88879/millennial-single -statistics#.ec2p0j:T08n

New York Post article by Reed Tucker, "Sorry, ladies, there really is a man shortage."[169]

It's not your fault. It's the ratio. . . . According to author Jon Birger, you're not imagining things . . . Birger [in his book, Date-onomics] . . . crunched demographic, census and other data to show that it really is historically rough out there for the ladies. After noticing that his single gal pals were always complaining that "guys were ignoring them or were toying with them," Birger decided to investigate.

When it comes to dating in Manhattan, the article continues:

The island is great for, say, watching a cheesy musical or spending $300 on a bottle of vodka. But for dating? Not so much. "Because women have been graduating from college in 30-plus percent greater numbers than men for years, there are now four women for every three men nationally in the marriage-age, college-educated dating market," Birger says. In Manhattan, the numbers are even more dire, with 38 percent more young female college grads than male. Birger says the imbalance is also exacerbated by New York's large population of gay males. Some 9 to 12 percent of men in Manhattan are gay, according to Gary Gates, a demographics expert at UCLA's Williams Institute.

He goes on to explain the dilemma for Christian women:

"People who leave organized religion are disproportionately male," Birger says. "Atheists and agnostics are also disproportionately male. An atheist meet-up would be a really good place to meet men."

---

169 Reed Tucker, "Sorry, Ladies, There Really Is a Man Shortage," *New York Post*, August, 25, 2015. http://nypost.com/2015/08/25/hey-ladies-here-are-8-reasons-youre-single/

And the old idiom evidently still rings true—why buy the cow when the milk is free? The article concedes:

> *And as reported by numerous publications, dating is out . . . and hookup culture is in. No need to wine and dine a potential mate when you can just swipe right. With the gender imbalance on college campuses, men are having a field day, and they may see no need to end their winning streak by settling down. For women, however, the longer a girl settles for casual sex as opposed to a long-term relationship, the more chance she has of ending up alone.*

You certainly won't be alone if you buy yourself roses on Valentine's Day in celebration of the happy life you have being single. Did you know that one in five women buy Valentine's gifts for themselves?[170] Have a girls' night out; visit a museum or treat yourself to a massage. Send your mother some flowers. It is not just a day for sweethearts. Do something loving for someone who needs love, and the love will come right back to you.

HOMEWORK

Homework for this tip is to read the book, *Date-onomics: How Dating Became a Lopsided Numbers Game*, by Jon Birger,[171] and stop feeling sorry for yourself on Valentine's Day if you don't have a man. Go make the most of it!

Given how there is a world of lonely people, far lonelier than you have ever been, you can use Valentine's Day as an excuse to do something nice for someone you would not otherwise do. There are women who

170 Brad Tuttle, "6 Totally Unromantic Truths About Valentine's Day Spending," *Time*, Feb. 9, 2015. http://time.com/money/3699604/valentines-day-spending-history-truth/
171 Published by Workman Publishing, 2015.

have it much worse than you've ever imagined. Bring gifts to those in need; volunteer at a battered women's shelter, and so on. Then, after showing love to somebody who needs it, go buy yourself some roses to celebrate God's love for you. Happy Valentine's Day! And, happy, indeed, it can be for you.

"So, whether you eat or drink, or whatever you do, do all to the glory of God" (1 Corinthians 10:31).

Good Men Still Exist

When I lived in Santa Monica, I was set up on a blind date with a man who met me at the popular Casa Del Mar for dinner, overlooking the ocean. I was told that he was a successful businessman from Dallas and also a Christian motivational speaker. We definitely clicked right away as friends. Over dinner, he said he had been married twice before, explaining that it was just very hard to find the right person with enough chemistry *and* compatibility. The evening seemed promising as we watched the sunset, both feeling camaraderie from our similar experiences speaking in Christian circles. He asked why I was still single, and I answered, "For the same reasons you have said your marriages did not work. I could have easily been married and either divorced or wishing I was divorced. I have actually not found enough chemistry, along with compatibility, either, so that explains why I never married." He responded, "Well, if God can part the Red Sea, He certainly knows how to bring two people together when it is His will."

It was the last time I saw him. After that dinner, we began keeping in touch by email. My attraction for him grew when he sent me his motivational lectures based on Christian principles. He was an exceptionally gifted and articulate speaker. Within a month, I put some strange things together that he had written to me in his emails . . . and realized he was gay. When I respectfully and gently confronted him on it, he did not deny it. I cried and cried, and that was that. He did not even want to stay in touch with me anymore as friends. He knew I knew him. Running from all that God had revealed to me about him seemed like the easiest thing for him to do, I guess. It was really God's faithfulness in my life that cut it off, because there was no more reason for us to stay in touch. I think he was hoping the right woman would *change him* through marriage. It was the only time I have ever felt attraction for a man who was gay, to my knowledge. Working in music, I have many gay friends, both men and women, but I had never before encountered someone gay pretending not to be gay, as far as I know, in order to mislead me. He was aiming to keep up a veneer for himself in general, because he also spoke in churches. I was honest. He was not. As it turned out, we were not so compatible after all as friends.

He had built a life on maintaining a false appearance for himself. Though the chemistry we shared had been rooted in deception, I actually never forgot what he said about how God can put any two people together at any point in time. That part was true. With our culture like it is today, I believe many Christian women have gotten to the place of thinking that meeting the right man would be akin to a miracle. Well, good news! If God could part the Red Sea, heal the sick, and raise Jesus from the dead, it is not at all hard for God to bring a good man of His choosing to you.

If you are His child, He has already saved you from all of the jerks out there if you will just trust Him. He made you. He knows exactly what you like. What's even better is to realize that God knows how to make us desire with all of our heart what He wants for us. Part of our salvation is the supernatural satisfaction God gives us when we are in His will. Think about it. When you have given your heart to Him, He cares more about your life than even you care about it. You are His property, purchased by the blood of Jesus when He died for you on the cross.[172] The Bible says He has declared "the end from the beginning," and He is the one who

---

172 1 Corinthians 6:20; Acts 17:11

"orders your steps."[173] He is obligated to accomplish His purpose in your life, and that certainly includes whether or not you are meant to stay single or get married. He has never failed one of His children, and He is not about to fail you.

God knows all of the good men out there, and He is more than capable of bringing the right one to you if His plan for you includes such a thing. Lest you think you have some problem when it comes to not being able to be attracted to a good man, just focus more on growing in your relationship with God as His child. Don't you think He has the power to overrule you if you are about to miss out on something He has planned for your life? Of course He does! Chill out and enjoy every single minute of your lifespan. Make the most of each day as a single woman! Realize you are too special for run-of-the-mill hookups with men. Find rest in the fact that God can certainly make you attracted to a guy with good character, if it is His will for you to be with someone.

I have heard men joke about how women do not want nice guys. That is not correct. We want a man we can *truly* respect. Any normal woman would love to have a man who could be there for her, which requires a man being wise enough to *be able* to lead her. As I have written previously, respect for a man goes much deeper than power, fame, education, status, talent, or looks. I hate to say this, but character worthy of a good woman's respect is not contingent on whether or not the man is a pastor, deacon, elder, Bible teacher, or so-called Christian leader. Falling in love comes as a mysterious gift from God when it is meant to be. You really cannot find such mutuality on your own. God has to give it to you. Chemistry grows when a woman finds herself enjoying hanging out as friends with a man on whom she can rely. It may seem like you have found this really nice guy and just do not feel attracted. I have discovered, through my own experience, that the feelings of attraction run much deeper. Marilyn Brown has made me more aware of this. In

---

173 Isaiah 46:10; Psalm 37:23; Proverbs 16:9

fact, when the attraction is not felt, there is not enough respect in true compatibility for the chemistry to grow. The root of a lasting attraction is compatibility and a woman's respect for a man.

Don't misunderstand. A good man is not a wimp. What does it look like to be a good man from a Christian perspective? A Christian man's loyalty is first to God, then to his wife, and then to his children. A good husband is not defined as pleasing his wife over God, rather, he accepts spiritual responsibility by lovingly guiding her in the right direction. A good woman not only welcomes such loving leadership, but longs to respect it in a man.

The Authentic Manhood Movement was launched by Dr. Robert Lewis to inspire Christian men to become better husbands and fathers.[174] Here are twenty-five characteristics of a husband who truly loves his wife, as identified by Dr. Lewis:[175]

1. Includes his wife in envisioning the future
2. Accepts spiritual responsibility for his family
3. Is willing to say "I'm sorry" and "Forgive me" to his family
4. Discusses household responsibilities with his wife and makes sure they are fairly distributed
5. Seeks consultation from his wife on all major financial decisions
6. Follows through with commitments he has made to his wife
7. Anticipates the different stages his children will pass through
8. Anticipates the different stages his marriage will pass through
9. Frequently tells his wife what he likes about her
10. Provides financially for his family's basic living expenses
11. Deals with distraction so he can talk with his wife and family
12. Prays with his wife on a regular basis
13. Initiates meaningful family traditions

174 http://www.mensfraternity.com/
175 All Pro Dad, http://www.allprodad.com/25-characteristics-of-a-husband-who-truly-loves-his-wife/

14. Initiates fun family outings on a regular basis
15. Takes the time to give his children practical instruction about life
16. Manages the schedule of the home and anticipates pressure points
17. Keeps his family financially sound and out of harmful debt
18. Makes sure he and his wife have drawn up a will
19. Lets his wife and children into the interior of his life
20. Honors his wife in public
21. Explains sex to each child in a way that gives them a wholesome perspective
22. Encourages his wife to grow as an individual
23. Takes the lead in establishing sound family values
24. Provides time for his wife to pursue her own personal interests
25. Is involved in a small group of men dedicated to spiritual growth

I have some male friends who are so good that they make up for the bad men in this world. I can attest they are good without a doubt, because I know their wives. Their wives have nothing but good things to say about them, because they treat their wives so well. One man comes to mind who works with me sometimes in my nonprofit organization. He never emails me without copying his wife on it. This is not because she has asked him to do it. He says he determined, even when he was dating her, to bring God glory in their marriage. "And God has honored that," he says. He copies her on the emails out of respect for her, to include her in any friendship he has with a woman. He's a good man. They are both beautiful people, inside and out, with a home that is a reflection of God's love. Another friend comes to mind whose wife is very ill. He says all he has to do is outlive her so that he can take care of her before going on to heaven to be with her. She has been the love of his life. Though she now requires round the clock care, he communicates with tenderness as he feeds her, bathes her, and is there for her in every way. I knew them both before she got sick, and their love was still like that of teenagers. That is how compatible they still were. After a lifetime together, they were still gushing over each other. Now it is difficult for her even to speak. At their home in Tennessee recently, watching him feed her, I couldn't help but brag on what a great husband he was. After feeding her, he just smiled and said, "I know as much as I love her, she loves me even more."

Some people can stereotype an impressive Christian man as some sort of pious, religious figure dressed in a robe. It could not be further from the truth. All any Christian woman needs is a normal, hardworking man with good morals, to whom she is attracted, who shares her faith in God enough to not make her feel lonely in a marriage because of spiritual incompatibility. If finding such an impressive guy was easy for Christian women, there would be no need for this book.

HOMEWORK

Homework for this tip is to tune in to one of my favorite television programs, *The Profit*, on CNBC.[176] I enjoy learning about business, and I have seen every episode at the date of this book's publication. Marcus Lemonis is a very smart guy with no hint of male chauvinism. I have watched him turn down deals with men who are disrespectful toward women and stand up for the women involved. It is refreshing to see a savvy businessman who is not the least bit threatened by smart, strong women. It is an encouraging reminder that good men still exist in every walk of life.

Listen to the International Living Center Broadcasts from Family Life Communications[177] to learn more about the healthy structure required for a good marriage. Men who make good husbands are hard to find these days. But they are out there! They will never come along, though, until we learn how to stop settling for less.

---

176 http://www.cnbcprime.com/the-profit/
177 http://www.theintentionallife.com/broadcast/broadcast-highlights/

Do a Background Check

All it takes is watching a few episodes of *Dateline*, *20/20*, or movies based on true stories about psychopaths on the Lifetime Movie Network to know that you have to be on guard before giving a man your heart. With the world like it is today, a few research skills on your end won't hurt. Love is blind. Do your homework. If you find yourself going from writing songs and poetry off in La-la Land in the beginning of the relationship to thinking, *What's wrong with him?* in a few short months, it may be past due for a little background check. If things have gotten weird and you feel in your gut something is off about him, it probably is. Everything hidden shall be revealed at the click of a few buttons online. You won't even have to leave your house to discover a whole other side to the guy if he has been dishonest. And what a relief it will be to learn nothing new about him if he is a keeper.

A friend of mine in Manhattan was willing to risk her future on believing she had finally found the right man. A co-worker convinced her to do a background check before getting engaged. She was shocked to discover he had a criminal history. She broke it off with him, not just for herself, but also for the sake of her child. I did a background check once on a man I was dating to realize he had been charged with assault and battery. I told him I had done a background check and knew about the charge and wanted to give him the chance to tell his side of the story. I can still picture how he was squirming around, caught off guard, when I confronted him in person about it. I was grateful to his ex-wife for reporting him as a warning for me. After I listened, I replied calmly, "I appreciate your perspective on it, but I'm afraid I can't get past it. Assault and battery is too serious. It's over with us." When I left his house that day, he said, still with a dazed look, "I have to somehow get that off my record." Yes, a background check can certainly leave a girl smarter for the road ahead with a clean slate for a brighter future.

Background checks are so common that you may see offers for them popping up on the first or second page of a Google search on someone's name. These background checks are affordable, and it pays to do them. The cold truth for women today is that we cannot fall in love without first making sure the guy is not a psycho. Although there is no shame in him finding out about the background check, these sites are confidential, sending results only directly to you. Even if you let him know that you are going to do it, there should be no reason for him to fault you unless he has something to hide. It is sort of like an AIDS test was in the nineties. Any stranger you meet on the street should expect to have it done before things get carried away.

You can pull up a little information from just his date of birth, address, and phone number. Try to get his Social Security and driver's license numbers for the best searches, which will include any criminal and marriage records plus pertinent financial history. If you are going to assume his debt after marrying him, it does not need to come as a surprise. You can check his background to your heart's content for as much information good money can buy about him online.

"And you will know the truth, and the truth will make you free" (John 8:32).

HOMEWORK

Homework for this tip is to watch the documentary series on CNBC called *American Greed*,[178] and do not trust any man without doing a background check. I recommend Intelius, the site I have used the most. When the Internet fails to let you see his true colors, as you are chatting with him on social networking sites, don't underestimate the power of Google when it comes to happy endings. Go online and do a background check on him before letting him squander your hard-earned nest egg. Crimes of the heart hurt but not as much as crimes of the heart *and* bank account.

"The secret things belong to the LORD our God, but the things revealed belong to us" (Deuteronomy 29:29).

"But there is nothing covered up that will not be revealed, and hidden that will not be known" (Luke 12:2).

---

178 http://www.cnbcprime.com/american-greed/

Tip #10

An Abuser Will Still Be Abusive Even If You Are Perfect

Living in Santa Monica, CA back in 2005, I found myself for the first time in my life attending a support group for women who left abusive men. I had met a man via an online Christian dating site who turned out to be abusive, and I was determined to let him go. He said things such as, "Men like respect from their women," as if *their* women have no need of being cherished by *their* men. He selfishly interpreted verses in the Bible about a woman being submissive, portraying God as misogynistic when He is not. It did not take long for me to discover that while this man called himself a Christian and was in church every Sunday, what he had found was empty religion, no life-changing relationship with Jesus at all. The only problem was that by the time I found out, I was stuck in a web of confusion. I was having a hard time keeping my mind straight about the abusive man he really was compared to the kind man I had seen in him when we first met. In the beginning of our relationship he was writing me daily and suggesting, much to my delight, a future with me. I found him charming and funny. One day he admitted, "I hate to get my hopes up about you and me." I asked, "Why?" He answered, "You've not seen me lose my temper yet."

As more was revealed about him over time, I knew in my heart that if I did not want to end up with a man who had it in him to hit me, I had better do whatever it took to break away. I wrestled with whether or not I could control his abuse, thinking that maybe he was right, and if I "showed more respect," we could live happily ever after. Perhaps I could pray enough for God to make him into a nice man. He had a good position writing code for a major tech company and was considered to be a genius. Disagreements with him were really not allowed in our relationship.

One day after I had disagreed with him about something, he told me that he wanted me to write him an essay about how I will respect him. He was not kidding! I said, "I'm not writing you an essay." In my own defense, I did not know much at the time about the signs of abuse, so it took awhile for me to realize he was an abuser. His church-going image, with his German-made car collection and the beaucoup money he earned in his executive job, was all he really had—that, plus the ability to make me laugh a lot with his quick wit when he was not making me cry. At first I felt sure I had met quite an impressive Christian man, who could offer me love. I found myself second guessing my instincts at times about his moodiness, wondering if I was just being too hard on him. After all, no one is perfect.

Because we were living in different states, we began a long-distance relationship by email and phone calls. He managed to hurt me enough before meeting me in person that I told him I had changed my mind about keeping the date we had set to meet. He stormed back at me with quite a tongue lashing by phone. I remember I stayed up all night and could not sleep, so shocked that things were ending like they were with us. I gave in at the last minute and flew to meet him in person as originally planned, at a Christian conference in Phoenix. When he saw me, though he had millions of dollars, he said, "I would pay for your room, but I don't like all of the acrimony, so you can pay for it." He left me alone right after we met the first night to go be with another woman, excusing it by saying that she meant nothing to him. He did not want to take me with him, though. There I sat in the Jacuzzi at the hotel all by myself that night thinking, *I need to go to that support group for the women who left abusive men when I get back home. One of these days, when he least expects it, I'm leaving.*

I realized somewhere along the way in the year I was involved with him that he was aiming through his insults to make me less than him. That plan failed. I attended the support group when I got back home to Santa Monica and just listened. As the women talked about the red flags they chose to ignore before marrying their abuser, I thought, *This will be your story if you do not leave.* One afternoon I finally decided to speak to the group about it. I began to cry as I shared how I knew I had to let him go. I had found myself wanting to keep in touch with him to try to help him out of pity. He had manipulated me to feel responsible for his abuse toward me. A woman in the group got my attention when she said, "Dwayna, if you were perfect, he would still be abusive." All of a sudden, I knew she was right. His problems had absolutely nothing to do with me, never did and never will.

That group, along with some professional counseling, taught me that abusive men are abusive by character. When a woman is abused, it is never her fault. I learned the signs of abuse, such as excessive charm in the beginning, followed by crazy-making behavior stemming from his inconsistency, jealousy, control, manipulation, mind games, mirroring for manipulation, and projection of his own problems onto me. Within that group, after listening to some of the smartest women on the planet speak about abusive men, I found the power to let him go. The last time I spoke to him I calmly said, "You would end up hitting me if I stay with you. It wouldn't be my fault, but you would tell me it was." That guy was stupid enough to say in response, "When men hit women, the women provoke it. You are very provocative, Dwayna." That was our last talk. I hung up the phone with no looking back. It didn't even hurt anymore. It was like God had given me a gift when that charmer actually verbalized his awful, abusive thinking toward me. That was all I needed to finally leave for good.

He was surprised. He sent me cards, and he called. I did not respond. Thanks to those women in that support group and to God answering my prayers, I broke away and never, ever went back or gave him the time of day again. Still, to this date, I have had zero communication with him since 2005. Through the grapevine, I heard that he was engaged a few years later. Our mutual friend attended his wedding and told me he would not *allow* his new wife to dance with any other man at their wedding and so on. What a nightmare for that poor woman!

I used to write on my public blog about where I was going to be sometimes in my travels, never assuming that this man was stalking me digitally after all these years. I had posted on my blog in 2009 that I would be at a certain Bible study in Atlanta. I attended and got back home to receive a phone call from the Bible study teacher. The teacher said, "Someone came to the Bible study late, right after you left, who knows you." As it turned out, it was him! He had shown up at that particular Bible study after reading my blog! When the teacher told me, I began to tremble. I could only thank God that I left early that night before he arrived and missed him. It was extremely creepy. I realized he had never stopped reading my blog to keep up with my life. When the teacher asked him how he knew about the Bible study, after admitting he had travelled cross country to attend, he began to squirm. Because I had been widely recommending the Bible study teacher's books on my blog and on Amazon, he asked this man point blank, "Do you know Dwayna Litz?" The teacher said he looked perplexed and paused. He nervously answered, "Yes, I think I do." His scheming was getting exposed. He got no response from me for his appearance in Atlanta at that Bible study, except for my warning the teacher that he was a dangerous person. I stopped sharing anything personal about my life on my blog.

Last summer in 2015, I got a direct email from him for the first time in ten years while I was in Vail, CO. I had posted on my Facebook public fan page that I was in Vail. He sent me an email as if we were close friends, like we had never said goodbye and he had never gotten married.

He simply wrote that he knew I was in Colorado and wanted to meet for coffee. You would have thought from the email that he had never hurt me. It was a warning for me to keep my whereabouts off of social media sites. After I did not respond to his email, I began getting crank calls for the first time on my cell phone. I knew they were from him, though they were coming from a number with a fake area code. I simply blocked the number from my iPhone. I told my family about it, and they were concerned for my safety. I spoke to the front desk where I was staying in Vail, and they assured me that they never give out information about their guests to inquiring strangers, which was a relief.

Thanks to my experience with him and the books I have read on abuse after dating him, I can now tell the difference between a good man who makes mistakes every now and then and an abusive man who is abusive by character. One difference between a good man and an abuser is that when a good man hurts you, he is sorry. When an abusive man hurts you, he is not. As a matter of fact, he keeps on doing the very thing he knows hurts you. Hurting you and putting you down is, sadly, a big part of his happiness. Being an abusive man is sort of like having a mental problem, and that is why abusive men rarely change, *Bible study* or no *Bible study*. They feel justified in their abuse toward women. Some men, either consciously or subconsciously, pick strong, confident women to subjugate with insults in order for them to feel more powerful. They target dynamic women with a depth to their character that these bad men know they themselves do not have. It is as if abusers are jealous of a genuine person, because they are so depleted on the inside.

An impressive woman, who has been one of my best friends for over a decade, called me last summer to get my advice. She said she had just returned from a Christian women's conference where the women were essentially taught, "If you have a bad marriage, just show the man more respect, and it will get better." There is just one problem with that. My friend is married to an abuser. I asked, "How does God define *respect*? If your husband were to beat you upside the head one day, do you really think God is glorified by your mustering up some sort of respect for him as an abuser? Is that honoring to your marriage in God's sight? Wisdom says the best way to show an abusive man respect as a human being is to let him know you have enough respect for yourself not to keep allowing his abuse toward you."

Jesus never died on the cross for a woman to be killed by her husband. I told my friend to set boundaries and to somehow give him consequences when he violates her boundaries. I reminded her that her responsibility is first to God. It hurts God when she is abused. The Holy Spirit is grieved within her, and she has to somehow take herself out of the danger when the abuse strikes. I told her that, obviously, the women leading the conference were not giving advice to women in abusive situations.

Yes, men need respect, and women need to be cherished in order to have a good relationship. The structure God has given for the home is beautiful; hence, the Bible teaches, when a man mistreats his wife, he hurts himself. He has no respect for himself when a man abuses his wife, because they are one. The verse in the Bible that teaches a woman to submit to her husband has to be taken into context with how the husband is also supposed to love his wife as Christ loves the church, even as Jesus is the Savior of the woman's body, not her destroyer.[179]

"For you have not received a spirit of slavery leading to fear again" (Romans 8:15).

HOMEWORK

Homework for this tip is to read *Why Does He Do That?* by Lundy Bancroft. Check out his website at LundyBancroft.com. I first found out about this author in the support group I attended for battered women back in 2005 in Santa Monica, CA. The women in the group

---

179 Ephesians 5:22-25

recommended *Why Does He Do That?* as the most insightful book on abuse they had read. I bought it immediately and could not put it down. I have given away many copies over the years to women who need it. Lundy was a counselor to men who were required to get therapy after being incarcerated for domestic violence. He shares what he has gleaned from getting inside the minds of angry men in this captivating book for abused women. Read all of his books, including *Daily Wisdom for Why Does He Do That?, When Dad Hurts Mom, Should I Stay or Should I Go?* and *The Batterer as Parent.* Keep reading until you find the way back to yourself again, with or without him.

Hold On to Your Money

When I was twenty years old and living in Nashville, I began doing music showcases for producers and A&R people on Music Row. I wanted to look my best for the shows, so although I did not have much money, I bought the finest outfits for my shows and paid for them with credit cards. The more I charged, the more credit I was offered for additional cards. People in the music business assured me I would get the record deal. Though it did make me a little nervous with every purchase, I presumed I would easily pay off the debt as soon as the deal went through. I was left with a cloud of credit card debt hanging over my head. It took me five years of working three jobs to get out from under it. It was a little like being in jail.

That was a long time ago, and I have never been in debt since. Now my credit report says I am in the top 3 percent of people in America with good credit. I am not saying that to brag, only to point out that I did not get there by spending money out on the town every weekend and buying anything I want, whenever I want it. I learned the hard way what the Bible teaches about *not* presuming on God to easily bail me out of cumbersome debt, when it was no one's fault but my own for letting myself get in over my head in the first place.[180]

There is nothing like the happiness and freedom of living debt free.

---

180 Psalm 19:13

I maintain that freedom by keeping my bank account at a certain level, and when it gets below that level, I stop spending, period, to build it back up again. It is not so easy when you love fashion as much as I do. When I am going through a period where I know I have to save my money and see something I feel I just cannot live without, I remind myself that after I catch up financially, I will have the money a little later when the next latest thing in fashion comes along. There will always be something beautiful to buy months from now or years from now. When I stay away from the fancy stores in order to save money, the world goes right on revolving, and I am fine with all that I already have. I have learned the hard way that nothing on earth is worth buying unless I can afford it.

If you use a debit card connected with your bank account to stay out of debt, the danger is that if someone hacks the debit card, they can hack into your actual bank account. I put every single purchase either on American Express or a Visa or MasterCard connected with airline miles. Because I pay everything off in full at the end of each month, I rarely ever have to pay for plane fare when I travel. Though it has worked to my advantage, I have gotten about one call per year from American Express alerting me to fraud. At least, they send me a new card and take care of everything. The hacker never gets my actual money, because the hacking is not associated with my bank account. This is not the case with bank debit cards, so paying by debit card requires more caution.

It is crucial to protect yourself against identity theft and fraud with the world like it is today. The top three companies that monitor credit are Experian, Equifax and TransUnion. Banks can help you acquire and monitor your credit report with a small monthly fee. I now use Lifelock, which protects me from identity theft and monitors my credit reports, because I have found it to be the most thorough.[181]

I hate owing money so much that it is difficult for me to let a girl-friend who is in debt buy me dinner when we go out. I told a friend

181 https://www.lifelock.com/

recently, "You can buy me dinner when you get out of debt," as I insisted on buying my own meal. I told her to take the money she would have spent on my meal to help pay off her credit-card debt. I've been there. Now, I stay about as far away from debt as possible. Speaking of that, as you get to know a man, keep in mind that if he is in financial debt and you marry him, his debt will become yours. To me, it would not be worth it. I would let him get out of debt first on his own. On the other hand, I would not want a man who is parsimonious, especially when it comes to giving to me or to others in general. How we spend our money says a lot about us. Just as the Bible teaches, where your treasure is, there your heart will be also.[182]

I know married couples who have joint bank accounts and are very happy and couples who have separate bank accounts who are also happy. It can work either way. I have a friend in Manhattan who has her own business, and her husband stays home with the kids. It works for them. What is important is not being caught off guard by a man's intentions when he fails to disclose that he plans on being supported by you financially after you marry him. Some men simply do not want to work. It has to do with their character. It is really something how so many men *just so happen* to lose their jobs after getting married, with their wives surprisingly left to financially support them for years. The notion of finances becoming your responsibility for the both of you is something that needs to be discussed before marriage.

Nothing is a bigger turnoff for me than when I hear a sad tale about a man asking his girlfriend for a financial loan. Don't ever, ever loan a guy money because, odds are, you will not see it again. I have heard many stories about women lending men money and not one single story of them ever getting the money back. Let him borrow money from his family, another friend, or the bank. If you are the only one he can turn to for money when he is broke, what does that say about him? It is not

---

182 Matthew 6:21; Luke 12:34

your responsibility to take care of him when he cannot even take care of himself.

I have to laugh now thinking back to the nineties when a friend of mine told me she had signed a prenuptial agreement before her marriage. I told her that it seemed so unromantic and bordering on dishonest, entering into a marriage as if she was already planning for a divorce. Well, I was wrong, and she was smart. She is still married today, and the prenuptial never came into play as husband and wife. To the contrary, I had one girlfriend who did not have her fiancé sign a prenuptial before marriage, only to end up paying him money in a divorce settlement. Now, with all I have witnessed over the years, I am all for prenuptials. I believe most couples who marry are sincerely vowing for it to last forever. Yet, without a prenuptial, if the husband cheats on his wife and the marriage ends in divorce, he may exercise his right to much of his wife's income and even her family's. In many states, when or if the wife wants a divorce, even with adultery as grounds for divorce, she has to pay him to leave! No matter how dedicated one spouse is to making the marriage work, if the other spouse wants out, the marriage is over. No one is capable of forcing another person to stay. I know of one Christian man in New York who used his life's savings to put his wife through college, only for her to cheat on him while she was in school and leave him for another man after her graduation. Just because he never wanted the divorce was not enough to keep him married to his wife. Not only are they divorced today, but he is in credit card debt, still paying off her schooling, without any obligation from her to pay him back. She is rolling in the dough with her new life, which he helped bankroll, and he is in the poor house. It wouldn't have been the case necessarily if they had signed a prenuptial agreement before they married.

Lately, I have been researching the hardworking ethics of financially successful people, such as Andrew Carnegie, the Rockefellers, and Warren Buffett. Hard workers who have made an impact in this world for the better all have something in common. When the weekend rolls around, high achievers never think, "Hey, it's Friday night. It's time to go party." They work far more than eight-hour days. At the end of the day they go to sleep and get up to work more the next day. They enjoy their work. They would rather be working than wasting time being idle. The Rockefellers did not build a financial empire hanging out in bars. We can thank the Rockefellers for much of New York City, from the Museum of Modern Art and the United Nations acquiring a place to meet alongside the East River, to their largess in funding the Lincoln Center and the Metropolitan Museum of Art. What would the Manhattan skyline be without the Rockefeller Center in Midtown? Nelson served a whopping four terms as New York's governor. When people asked Nelson Rockefeller why he did not go out on the town more at night, he told them he didn't have to go out on the town at night. He owned the town.[183]

Some people feel they are missing out on life without going out every weekend. Well, having money in my bank account when I balance my checkbook makes me feel like I am not missing out on life. I like going out and having fun as much as anyone else, but too much pleasure would not be pleasurable for me. There is no greater reward than working hard to make this world a better place. Saving up for a rainy day, not just for myself but for the sake of giving to others, makes me happy—as long as the man I am dating is not the one with his eye on the hard-earned money I've saved.

"The desire of the sluggard puts him to death, for his hands refuse to work" (Proverbs 21:25).

"Here is what I have seen to be good and fitting: to eat, to drink and enjoy oneself in all one's labor in which he toils under the sun during the few years of his life which God has given him; for this is his reward" (Ecclesiastes 5:18).

---

183 Richard Norton Smith, *On His Own Terms: A Life of Nelson Rockefeller*, (New York: Random House, 2014). Reference is not a verbatim quote.

HOMEWORK

Homework for this tip is to get out of debt if you are in credit card debt, and then put some money away in savings. Learn how to bring yourself financial peace.

Dave Ramsey is an expert on responsible spending and investing. Peruse his website at DaveRamsey.com. Listen to his radio show for inspiration.

Shopping can become an addiction like anything else. When you are sad, call a friend, take a walk, read a book, write a song, but stay away from the shopping malls. Taking control of our spending enough to invest in charity, in work that brings God glory, is the most rewarding. The greatest life any woman can build for herself can only be attained through sacrifice, not self-indulgence.

Don't Date "As Friends"

I am a little embarrassed to admit how naive I used to be at age twenty-four when I began going out with a man on a regular basis *as friends*. There was not even a hint of attraction on my end, and I said nothing to mislead him to think there would ever be anything more. I sincerely never intended to hurt him. But I did hurt him in the tricky foray of dating as friends.

He was a high-profile attorney in Nashville. It just so happens he was also old enough to be my grandfather, but that was beside the point. Since my mother was divorced, I actually had in mind setting him up with her. It was fun borrowing his brand new Porsche, which he insisted on loaning me to drive. I should have known something was up when he took me to the Mercedes dealership in Nashville and asked, "If you could have any car on this lot, what would it be?" I truly wondered why on earth he would ask me such a question. I honestly did not have a clue. One day he took me for a drive on the prestigious Belle Meade Boulevard, as we were enjoying what I thought was a special friendship. I remember him saying as we drove through one of Nashville's most affluent neighborhoods, "When I get married, I am going to have my wife just pick out her mansion." Clueless, I replied, "Well, she will be a lucky woman." I was oblivious to his intentions toward me. One day my brother said, "Dwayna, he is calling you every day. He says he has told his whole office about you. When a man calls a woman like that, he wants to be more than friends." Well, my brother was right.

One night after a dinner that seemed like any other, he pulled me close and kissed me. My goodness! I pulled away and left without even knowing what to say. I felt so sickened by it, because I was not attracted to him or romantically drawn to him at all. I had no desire to be friends with him after that. The next morning, I showed up at his condo bright and early, rang his bell, and gave him back the keys to his Porsche. It was the last time I ever let myself get close to a man as a friend without any romantic possibility for the future. It was a shame, because this man had always been good to me. If I had known then what I know now, I would have never allowed the relationship to begin, realizing when a man wants to take a woman out *as friends*, he wants to be more.

A date is when a man takes a woman out. That's a date. It does not matter if you do not consider it a date. By definition, a date is a date. It is not fair to the man, over time, if you do not want to be more than friends. He does, or he would not be taking you out. When I meet someone new, and there is no chemistry or attraction initially, I give it only three dates. After three dates, I feel I am beginning to mislead him if I do not cut it off. Three dates gives the chemistry a chance to grow. Having enough chemistry for a relationship with a man is based on many factors, including a compatible future with him. I have known some great guys, but our backgrounds and futures were not enough of a match for a serious relationship. After three dates, when that is the case, I show a man enough respect to stop going out with him. It is the least I can do in memory of that attorney in Nashville who I never meant to hurt but did.

When I was living in California back in 2004, I did a magazine interview with a guy who actually said he fell in love with me, to quote him, after only interviewing me for the article. All I did was meet him once for lunch as he asked me questions and recorded the interview. It took him a few weeks from the time of our interview to write the article. I noticed over this period he began calling me a little too much for a guy who only wanted to be my friend. Since I was not attracted to him in any way, I called back only enough to be professionally cordial. After the piece about my work came out in the magazine, he actually got mad at me when I would not date him. I responded to his anger by kindly asking, "Have I ever said anything or done anything to mislead you, to make you think I want to date you? Have I ever said or done anything to insinuate I was attracted to you?" I went on to add, "Because, if I have, I'm sorry." Gathering his emotions, he answered, "No, you have not." He ended up apologizing to me, explaining that as he heard my voice and listened to me speak about my life for the article, he found himself very drawn to me hoping we could have a relationship.

Unfortunately, over the years I have had to ask several men who were only friends of mine those same questions, "Have I misled you in any way? If so, I am sorry . . ." I have found it is all too easy for a guy, with the best of intentions, to muster up some sort of unrealistic future with me without ever dating me. I have learned to be very careful with men who are only meant to be friends. I have lost all desire to let myself become close friends with a man, except when it comes to a man I am dating for real. I do not want to hurt anyone. If I know within myself I will never fall in love with a guy, who would otherwise make a good friend, I am much better off turning to one of my girlfriends when I need a friend. Things get too complicated with men and too easily misunderstood otherwise.

I have been clear throughout these tips about how I want to fall in love with my best friend. That being said, a woman knows after a few dates if there is absolutely no chance of falling in love and needs to respect the man enough, in such a case, to let him go. It is just not fair to him to keep going out when he is hoping for it to develop into more than just a friendship. I have some men in my life as friends who are wonderful people, but I intentionally keep them at a distance. We have mutual respect for one another, and we work together well. We are connected on social media sites. If we go out, it is not often, and I always pay my own way *when I know for sure I only want to be his friend.* I realize that if things get misunderstood, I will lose the nice guy as my friend, and I do not want that to happen.

Since I have a nonprofit organization, I have also experienced men who have made donations to my work for the intent of dating me. I used to feel that when a large contributor asked me out to dinner, I owed him a date in thanks for his contributions to my work. I began noticing as I went out on all of these *business dinners* that I was not happy afterward. It did not feel right. The dinners were long. I would have never been having dinner with any of them if they had not given to my work. Marilyn Brown, my counselor, asked, "Are you willing to risk them no longer donating to your work if you stop going out with them?" She made a comment about how I needed to be true to myself. I had not even realized that going out with a man who was donating to my work, on what was by definition a date, was not being true to myself unless I was attracted to him. God bless the day I finally said to a man who was a major donor and wanted to date me, "I do not think that God expects me to date a man just because he donates to my work." Ever since then, I have made it clear to men who make donations to my nonprofit organization and ask me out, that I do not date men who contribute financially. If I meet them in person for some reason, it is usually only for coffee, and I pay for it myself. Marilyn was right in that I never owed a man a date for making a contribution. Though every single one was platonic, it really was not fair to them or to me. I am thankful for donations of any amount, but no more donations come with the bonus of taking me out to dinner. I save my dates for the men I actually consider dates, and it feels good.

A horrible scenario for a *friendship* is when you are attracted to a bad guy. After you break up, the men usually come back saying, "Let's be friends." It may cross your mind to fall for it. Don't. When you realize that a real relationship with him would certainly never work due to your incompatibility in character, go ahead and put the thought out of your mind when it comes to the possibility of being friends. The chemistry won't wane, especially when a better man has yet to come along to date (for real). If you became addicted through chemistry to a guy who was not good to you, don't try to pretend you can date him again after time has passed *as friends*. If he had been your friend in the first place, he wouldn't have hurt you. Men who hurt women do not make good friends.

You can't make friends with an addiction. Just as true love lasts forever, addictions are also for life. Addiction is rooted in inconsistency and humiliation, not love. When a former boyfriend wants to be your friend, if you look back and realize you gave far more than he did in your past relationship, keep pouring your heart into your new beginning without him. Move on in your quest to become your own best friend, as a person you really like. After losing his baggage that was weighing you down in life, let it stay lost in all of its confusion. Don't go losing yourself again chasing after it. That way, when a best friend comes along for real in a nice man, you are free to fall in love and never let him go. Until then, trust me, call a girlfriend.

HOMEWORK

Homework for this tip is to watch the romantic comedy *When Harry Met Sally*.[184] The premise for the movie is that while best friends can fall in love, men and women cannot be just friends. This is because either the man or woman is hoping to be more than just friends most of the time. The movie makes a valid point.

It's just how it works with the birds and the bees. Keep your dates for the men you actually want to date and stop dating men you only want as friends.

---

184 *When Harry Met Sally*, 1989, written by Norah Ephron, produced by Rob Reiner, Columbia Pictures; https://en.wikipedia.org/wiki/When_Harry_Met_Sally . . .

Beware of Dangerous
Men in Church

*I*t was the late nineties, and I was at the end of broken dreams. It felt like God's love was all I really had. Every day I would wake up with the same prayer, *Hold my hand, Lord, and help me make it through.* At least I had finally found a good church where I could make new friends and learn more about living for Jesus during a time in my life of brokenness and pain. It was a large church of about three thousand members. The music director and I really clicked, and I began singing in the worship team. He said he planned on featuring me as a soloist. To say I was happy with my church home was an understatement. It was the greatest joy of my life at the time. I looked forward to going there every Sunday, along with attending Bible studies throughout the week. I thought about how I hoped to spend the rest of my life as a member of that church with Christians I loved, in a place where people cared for my soul. All was going well until the pastor decided he wanted to have an affair with me.

I had visited the church for only about two Sundays when I knew I wanted to become a member. Everyone who joined the church had to first attend a few weekly meetings about the church's core beliefs. The pastor led the membership meetings. He was clever and made everyone laugh at his rote illustrations and anecdotes. He had it all down pat.

People praised his sharp wit and complimented him for being such a whiz with names. I should have known something was off when he said during a membership meeting that he used to work for the CIA. He went on to confess that he had never really wanted to be a pastor. He joked about it, as if he had left his heart with the CIA. Well, as it turned out, the CIA would have been proud. He certainly knew how to lie and pretend to be someone he was not.

The pastor had a little, old, humble car he drove to church. Judging from the car, his church members could assume he either had no money or had no desire whatsoever for material possessions. What I found out later was that he had a brand new Cadillac for other outings around town. Before I became a member, I had joined the choir. I noticed that when I was a featured singer in the worship team, the pastor was abnormally staring at me. Pretending to be in praise to God, he raised his hands above his head in the air. The problem was, with his hands raised up in the air, his eyes were staring straight at me. As I was singing in front of the church, when I glanced at the pastor from the worship team, I realized something strange was happening.

He began flirting with me. He once hugged me and said, "I love you, Dwayna," but it felt weird. The more I went to church, the worse it got. One day, when I shared my testimony with the pastor and his secretary, I could not help but get tears in my eyes when I talked about how much God had done for me. When the pastor ended up wanting to have an affair with me, I promised myself I would try my best never to cry in front of a pastor again. I figured it was my tears that made him move in for the kill. After I survived the whole ordeal, I decided to keep my distance at future churches so as not to allow myself to be that vulnerable again with a pastor. It was by no accident that I chose women to counsel me instead of men a little later on when I began in-depth counseling. When I cried in front of the pastor, it did not mean I wanted to have an affair with him! He must have mistaken my crying for weakness, and as the head pastor of the huge church, he decided to see how far he could exploit the respect he knew I had for him at the time.

I began noticing when I was around him at church that there was something amiss in the air. I found myself trying to avoid him. After a little over a month, I was brazen enough to confront him. I set a time to meet with him in his church office. How I wished I had taped our conversation. Since then, I have noticed that honest pastors either meet with me with someone else present or at least leave the door open for their secretary to enter. This pastor closed the door.

The first question I asked was, "What is going on?" He seemed very uncomfortable. He began flirting. I let him know without any doubt that I had no desire to have an affair with him. He responded, to quote him, "You mean, you would be disappointed if I said we could get it on right now?" and shook his hands as he said it, as if he was ready for exactly that right there in his church office. With a disgusting look on my face I answered, "Not only would I be disappointed if you told me that, but I would have to wonder if you were even a Christian!" Realizing I did not want to have an affair, he looked down and confessed verbatim, "Pray for me, because I have struggles." As I left, he helped me put on my coat, and he kept his hands on my shoulders for about ten seconds afterward like he did not want to stop touching me. I left in shock. What I had feared he was thinking, he actually had been thinking all along. No wonder a member of the church had come up to me the previous Sunday to tell me she was praying for me. She said that my singing had been such a blessing to her. "For some reason, God has put it on my heart to pray for you," she said seriously. It was a sign God was with me through the ordeal. I thanked her. God certainly knew why I had needed that woman's prayers.

Confidentially, I told my best friend about my meeting with the pastor and the details of every single word he said to me. Before I told my best friend, who was also attending that church, I made her promise not to tell anyone. I understand now that despite that promise, she had to do what she felt was right, so she told our Sunday School teacher about it. Looking back now, I am glad she did, but I certainly did not feel that way at the time. The next day I got a phone call at work from the Sunday School teacher. He said he had talked to my friend, and he knew about all that the pastor had told me. I almost started crying right there on the spot. I thought, *This is a nightmare!* The teacher said I was obligated before God to tell the elders of the church about the whole thing. Looking back, I know that God chose me, of all people, for this purpose, but it was one of the hardest things I have ever had to experience in my entire life.

I sat in front of *The Elders* in a private meeting. They made it out to be akin to my standing right before God Himself. But if I had been standing before God, God certainly would have been more loving. They asked me about everything, and I told them the truth. With every answer I gave, tears rolled down my cheeks. I just could not stop crying. I could tell that the women in the meeting believed me, but the men did not. They said they would talk to the pastor about it, and we would meet again.

They spoke with the pastor, and someone called me to arrange my second, follow-up meeting with *The Elders*. When we met again, they declared, "He said you are the one who is lying. He said you are the one who wanted to have an affair with him." I sat in silence with tears streaming down without trying to defend myself. I told them that I was planning on leaving the church. None of these elders asked me to stay. They were relieved to see me go. In that last meeting, the elders said, "We are going to swear you to secrecy." I was crying too much to tell them that such a decree was not biblical, that *swearing me to secrecy* was not at all taught in the Bible. They reiterated how the pastor had said I was the one who had wanted an affair. They grilled, "Now, what is your response?" I answered, after pausing. I looked up into their eyes with my make-up-streaked cheeks and had only one thing to say. I said, "I'm glad I am a Christian, because I don't know where I would be today if I were not a Christian." That elder meeting was the last time I ever stepped foot in that church.

I called the music director to tell him goodbye. He asked why I was leaving. I answered, "I cannot tell you." I cried more. The music director kept asking for details, and I finally said, "Someone at the church has hurt me." The music director argued, "Well, he should be the one to leave, not you." I answered, "I can't avoid this person. This person won't be leaving." I hung up the phone in pain. This time *church* had broken my heart. My mother (who had recently moved to Nashville) knew about it and was also heartbroken. For hours that day, my mother and I sat at the piano singing the hymns. I knew Jesus was with me, and I could feel His love. The tears of sadness turned to tears of joy as I sang those old hymns for the rest of the afternoon accompanied by my mother on the piano as the Holy Spirit encouraged both of us. What else could I have done? Where else did I have to go in my sadness? *Whom have I in heaven but Thee?*[185] God was listening.

The word spread to the entire Presbytery. So much for my brief time as a Presbyterian! The leader of the Presbytery called me. He met with me. Though no one else was around, he whispered, "None of the Presbytery can believe this, but we cannot stop thinking about what you told us! I mean, this man is just so well loved and respected. Would you be willing to take a lie detector test?" Without hesitation, I answered, "Absolutely! I am not lying."

About a week later, there I sat hooked up to wires for what I hope will be the only polygraph exam I will ever take in my life. Before I took the lie detector test, the administrator asked me to uncross my legs and sit with both feet level on the floor. I told him I had just one request. "Please

185 Psalm 73:25

let me hold my Bible as I take the test." He agreed, even though I could only rest it on my lap, as my arms were connected to the wires. The man administering the test asked, "Did the pastor say, 'We could get it on right now?'" I answered, "Yes." He asked, "Did the pastor say . . . ? Did the pastor say. . . .?" When I passed the test, the nice man said, while unhooking me from the wires, he knew I would pass it all along. He smiled with sympathy. He said he could tell I was telling the truth from the very beginning. I thanked him and left with my Bible.

I gave the results to the Presbytery and moved on with my life. A Presbyterian counselor affiliated with the situation called a few months later to tell me that the elders had decided to replace the thick wooden door to the pastor's office with a glass one. "They must have believed you after all," she said. I told this person that it did not even matter to me anymore. The pastor was asked to *retire* about a year later. I was a member of that church for a total of two months and have never had a desire to visit it again or look back since the last tear-filled elder meeting. Though I have known some really good men who have been authentic pastors, it was the last time I ever assumed, before knowing someone's character, that just because a man was a pastor, he was good.

HOMEWORK

Homework for this tip is to research what actually defines a Christian man. A man is not a Christian just because he says he is. Going to church every Sunday does not make a man a Christian any more than walking in a barn would make him a horse. Pagan spiritualities offer belief in a very strange *Jesus* that is totally contrary to the Jesus of the Bible. An atheist can *believe* that Jesus existed historically and died on a cross; an atheist just does not believe He is God.[186] Mere belief in Jesus is not enough for salvation, if someone believes in the wrong Jesus.[187] A man is a Christian

---

186 John 10:30
187 2 Corinthians 11:4

when he agrees with what the Bible teaches about Jesus being God; he
submits his will to God's and is willing to live in "newness of life," as the
Bible calls it, for God's glory.[188] Jesus also teaches in the Bible that unless
a man takes up his cross, he cannot be His disciple. The Christian life is
one of self-denial for the greater joy of a close relationship with Incarnate
Love who died for us on Calvary.[189]

If you hate hypocrisy, rest assured that God hates it more. The Bible
actually teaches that hell was created for the hypocrites.[190] Hypocrites
are actors; people pretending to be Christians who are not.[191] The Bible
also calls such actors wolves in sheep's clothing.[192] In contrast, the word
Christian means Christ-like, not counterfeit.[193]

The most important book that explains what it means to be a Christian is the Bible: "Therefore, by their fruits you will know them" (Matthew 7:20). "Even so faith, if it has no works, is dead, being by itself"
(James 2:17). "Woe to the world because of its stumbling blocks! For it
is inevitable that stumbling blocks come; but woe to that man through
whom the stumbling block comes!" (Matthew 18:7).

To understand more about living an authentic life for Jesus, read
the books *Humility* and *Absolute Surrender* by Andrew Murray. Here is a
favorite quote of mine from Murray to better explain what it means to
be a Christian:

"Pride must die in you, or nothing of heaven can live in you. . . .
Humility is perfect quietness of heart. It is to expect nothing, to wonder
at nothing that is done to me, to feel nothing done against me. It is to
be at rest when nobody praises me, and when I am blamed or despised.

---

188 Romans 6:4
189 Matthew 16:24; Luke 9:23
190 Matthew 24:51; Matthew 13:41-42
191 Rich Deem, "Hypocrites Defined: What About Hypocrisy in the Christian
    Church?" Evidence for God. http://www.godandscience.org/apologetics/
    why_are_christians_hypocrites.html#n16
192 Matthew 7:15
193 See http://www.christinyou.net/pages/what2bxn.html and http://www
    .bygodsgrace.org/

It is to have a blessed home in the Lord, where I can go in and shut the door, and kneel to my Father in secret, and am at peace as in a deep sea of calmness, when all around and above is trouble."[194]

If you enjoy reading inspiring thoughts each day, you will love the timeless devotional *My Utmost for His Highest* by Oswald Chambers. Chambers teaches that to live for Jesus in the utmost for His highest means: "You will never cease to be the most amazed person on earth at what God has done for you on the inside."

194 Andrew Murray, *Humility* originally published in 1895. Multiple modern editions available.

Report Him for the Protection of Others

*A*s I write this tip in the fall of 2015, it is hard to keep track of the number of women who keep coming forward to report being drugged and sexually abused by the actor Bill Cosby. The latest count is roughly fifty.[195] Thanks to the work of attorney Gloria Allred and articles including "I'm No Longer Afraid: 35 Women Tell Their Stories About Being Assaulted by Bill Cosby and the Culture That Would Not Listen,"[196] the statutes of limitations are on the verge of being changed in support of women's rights. Cosby's victims are finally given a voice on behalf of any woman in the future who alleges rape.[197]

One brave woman is suing Cosby for his reaction to her initial report last year that he raped her back in the eighties, claiming that Cosby's retaliation alone defamed her with even more emotional abuse. For going public with her story, she has suffered the backlash of accusations on

195 Richard Winton, "Bill Cosby, Gloria Allred to face off in deposition over molestation claims," *Los Angeles Times*, 20151009-story.html

196 Noreen Malone and Amanda Demme, "'I'm No Longer Afraid': 35 Women Tell Their Stories About Being Assaulted by Bill Cosby, and the Culture That Wouldn't Listen," *New York Magazine*, July 26, 2015. http://nymag.com/the cut/2015/07/bill-cosbys-accusers-speak-out.html#

197 Winton, "Bill Cosby, Gloria Allred . . . ," *Los Angeles Times*, Oct. 20, 2015. http://www.latimes.com/local/lanow/la-me-ln-bill-cosby-faces-tough-questions -protest-20151009-story.html

her character from Cosby and his legal team as her integrity has been called into question. Here is an excerpt about it from the *Pittsburgh Post-Gazette*:[198]

A . . . woman who appeared on TV with Bill Cosby three decades ago while an aspiring actress and model today sued the comedian, alleging as have dozens of other women around the country that the once-beloved and influential entertainer drugged and molested her. Renita Hill, 48, claims that the star . . . gave her a bit part on television, funded her college education and pledged to assist her career, all while sporadically sexually abusing her from 1983 to 1987. . . . While the complaint . . . accuses the TV star of plying Ms. Hill in the 1980s with spiked drinks and assaulting her at various hotel rooms in Atlantic City, New York City and Denver, the counts alleged do not directly pertain to any sexual misdeeds.

Instead Ms. Hill is claiming that Mr. Cosby last year defamed her, cast her in a false light and intentionally inflicted emotional distress. She is seeking a jury trial. Those counts stem from allegations that the celebrity, his wife and business manager, Camille Cosby, and his attorney, Martin Singer, made statements that portrayed Ms. Hill as a liar and extortionist. . . . The complaint says Ms. Hill kept quiet for decades about the alleged abuse by Mr. Cosby. But after learning that other women claimed to have had similar experiences, she felt comfortable coming forward.

Bill Cosby's denial is the perfect example of what usually happens when a woman reports a man for abusing her—he becomes the victim. His aim is to manipulate her to pity him and anyone she tells, while he

---

198 Jonathan D. Silver, "Baldwin Woman Files Suit Against Bill Cosby," *Pittsburgh Post-Gazette*, October 14, 2015. http://www.post-gazette.com/news/nation/2015/10/14/Baldwin-Borough-woman-sues-Bill-Cosby-alleging-that-comedian-drugged-and-molested/stories/201510140194

remains calloused toward her as his accuser. It is his word against hers; instead of addressing the accusation against him, he insults her, taking the focus off of himself and onto the victim with ad hominem attacks against the victim's character.

For this reason, any woman who is a victim of abuse has to care more about the truth being known than her own reputation. When the truth is on her side, so is God. God will vindicate the truth in His timing. But the truth can only prevail if it is reported. If each of Cosby's victims had found the courage to report him to the police years ago when the abuse happened, he could have been charged for his crimes and been prevented from abusing so many other women. Abusers will continue to abuse until they are caught. When I think of the scores of women who have come forward to report molestation by Bill Cosby, I picture the faces of women who have finally won by simply telling the truth.

There is a difference between reporting someone out of vengeance and reporting a dangerous person for the good of society. Having the courage to report someone who has abused you requires caring more about others than yourself. It is the light at the end of the tunnel, no matter how it hurts. Preventing the abuse of other women is the good that can come out of your pain. If a man shows signs of being a threat to the safety of other people, we have an obligation as women who are good citizens to report him for the protection of others. Don't let any threats or intimidation let him continue to hurt you by keeping you silent.

HOMEWORK

Homework for this tip is to watch the documentary *Anita* on the landmark case of Anita Hill and her astonishing testimony against Supreme Court Justice Clarence Thomas. I also recommend reading the book by Anita Hill, *Speaking Truth to Power*.[199] Though she had

---

199 Anita Hill, *Speaking Truth to Power* (New York: Doubleday, 1997).

never set out to make Thomas's sexual harassment toward her public, FBI interviews were leaked. As a result, she garnered empowerment for all working women. She had both the fortitude and grace to walk into a political lion's den and hold her own. Any intimidation efforts from the men who questioned her failed. She was articulate and strong. The confidence she displayed in telling the truth in front of a committee biased against her politically, racially, and sexually was a turning point for the rights of all women in the workplace. All she had to do was tell the truth, and her truth became the focus of national debate that changed the course of history for women.

God is the God of light. The light exposes, unlike the darkness that keeps everything hidden away. There is biblical basis for letting the truth be known about a dangerous person. The Apostle Paul warned publicly about a guy named Alexander who had the potential to hurt others.[200] Paul set forth an example for us to follow by publicly mentioning Alexander by name when he said, "Alexander the coppersmith did me much harm; the Lord will repay him according to his deed" (2 Timothy 4:14).

As a rule, learn to keep your emotions regulated around strangers. You won't regret it. This is very important in professional settings. Keeping your composure is a testament of strength that no adversary can take away. Being real is a component of a *real* relationship, in a place where you know you are loved. Save it for personal relationships. Distance yourself emotionally as a businesswoman in a man's world where you are due a man's respect.

Crying is cathartic, but only when it is safe. I've found that when we cry as women we give our power away. Don't let them see you sweat. They don't deserve it. Strangers, business contacts, and certainly predators have not earned the right to know you to that degree. So, when you do report him, try your best not to cry. When his criticism of you

200 BibleStudyTools.com, "2 Timothy—Introduction," http://www.biblestudytools.com/commentaries/jamieson-fausset-brown/2-timothy/2-timothy-introduction.html

comes as a consequence, don't be intimidated. Keep looking up, and stay poised. Be tough, and take it like a man on behalf of all women.

"All tyranny needs to gain a foothold is for people of good conscience to remain silent."—Edmund Burke

"The truth is incontrovertible. Malice may attack it, ignorance may deride it, but in the end, there it is."—Winston Churchill

Stop Looking

Have you ever stopped to think of all of the meaningful things you could be doing with your life instead of frantically running around trying your best to find *the one*, only to be hurt time and time again? The process of looking for a mate can be one of the loneliest experiences on earth. Do yourself a favor. Stop looking. I am convinced that some women believe if they stop looking by giving up on the dating sites or going out all dressed up in hopes of meeting a new man, that somehow finding the right match for them will never happen. It is as if they believe the right person will not come to them unless they directly work at it. This outlook is unrealistic. We are not in charge of what is meant to be for our lives. God is. Our control is limited. Destiny is more powerful than any attempt we can make to overrule it.

One way God leads us into His predestined plan for us is through our desires. He can certainly put the right two people together, where both the woman and the man have a meant-to-be compatibility and mutual attraction. That is absolutely no problem for God. If you have the desire to *keep looking*, go ahead expending all your energy on the quest to find your perfect match. But should you lose the desire to continue over time, don't feel like you have let yourself down. The bottom line is you have to get to the place of leaving it all in God's hands, one way or another. There is no harm done in surrendering the effort. The more unique you are as a person, the less likely you are going to find anyone compatible through speed dating or Internet dating sites anyway. Even if you spend countless nights dating the wrong men, a myriad of lunch dates with the wrong ones, and hours communicating on dating sites with all of the men out there who are not meant to be, you may only find yourself exhausted without the right one by the time you are done. If you do find the love of your life (as many people have online who are married today), of course, it was worth it. If you don't, it will probably feel like a big waste of time, time you could have been spending doing far more important things. The point is, no matter how many men you date or don't date, serendipity has a mind of its own.

Back when I was on several Internet dating sites at once, around 2004, I can remember meeting with my accountant in Los Angeles for a business lunch. He and his wife were personal friends of mine, so I felt comfortable sharing some of my dating experiences with him over lunch. Before I knew it, he made an observation about all of my dating fiascos. "Well, finding the right man must be important to you. It's all you have talked about," he said. It came as a surprise to me at that moment how the dating sites had been consuming my thoughts to such a degree. How could it really be any other way when I had paid good money to find the right match, much less the fact that the *matches* were being sent to me all hours of the day and night by email? I replied, "I don't mean for it to be the most important thing in my life," and quickly changed the subject. I have certainly met many women and men since then to whom I could say the same thing. It seems when most people join dating sites, finding a match tends to become their number one priority and always on the forefront of their mind. The whole ordeal can bring unwarranted sadness to them if, hundreds of dates later, they are still single.

Many women are too fed up, after so much heartache from men, to endanger themselves more by continuing to look for someone new. It does not matter if that description fits you. God can certainly turn your heart around if He has someone designed for your future. Part of

His plan for you, obviously, is the fed up stage you are in today, or you would not be feeling like you are. A vast gamut of emotions makes up who you are, even when discouragement is one of them. The important thing is to get out there and make the most of your life's calling and purpose, either way.

A Christian pastor gave me some advice years ago, which I thought was foolish at the time. He said, "Move out in your plans as a single person, and let God interrupt those plans if He has someone prepared for you to marry." I certainly disagreed with that. It made no sense. How could I not try my best to make something happen when it meant so much to me? Now I know that pastor was right. It was wise advice. If God cares for the birds of the air, He cares for me.[201] He knows what He wants to do with my life. As the Bible teaches, live in the moment. Don't worry about tomorrow. When you live right by being true to yourself through faith in the Lord, tomorrow will take care of itself just fine.[202]

Thanks to God's existence, you can rest assured that your life is in more powerful hands than luck. I have been told, "It happens when you are not looking." But *it* has only been Mr. Wrong instead of Mr. Right I have found thus far, *when I was not looking* for chemistry to sweep me off my feet. At the same time, I have also met an array of really nice people—both men and women—who are friends of mine today when I was not looking to meet anyone. I was just out doing my thing, busy either at work or at play. In other words, I was living my life to the fullest when some of my best friends have come along. God is sovereign over everyone we meet and every relationship. When you stop to think about it, you may very well agree that most of the closest relationships with men you have had in your life have not necessarily come from the Internet. They come along, just like the girlfriends do, when you are busy just being you.

---

201 Matthew 6:26
202 Matthew 6:34

HOMEWORK

Homework for this tip is to let God's love fill up your heart through the art of Scripture memorization. As I was being raised, it was very common for Christians to memorize Bible verses. It is unfortunately not as commonly taught now in churches. As our society has changed, we have far more adults today addicted to antidepressant drugs and fewer people turning to God's Word on a daily basis to overcome depression. If you are a Christian struggling with thoughts of defeat, how much time are you spending reading the Bible each day? Taking the *simple* step of putting a holy God who is a Healer[203] on the throne of your heart can do wonders to make you better.

The Bible teaches, "Thy Word have I hid in my heart that I might not sin against Thee."[204] When you memorize a Bible verse, it becomes part of who you are as God's promises go with you through your trials. If you are feeling lonely, I suggest writing down a Bible verse on an index card to carry around in your purse to read throughout the day.[205] Let God sustain you every time you read the verse, one moment at a time. Did you know that if you read the same Bible verse every single day, each day it will mean something different? God will apply it to whatever you are going through in the midst of your changing circumstances. Here are some of my favorite verses, which I have memorized. God continues to bring them to my mind to encourage me. Scripture verses like these are in my heart to stay, because I took the time to memorize them:

"And my God will supply all your needs according to His riches in glory in Christ Jesus" (Philippians 4:19).

---

203 Mark 6:56; Psalm 103:1-3; Acts 10:38
204 Psalm 119:11
205 When I was sixteen, my mother gave me a New American Standard Bible (NASB), and I have done most of my Scripture memorization from it through the years. I also like the English Standard Version (ESV), the New King James (NKJV) and the King James Version (KJV). The majority of the Bible verses in this book were taken from the NASB.

"He heals the brokenhearted and binds up their wounds" (Psalm 147:3).

"I can do all things through Christ who strengthens me" (Philippians 4:13).

"Blessed be the God and Father of our Lord Jesus Christ, who according to His great mercy has caused us to be born again to a living hope through the resurrection of Jesus Christ from the dead, to obtain an inheritance which is imperishable and undefiled and will not fade away, reserved in heaven for you . . . and though you have not seen Him, you love Him, and though you do not see Him now, but believe in Him, you greatly rejoice with joy inexpressible and full of glory" (1 Peter 1:3-4, 8).

Greater knowledge of God builds greater faith in God. Before you trust someone you want to know the person. We get to know God by reading the Bible. When you put your faith in Jesus and decide to live for Him, He promises to be your friend.

Jesus said in John, chapter 15, verse 14, "You are my friends, if you do what I command you."

"Whoever believes in Him will not be disappointed" (Romans 10:11).

Men Who Are Alcoholics and Addicts Are "Girls"

*I*t is a man's place to chase a woman. The man gives, and the woman *gives back* as he pursues her. Courting a woman like a real man means he is willing to take action on his end such as calling her, bringing her flowers, and working in general to earn her respect. This requires vulnerability. He must risk rejection in order to go after her and let her know how much she means to him. Should it not work out, he has to be confident enough to handle the disappointment and move on to chase the next girl until he finds the right one. It is a beautiful picture as a man places a woman high on a pedestal above himself, willing to do whatever it takes to merit her love. Real men do this naturally. If the man is an alcoholic or addict, however, you can forget it. He will be too emotionally impotent to allow himself to fall in love like a real man.

Alcoholics and addicts cannot be vulnerable. They get terrified of feelings, which drive them to the drinking and drugging in the first place. They must maintain the illusion of being in control at all times; therefore, they only pursue when it is easy for them. The minute they start to feel, they numb the feelings by doing what addicts do. From an emotional standpoint, they run away. This type of guy is most comfortable on the receiving end of admiration when the woman assumes the role of a man and chases after him. (This includes a man addicted to porn, who is

incapable of intimacy as a result of the porn addiction.) The man who is
an addict wants the woman to lead. As she is the instigator, she is by far
putting more energy into the whole thing than he. He likes it like that.
This is because, when it comes to having a relationship, he is a *girl*.

I am not talking about anything that has to do with effeminate characteristics, cross-dressing, or being gay or transsexual. This has to do with
old-fashioned gender roles in a relationship and how those roles get confused when the man is emotionally unavailable due to drugs or alcohol.
I am referring here to the heterosexual man who is an addict, not exclud-
ing love and sex addicts who confuse lust with love. Masculine men on
the outside can be girls on the inside—men who want to be pursued by
women instead of being the pursuer. Although not all abusive men are
alcoholics, all alcoholics and addicts are abusive to a degree. There is a
reason drug addiction is called substance *abuse*. Selfishness is one of the
biggest characteristics of addiction, beginning with how the addict is
abusing his own self, much less the people in his life closest to him. Addicts have trouble staying connected to feelings, because feelings are too
scary. This includes not only negative feelings like fear but also positive
feelings like love. Ironically, they induce more pain into their lives by trying to escape their painful feelings, such as the component of attachment
that makes them feel so out of control. They cannot stay connected emotionally to themselves, much less anyone else. I have known alcoholics in
recovery, even after years of sobriety, who are still too terrified of feelings
to let themselves truly fall in love. Addicts become overwhelmed with
fear when they begin to feel vulnerable. Falling in love requires vulnerability; therefore, they are severely limited when it comes to experiencing
love. It is too scary. Flirting and making women laugh is much easier for
them than love.

It has been said that alcoholics and addicts are arrogant with no self-
esteem. They feel terrible about themselves down deep but are too con-
ceited to get honest and do what it takes to get well. They certainly do
not care about loving God enough to think of how they are hurting Him

as they continue to hurt themselves and others. All they care about is whatever makes them most comfortable. In the beginning, they seem so full of life, but they are incapable of being genuine men. Their quick wit can turn to silliness pretty fast when the selfishness comes to surface.

Normally speaking, a woman works well when she feels good. A man feels good when he works well. But, a man who is a girl has trouble even working at all when he does not feel well, which is usually whenever he *feels*. A real man wants to make a woman feel good. The men who are girls want the women to make them feel good. They struggle with feelings on every end of the spectrum.

A man who is a girl cannot recover from stress the same as a real man. For instance, when a man begins abusively raging at a woman, he is overwhelmed in that moment by fear. A real man knows how to get a grip on his emotions. A man who is a girl doesn't. He gets overly emotional, throwing a tantrum and pouting afterward, unable to recover from hurt feelings like a responsible man who knows how to lead. The longer the alcoholic drinks or addict acts out in his addiction, the more he becomes incapable of true feelings while remaining overly emotional at the same time.

If you are a family member of an alcoholic or addict, you know all too well about their larger-than-life personality turning to broken promises, disappointments, and heartache. The drama of his unreliability can be itself addicting. A woman cannot love a man enough if he does not love himself to the point of sobering up. Otherwise, he will never be the person he was born to be, as alcohol and drugs affect his brain and alter his personality. Cooing a woman one minute with flattery and then flying off the handle in anger like something is off-balance hormonally is not the picture of what you are hoping to find in a man.

If you are in a relationship, here is some advice: be the girl. Experience how good chivalry can feel with a man who is capable of giving it to you. Let him chase you. He can only prove how much he cares when you decide to give him the space and challenge of doing just that. He can't chase you if you are standing still. Get busy living your life to its fullest. Don't be the one to pursue him. If it is meant to be, a real man will pursue you and love every minute of it. Staying in your place as a woman is the best way to see who he is as a man.

HOMEWORK

Homework is to watch the reality TV show *Intervention*[206] on the A&E network. See how the addict actually becomes a new person, more empathetic toward others and confident, after rehab and detoxification. Relief from anxiety, which drives addiction, begins with turning your life over to God. Whatever your struggle, God's love is available to see you through. So if you feel like God is far away, ask yourself, "Who moved?"[207]

Never mistake humility for weakness. God promises, "I live on a high and holy place, but also with him who is contrite and lowly of spirit."[208] Only the most confident men are able to have the humility necessary to treat a woman well. It requires humility on the woman's end to give the man room to come after her and let him lead. Resist trying to control or manipulate a future with a man if it is not meant to be. After all, if he is a *girl*, better to find out sooner than later. If you want something a little deeper than nights out drinking in a bar, best to move on and find a real man.

206 http://www.aetv.com/shows/intervention
207 *Celebrate Hope*, Christian Drug Treatment and Rehab Blog, http://blog .celebratedrugrehab.com/
208 Isaiah 57:15

You Reap What You Sow

*D*o not be deceived, God is not mocked; for whatever a man sows, this he will also reap" (Galatians 6:7).

It doesn't matter whether or not you believe in gravity. What goes up must come down. It doesn't matter whether or not you believe in God. We all reap what we sow. Reaping what we sow is a moral law of the universe. When we make mistakes, there are always consequences. We are left with the regret of time wasted, at least. Too much time spent with wrong men creates memories of heartache you are left to carry around, which you would not otherwise have. There are much more important things to do with your time, such as heeding that little voice in the back of your mind saying, "This is not right. Stop." This is true especially if you are dating a man of bad character who has it in him to hurt you, hurt members of your family, and most of all take you away from feeling at peace in your relationship with God. When you begin dating a new guy who wants you to move too fast, listen to your common sense and slow down. This undeniable mechanism we have to steer us in the right direction is distinct to humans. It is called the conscience.

Thanks to Adam and Eve, divine morality is written in the heart of every human being to the degree that every single person in the world knows right from wrong.[209] As for those who seem unconscionable in

---

209 Genesis 3:22

their evil actions, well, there is an explanation. They have tampered so much with their conscience that it has become confused. Some people have lived with a guilty conscience so long that the innate morality they were born with has been reversed where it feels right to do wrong and wrong to do right. [210] They have seared their conscience to behave as if this universal moral law on planet Earth doesn't apply to them. Yet their day of reckoning is coming when they will have to pay for their sins. We will all reap what we sow without exception.

The human conscience works as a restraint so that we can live in happiness and peace. Guilt and pain in the moral conscience is a gift of limitation. It dictates the right path for us, away from harm. The only way to know peace when we are all alone is to keep a clear conscience. It is no accident that the moral principles set forth in the Bible agree with our conscience. Because we each reap what we sow, the Bible is packed with many promises from God conditional on whether or not we choose to live in obedience to His moral character. An example of this is Proverbs 11:25: "The generous man will be prosperous, and he who waters will himself be watered." It is clear throughout the Bible that God's greatest blessings are contingent upon our obedience.

Some people are hell-bent on making their dreams come true when it comes to *living happily ever after in marriage.* In the Bible, Jesus commands that His own love Him more than a spouse, children, or even the desire for these gifts.[211] Especially if you are a Christian, if you put marriage over pleasing Jesus, God may just let all hell break lose in your life to get your attention by allowing you to marry the wrong person. He won't be to blame if that happens, if you reap misery as a result of being out of His will. Obedience is painful, but disobedience is even more painful. I will take reaping what I sow for a good life through the pain of obedience to God any day over what denying Him could offer in momentary pleasure,

210 John MacArthur, "How God Restrains Evil in Society" video, Feb. 22, 2015, http://www.gty.org/video/Pulpit/V8280-419?Term=restrains
211 See Matthew 10.

resulting in long term regret. We can't hold on to our plans for our life so tightly that God cannot change them to give us something better.

If you are dating a man who shows signs of bad character, listen to your conscience and break it off. If not, prepare yourself for a big battle on your hands if you marry him. In Matthew, chapter 10, Jesus said He does not come to bring peace in a house divided but a *sword*. [212] "For I came to set a man against his father, and a daughter against her mother, and a daughter-in-law against her mother-in-law, and a man's enemies will be the members of his household." [213] Only stay with a man who shares your definition of right and wrong, without the personality problems resulting from a confused conscience.

We are where we are today because of decisions we made yesterday. The Bible warns in Psalm 99:8 that although God is merciful, there are always consequences because of our mistakes: "You were a forgiving God to them, and yet an avenger of their evil deeds." Begin basing your decisions on the wisdom set forth in the Bible right where you are now for a brighter tomorrow, with or without a man. There is no reason to fear keeping your standards high, even if it means staying single. Fear, instead, being out of God's will by marrying the wrong one. *"For better or for worse, through sickness and in health, until death do us part"* may produce far more pain than reaping what you sow in the freedom of making the most of your life staying single.

HOMEWORK

Homework is to read the book by John F. MacArthur Jr., *The Vanishing Conscience—Drawing the Line in a No-Fault, Guilt-Free World.*[214]

Watch the movie *Unbroken*, based on the life of Louis Zamperini who became a Christian during World War II, and yet suffered extraordinary

212 Matthew 10:34
213 Matthew 10:35-36
214 Published by Thomas Nelson, 1994.

abuse as a prisoner of war.[215] He turned down the offer to betray America and get released from the Japanese prison camp where he was being tortured. At that time, he never thought he would even survive the war. Because he chose to live according to his convictions, he will never be forgotten as a hero for all ages. He kept his promise to give His life to God after surviving the war and became a Christian evangelist. He passed away during the making of the film. Now, in heaven, he has his eternal reward.

"But store up for yourselves treasures in heaven . . . for where your treasure is, there your heart will be also" (Matthew 6:20-21).

"Do not fear those who kill the body but are unable to kill the soul; but rather fear Him who is able to destroy both soul and body in hell" (Matthew 10:28).

"Do not forget my law, but let your heart keep my commands; for length of days and long life and peace they will add to you. Let not mercy and truth forsake you; bind them around your neck, write them on the tablet of your heart, and so find favor and high esteem in the sight of God and man. Trust in the Lord with all your heart, and lean not on your own understanding; in all your ways acknowledge Him, and He shall direct your paths. Do not be wise in your own eyes; fear the Lord and depart from evil. It will be health to your flesh and strength to your bones" (Proverbs 3:1-8).

---

215 *Unbroken*, based on the book by Laura Hillenbrand. Movie produced by Angelina Jolie, 2014. Read the rest of his story on Billy Graham's website at http://billygraham.org/landingpages/unbroken/?utm_source=bing&utm _medium=cpc&utm_content=SearchAd&utm_campaign=NN -Zamperini&SOURCE=BY14CZGGS

Never Stop Learning

*L*eaving a man who is wrong for you can feel like a part of you has died, as if the plug was pulled from your only chance for an exciting life when you said goodbye to him. This couldn't be further from the truth. Look at it like a new beginning for the rest of your future, as opposed to a new season of heartache, by pouring yourself into the adventure of learning. There is too much out there you have yet to discover to be bored, especially after a breakup. Staying gone after you leave him is like passing a test. Determine within yourself to keep active as you fill up the hours of the day without him. Focusing on him (like thinking about whether or not he is missing you or looking at his social media profiles) can lead to regretful moves such as getting back in touch with him, which will only hurt you more. God does not shut one door without opening another. Find zeal in proactively busying your mind with learning. Look at it as an opportunity to grow as a person in a way you would not have the time to do if you were in a relationship.

In addition to exercise and exploring new hobbies in general, here are some ideas for getting your mind off of him altogether through learning: take notes while listening to podcasts on subjects of interest such as health or Bible study; enroll in a new course to further your formal education; write down words from the dictionary you have never before used for a broader vocabulary; memorize new Bible verses, and look up what they mean in commentaries; unearth more about your ancestors by researching your family tree; read a book that can make you a better person.

I am now hooked on audio books. This is because I can learn while I am doing other things. I can devour a book on tape throughout the day, instead of just reading at night like I've always done before drifting off to sleep. Besides, I already have more books than I can fit on my shelves, and I only read from Kindle or Nook when I am traveling. In otherwise humdrum moments of everyday life, I am now learning by listening to recorded books.

A few months ago, I began downloading a different nonfiction audio book to hear every month. I am surprised at how much time I have re-deemed listening to historical biographies while in my car running short errands. I've noticed it can also make the time fly on road trips or traf-fic jams. Since I began this journey, I feel like a new person from the knowledge I've gained. I also stick regularly to my rule of never watching television unless I can learn something from it. I've found a pleasure like no other researching subjects of interest like health and studying to learn more about people I would like to emulate. The great thing about learn-ing is that it never ends. No matter how much we study, there will always be more we have yet to grasp. To live is to learn!

Of course, if you have just had a breakup, stay away from stupid ro-mance novels. Get your mind on self-help books that can encourage you, or leave the subject of bad men altogether and download biographies of men and women of great character. I recently downloaded the biography *Oswald Chambers: Abandoned to God, the Life Story of the Author of My Utmost for His Highest*[216] and could feel myself becoming a wiser woman as I listened to every chapter. It certainly put vanity in its place and made me want to live on a higher, more sacrificial plane of happiness. Whether or not you have a man is stupid in comparison to making the most of every day growing in the Lord. No one on earth can give that to you anyway.

---

216 David MacCasland, Discovery House Publishers, 1993.

If you do take a step back and begin communicating again with Mr. Wrong after a goodbye, it does not have to be the death of your dreams. No one is perfect. Slipups happen with any addiction. If you have a slipup, all you have to do is get back on track. As I wrote in Tip #42, addictions are addictions for life, and this includes addictions to the wrong men. If a guy to whom you have been addicted gets back in touch with you, don't fall for it when he suggests *being friends* or dating *as friends*. You cannot make friends with an addiction. If you slip up and begin communicating with him, it is never too late to detox. There is always *Day One* of sobriety waiting for you tomorrow, minus the confusion of his contradictions. It does not take long for a bad guy's toxicity to rub off on you.

The first step to your freedom is the one you have taken before— break off all contact with him. It will probably take only about a week to start feeling fine again, if all you did was email. The more you engage with him, the harder it will be to get back on track. You can do it, though. This is also true in the area of food, although addictions to men are harder emotionally. Slipups will never leave you feeling confident, so use them as a tool to teach you to stay away. Just like refined sugar, the wrong men upset the chemistry of your brain and body. Don't beat yourself up over a slipup, just learn from it and get back on track. Give up the poison long enough, and you won't miss it at all. No matter where you are, God's mercy is waiting to make you well.

When an employer sees potential in one of his employees, he says, "I'm going to promote you!" When God sees potential in one of His children He says, *I'm going to prune you.* Jesus taught, "I am the true vine, and My Father is the vinedresser. Every branch in Me that does not bear fruit, He takes away; and every branch that bears fruit, He prunes it so that it may bear more fruit." [217]

When we become saved, the Bible says a miracle happens. The "seed"

---

217 John 15:1-2

of Jesus abides in us.[218] When God's seed is planted in our hearts, we want to worship God as He is in three Persons—God, the Father; God, the Son; and God, the Holy Spirit. The seed manifests itself in our faith to believe God is who He says He is in the Bible. This seed implanted within us is as miraculous as the resurrection of Jesus from the dead. Far from mere religion, we have Him then living in our hearts through the Holy Spirit. The fruits of this seed are manifested, not only in our character, but in a supernatural love for Jesus and a hatred for lies about Him. As an overflow of His seed abiding in us, we are not comfortable living in sin; we will bear fruit of His character. (This is why not everyone who claims to be a Christian really is.) When someone wants to learn more about God, God is drawing that person. A seed of faith grows by a desire for reading the Bible and a love for God's people. We are born again spiritually as God's possession when He plants the seed of Jesus within our hearts. By this seed, the Holy Spirit living inside of us works to bring glory to Jesus through our lives.

The Bible symbolizes character as fruit, both good and bad. It depends on the source of the fruit, as to whether or not it comes from God. The Bible teaches to look at someone's character. "So every good tree bears good fruit, but the bad tree bears bad fruit. . . . So then, you will know them by their fruits." [219]

"Now the deeds of the flesh are evident, which are: immorality, impurity, sensuality, idolatry, sorcery, enmities, strife, jealousy, outbursts of anger, disputes, dissensions, factions, envying, drunkenness, carousing, and things like these, of which I forewarn you, just as I have forewarned you, that those who practice such things will not inherit the kingdom of God. . . . But the fruit of the Spirit is love, joy, peace, patience, kindness, goodness, faithfulness, gentleness, self-control; against such things there is no law."[220]

---

218 1 John 3:9
219 Matthew 7:18, 20
220 Galatians 5:19-25

As branches rooted in Jesus, our Heavenly Father takes full responsibility for our pruning. We are not the ones in control. God is the One who chooses our tests, and they differ person to person. Sometimes God prunes us through our mistakes. He does not kill us with His pruning but shapes us so we can bear more fruit and become stronger. It can hurt when he prunes us, taking out diseased patches for our growth to keep us healthy overall. But, it is all for our good. Like a tree, we could not become the people He saved us to be for His glory without being pruned. God won't be done pruning us until we get home to heaven. We might as well yield to the tests in faithfulness.

Whenever I feel disappointment, I have learned to pray, "God teach me what you want me to learn from this." I can trust He is working to make me wiser from any trial, even it hurts. In His timing, He never fails to take away the heartache in my life and replace it with something better as I trust in Him. Until, looking back, I wouldn't have had it any other way than His plan after all, even though He had to prune me in pain to accomplish it. I can only thank Him for every single hello and goodbye I've experienced in relationships with both men and women, learning not even to make my friendships idols. If God has happiness waiting for me with a man who is good for me, I welcome it, but, thanks to His pruning process in my life, I am bearing much fruit in Christ alone. And this includes the fruit of not being able to say I need more in my life than what the Lord has already given me. Where He leads me, I will follow, and that is good enough for me.

HOMEWORK

Homework for this tip is to be teachable. Especially after a breakup, stay busy making the most of your free time away from television shows and movies that cannot offer any nourishment for your soul. Historical literature can transport you to another place and time. You will find when you read or listen to an audio book that you must keep your mind fully engaged with it or else will miss it. It is impossible to concentrate on anything else, including thoughts about a man who is not right for you.

Take a break from all of the jerks you meet these days, and go back in time to learn from extraordinary Christian men like Oswald Chambers, Charles Spurgeon, and Jonathan Edwards. It will put everything in perspective to remind you that you have all you need already for happiness, if you have Jesus.

"How sweet it is to learn the Savior's love when nobody else loves us! When friends flee, what a blessed thing it is to see that the Savior does not forsake us but still keeps us and holds us fast and clings to us and will not let us go!" —Charles Haddon Spurgeon[221]

---

221 Charles Spurgeon, "Never Forsaken," *3-Minute Devotions with Charles Spurgeon: Inspiring Devotions and Prayers* (Uhrichsville, Ohio: Barbour, 2015).

You Are the Prize

A woman is like a fine piece of china, delicate and sensitive. She was made to be handled gently. She's a treasure, not meant to be thrown around like a football. If you have been involved with abusive men who have put you down, it may be hard for you to think realistically about yourself. Go back to when you were a little girl, happy and free. The role of a father raising a daughter is to nurture her femininity with tenderness. If you did not have that growing up, God waits to be your Father today with healing and restoration. Just give your heart to Him, and He promises to give your life back to you as a prize. We can find our life as a prize in Jesus, because our prize was in Him all along. The Bible teaches, "I press on toward the goal for the prize of the upward call of God in Christ Jesus."[222]

Jesus promises if you "lose your life," you will find it again in Him as a prize. You find it not in your reputation or positive thinking or communication skills. All of those things are important when relating to people and getting by in this world, but living for Jesus means far more. Only through *dying* to ourselves—meaning, our outward image, what others think of us, and the plans we have set for our future—can we surrender and present ourselves as an offering to the Lord for Him to live through us and accomplish whatever *He* wants.[223] It is all about the

---

222 Philippians 3:14
223 1 Corinthians 15:31

brokenness of the Cross. As we love Jesus and *be* who He calls us to *be*, He will *do* His work through us. Jesus said, "For whoever wishes to save his life will lose it; but whoever loses his life for My sake will find it." [224]

Being a prize has nothing to do with looks, age, money, or anything on the outside. Knowing that you are a prize has everything to do with how God sees you and how you see yourself. It has to do with who you are as a woman at the core. When you see yourself as a prize, you won't settle for any man who does not. You are a rare find, a precious jewel, too special to go on wasting your time in sorrow over any jerk who is not worthy of a woman of virtue.

Don't confuse being a prize with being a trophy wife. Google "trophy wife" and you will see the title is rarely used as a compliment toward a moral woman.[225] It promotes the image of a wife as only an object, as a status symbol for a man. The average trophy wife won't be his first wife. She will be much younger and anywhere from wife number two to wife number four or five. Any rich sugar daddy can get a trophy wife. Evidently now, a poor younger man can have one, too. Studies show there is another trophy wife up and coming. It's is the woman who is very wealthy, able to support a man financially. Supposedly, this is the new trophy wife of the 21st century.[226]

Most of the men with trophy wives know nothing of putting a woman up on a pedestal as a prize. It is only a man of good character who is willing to love unconditionally, for better or for worse, with a deep respect for what his family means to him. It is the other way around for a selfish man—he wants to be the prize! A man who sees his wife as a prize is a man who knows how to keep his commitment and loves her because of who she is, because it is right. And he is willing to work to have and keep her.

---

224 Matthew 16:25
225 "How to Be a Trophy Wife," http://www.wikihow.com/Be-a-Trophy-Wife
226 Kristen Houghton, "The New Trophy Wife," *Huff Post for Women*, Dec. 13, 2015, updated Jan. 25, 2015. http://www.huffingtonpost.com/kristen-houghton/the-new-trophy-wife_b_6207364.html

A prize implies an accomplishment, something earned. It is the motive behind chivalry. This is the reason real men are not intimidated by women who are hard to get. If you don't know how to let a man pursue you without chasing after him, stop selling yourself short. If you feel you cannot get to know a man without sex, odds are you were sexually abused as a child. Sexual abuse can result in a woman being oversexed. This is because the sexual exploitation leaves her not knowing *how* to relate to a man to whom she is attracted apart from a physical relationship. Her addiction may feel like a high sex drive, but there is actually more going on beneath the surface. Subconsciously, a survivor of sexual abuse can feel all too comfortable using a physical relationship with a man to control him. This is because she does not realize she is worth being loved apart from it.

Think of the best sex you have ever had in your life with a guy. Do you really believe that same person would have been a bad lover in marriage? The answer is, of course, no. I have had women tell me they have to have sex before marriage to make sure "everything is working well." Believe me, you will be able to tell if "everything is working well" when you kiss him. You don't have to go to bed with him. Wait, and you won't be sorry. God gave you a brain, and you need it in full capacity, instead of high on oxytocin, while getting to know a man in order for God to let you test if everything, including his brain, is working well. These days some men don't have a well-functioning heart because it is way too hard. If his heart is not right, trust me, nothing else will be right for marriage. Do yourself a favor, and wait. It is too scary in today's culture to let chemistry lead instead of love.

You may be thinking, "Well, I know many couples who have slept together on the first date and have lived happily ever after in marriage." I dare to challenge that, in general. Selfishness does not make for a happy life. If you think waiting is too difficult, my response would be this. Do you know what is too difficult for me? Oxytocin withdrawal, as explained in previous tips. By God's grace, I have lived a very happy life with no sexually transmitted diseases and no abortions as a result of not sleeping around. Of course, God can turn any mistake we make around for our good, but life is much easier when we just take God at His Word and not have to learn things the hard way.

Settling only for a "commitment" from a guy outside of marriage comes with a high risk. A commitment is basically easy for a man to give but much harder to prove. Playboys are pros at offering a *commitment*. It is just something said to get the woman into bed. Many guys today are only out to use women for sex, with *commitments* only lasting as long as they want them to last, maybe just for a night or two. A guy can mean it at the time, but not mean it tomorrow. With one more sexual relationship and one more antidepressant, the search goes on looking for love in all the wrong places.

Compare my advice to the popular "Do as thou wilt shall be the whole of the Law," which I referenced in Tip #22, warning that it is the creed of Satanism.[227] Satanism teaches, right out of the *Satanic Bible*, to do what is right in your own eyes, with boundaries only set by *you*. Satanism gives you license to gratify your desires, however you want, according to whatever *you* think is best. God offers to give you the desires of your heart *His way*, in purity. The two belief systems are opposed to one another. Satanism is all about rebellion from God, even teaching, "Say unto thine own self, 'I am mine own redeemer.'"[228]

Do you believe it is only a coincidence that Satanists mock, reverse, and twist verses from the Bible in their rituals instead of other books like the Quran, the Bhagavad Gita or the Book of Mormon? Obviously, it is because Satan hates the Holy Bible. He hates the blood Jesus shed on

---

227 Aleister Crowley, *The Book of the Law*, 1904, also known as *AL vel Legis*. Crowley wrote, "There is no law beyond 'Do what thou wilt,'" III:60; https://en.wikiquote.org/wiki/Aleister_Crowley; also see https://en.wikipedia.org/wiki/Thelema. For more on the satanic rituals that L. Ron Hubbard, founder of Scientology, practiced from Crowley, see http://www.bible.ca/scientology-satanism-Hubbard-jr.htm.
228 Anton LaVey, *The Satanic Bible* (1969) and *The Satanic Rituals* (1972).

the cross for you. Satan works to deceive you to believe you can have a relationship with God apart from His moral law and apart from Jesus as Savior. Satan wants to keep you in bondage to addictions, far away from the Bible. Satan does not want this God of love to have you, heart and soul. Satan does not want you to know that your life is a prize just waiting for you in God's mercy and love.

Be happy in a way that sets you free to soar in the life God created you to have. Learn to be thankful for what God has given you, and let it be enough. A man does not belong to you outside of marriage a bit more than you belong to him. If it is meant to be that he belongs to you and you to him, you will become husband and wife. Then you can have the real gift God has given to a man and woman, as opposed to the counterfeit. Wait to truly make love, and be someone's lover after a man actually proves his commitment and love to you by marrying you. With or without a man you win! God promises in the Bible to give your life back to you as a prize, if only you will put your trust in Him. "And do you seek great things for yourself? Seek them not, for behold . . . I will give you your life as a prize . . . in all places to which you may go."[229]

HOMEWORK

Homework is to read the classic allegory about how to have a victorious life as a Christian, *Pilgrim's Progress* by John Bunyan.[230]

In order to find your life as a prize waiting from God, don't be afraid to share your shortcomings at times with trustworthy people. To find the hidden treasure of your life as a prize, you have to have the ability to be real with yourself and others. After all, it is every bit of you, including the broken pieces, that makes your life in Jesus such a prize.

I also recommend reading the book by Sue Ellen Browder, *Subverted— How I Helped the Sexual Revolution Hijack the Women's Movement,* for

---

229 Jeremiah 45:5, ESV
230 https://en.wikipedia.org/wiki/The_Pilgrim%27s_Progress

more research on the theme of this tip from a secular perspective. Any sensible woman would champion the fight for equal rights for women, but, as this former freelance writer for *Cosmopolitan* magazine points out, the sexual revolution was something else altogether. It actually took away our standing in society as women. It cheapened us in the eyes of men to the point of them no longer having to earn our affection. We are still suffering the repercussions from the sexual revolution in our American culture today. The men now think they can have us for free.

Look up Proverbs 31, verses 10-31, to read about how God honors a virtuous woman. Become the woman described in Proverbs 31 in the Bible as the type of women God holds in highest esteem. Trust that if there is a right man for you, he will love you because of your virtue. The longer you live in virtue, the more you will feel good enough about yourself to know that if a man is worthy of you, he will cherish you like a prize.

Happiness Happens
When You Least Expect It

*I*t was not until the beginning of 2010 when one day I realized I was happy on my own. I was all alone when the moment hit me by surprise. I found myself quite comfortable within my being. I did not need a man to fix me or fulfill me. Somewhere along the way, when I hadn't even noticed, God had taken away my loneliness and made me happy, with or without a man.

My newfound satisfaction within continues to feel like a miracle from God. If I can cross through the rivers I thought would drown me in tears to finally arrive in the Promised Land, you can, too. Staying away from wrong men in this new existence of "comfortable within myself alone" is true freedom. There are trees of green and skies of blue. Every day is fresh and new. Though the right man is more than welcome to join me here, no man is required.

To get to this land of plenty, you will have to let God lead and finally stop running from feelings. On this road you must *learn to feel* by doing the hard work of overcoming addictions and changing your way of thinking. And, with one step in front of the other, you will find that disappointments won't kill you on your way.

When you arrive, you'll realize the Love you've been wanting so desperately has been there all along with God. I promise there is no man on earth needed for the discovery, and this experience is not too good to be true. If you are willing to come to God His way, He will heal you and grant you contentment, married or single. Not only is no man necessary, but no man on earth is even capable of completing you to such a degree. Men will only be bandages for the much deeper wounds of your heart until you learn to take your burdens to the Cross and leave them there. God is the only One able to heal you, and He wants to begin now. But you'll have to lean on Him intensely. Then you'll have everything you need to be happy in a life of service to others in Jesus' name, and you'll be healthy enough to recognize true happiness when you have it—with or without a man.

Some women reading this may believe that God owes them happiness, even when they are running as fast as they can away from Him. But to run away from God is to run away from the happiness and peace only He can give. You cannot have both your way and His at the same time, so you must choose. If you continue to refuse Him always, you will never know what you are missing. If you want Him right now, the Savior is waiting if you will ask Him to enter your heart. He wants to come in and make your heart His home. All you have to do is ask.

God understands exactly what you are going through, and He wants to help you. He has direct access to your conscience to make it clean and make you strong. His plan for your life is contingent on your relationship with Him coming first. He works through our obedience. He wants you to lean on Him in your loneliness as you go about your days and nights. This is because He cares for you. Unlike the other spirits of deception, you are safe giving your heart to Jesus and trusting Him with your future. Only then can you discover the life waiting for you in the One who died to give it to you. Let Him bring you friends, bring you accomplishments, and bring you Love in a life set apart for His glory. When your heart is right before Him, He will accomplish what He wants through you, married or single. He loves you more than any earthly man ever will or can anyway.

Jesus is called a Bridegroom for his own in the Bible, "and so this joy of mine has been made full," thanks to a Bridegroom, Jesus, who will never be done teaching me and healing me until I see Him face to face in heaven.[231]

If we stop worshiping our idols—which can sometimes be good things like marriage—we will always find more than enough affirmation in God alone. There is a vast difference from receiving a blessing of marriage from God vs. worshiping it. The institution of marriage is from God. You are not the one who can create it. He certainly knows how to make it happen in your life, if it is His will.

If anything you tried in the past had been able to secure happiness within you, you probably wouldn't have picked up this book. Since what you thought would bring you lasting peace time and time again has not, why not consider this new idea of surrender. God wants His will to be fulfilled more in your life than you could ever possibly want it. Give your life to Him, and you won't have to worry about missing out on something that is His best for you, because it is *His* job to make that happen in your life and not your own. Your job is only to stay close to Jesus by living for Him (instead of living for a man you have yet to meet).

Live each moment to the fullest. Don't keep running away from God's rest. Joy is yours for today, for tomorrow, and the next day, and the next. Don't let anything or anyone keep you from it, including yourself. It has more to do with your attitude within than with any man. After all, God is most glorified when we are most contented in Him.

HOMEWORK

Homework for this final tip is to take your eyes off of yourself and put them on God. Truly loving God is no killjoy, and truly loving a man in marriage is not some fairy-tale utopia. Let God fill up your emptiness,

---

231 See John 3:29; 2 Corinthians 5:8

because He is the only One who can. It may sound hard to believe, but there is no true and lasting happiness apart from the Cross. It matters not if you are single or married.

Relinquish control for God to be God over all of your hellos and goodbyes. Vow your allegiance first to God, and everything will work out just fine. Jesus waits for you at Calvary with His perfect plan, beginning and ending with Him for all of eternity. Don't let any far-fetched dream of *falling in love* steal it away. God has something better than what you've envisioned for your worth, as you learn to see yourself through His eyes. The reflection of a mere man to flatter you could be nothing in comparison.

Keep smiling at the men like you've never been hurt before. Good men are out there searching for a good woman just like you. Take care of yourself like the good catch you are. Drop a dud in a heartbeat and get on with your life, never settling for less than the best. Keep dating the good guys. But don't forget, while you are waiting on something real to last forever, there is someone who loves you so much He died for you. He wants you to be His chosen one. Whether you marry or not, it does not matter. The good life is yours for the taking today! Love has not passed you by.

Acknowledgments

Special thanks to my family. I thank my mother for being my best friend. I thank my dad for remembering the first essay I wrote in elementary school, saying that is when he first knew I had a gift for writing. I appreciate both of my parents for teaching me to be a servant to people in need and to love others without pretense. I'm grateful for a brother who is a marketing whiz and is always there to support me in business and offer advice, a brother who is my friend and a genuinely good man.

My mother, Claudette Litz, is a retired English teacher, and I thank her for pouring over the manuscript with me day after day for months. I appreciate my mother, not just for the content editing, but for the amazing woman she is. I would not be me without the unconditional love she has given to me all of my life. I thank her for being the strongest and greatest woman I will ever know.

It is one thing to write a book and yet another to surround yourself with the most prolific and talented people who know how to professionally guide the endeavor and bring it to fruition with excellence. I had the perfect team. Special thanks to my friend, Rose Yancik at Y Design, for the stunning cover and interior design. She went the extra mile, helping me in every direction to make these tips a transforming success in the hearts of women far and wide. Pam Shoup did the light copyediting and worked closely with Rose proofing the typesetting. I am convinced that no other editor could have been better for this project. She was thorough with an eye like an eagle and went over and beyond my expectations. She truly showed a respect and understanding for the message I hoped to convey. This book exists thanks to the extraordinary team of women I had working with me.

I thank Eli McFadden, the photographer who shot the cover photos, for always knowing how to bring out the best in me. Loren Turner at The Mirror in Nashville did my hair for the shoot. She is one rare stylist who knows how to give me the perfect cut.

During my time of living in Los Angeles, I received some great counseling. I thank Dr. Charles Browning, a Christian counselor, who told me that if a man could not say he is sorry when he hurts a woman or ever take any correction without getting upset, the man has a pride problem. I thank Dr. Sherie Zander, a dating and communications expert, for telling me years ago that it was to my credit I am still single after hearing about some of my dating scenarios. I thank countless women I have met in support groups for sharing both their pain and their strength with me. I love you, my sisters. I especially thank Marilyn Brown, a counselor specializing in addiction, who told me one day that she would rather see me get happy on my own than keep going out with the wrong men.

Last, but not least, I want to thank all of the men who have been disappointments. What a cast of characters! It's okay. The pain is far behind me now. At the end of the day, it all made for a good read. I had to laugh a time or two writing about some of them (without naming any names). And I sincerely wish to thank every single one who hurt me for every single penny this book will make.

About the Author

*D*wayna Litz is a singer, songwriter, founder of Lighting the Way Worldwide nonprofit organization, speaker, author, health coach, and entrepreneur. For more information, and to contact her for book signings and speaking engagements, visit her website at DwaynaLitz.com.

CPSIA information can be obtained at www.ICGtesting.com
Printed in the USA
LVOW10s0831090316

478270LV00002BA/2/P